MILESTONES OF AVIATION

MILESTONES

SMITHSONIAN INSTITUTION

EDITED BY JOHN T. GREENWOOD

CRESCENT BOOKS

OF AVIATION

NATIONAL AIR AND SPACE MUSEUM

NEW YORK

ENDSHEET:
In the spacious Milestones of Flight Gallery of the National Air and Space Museum, five historic aircraft and the Apollo 11 command module greet millions of visitors every year. The restored Wright *Flyer* of 1903 prominently occupies the central place of honor. To its left are Charles Lindbergh's Ryan NYP, the *Spirit of St. Louis*, and Bell Aircraft's X-1 *Glamorous Glennis*, in which Chuck Yeager broke the sound barrier in October 1947. To its right, Samuel P. Langley's *Aerodrome* No. 5 of 1903 is almost hidden by a North American X-15 rocket-powered hypersonic research aircraft. Below the Wright *Flyer*, visitors examine the Apollo 11 command module that carried Neil Armstrong, Michael Collins, and Edwin Aldrin to the moon in July 1969.

This 1991 edition published by Crescent Books, distributed by Outlet Book Company, Inc., a Random House Company, 225 Park Avenue South, New York, New York 10003

ISBN 0-517-06545-2

Printed and bound in Hong Kong

8 7 6 5 4 3 2 1

MILESTONES OF AVIATION

CONTENTS

PREFACE

John T. Greenwood

This book originated in 1987 in a stimulating discussion among Dr. Von Hardesty, then chairman of the Department of Aeronautics at the National Air and Space Museum, Smithsonian Institution; Ms. Trish Graboske, chief of Publications for the National Air and Space Museum; Mr. Martin P. Levin; and myself, editor and then consultant to the Department of Aeronautics. Our talks centered on developing a fresh approach to the fascinating history of flight that would enlighten readers about many of the little-known, fundamental advances in aviation and place the more well-known achievements in their proper historical context. We concluded that we would focus on the milestones marking the process of aviation since December 17, 1903, when Orville and Wilbur Wright first achieved manned, powered flight in a heavier-than-air flying machine. To organize such an undertaking, a chronological structure would follow a path trodden so many times before that we opted to look at aviation based on the principal objectives of aeronautics. In its essence, aeronautics and aviation is the quest to achieve and then improve upon four fundamentals; the attainment of sufficient speed and altitude, without which flight is impossible; the covering of distances, without which flight has little purpose beyond personal enjoyment; the development of size, which will satisfy societal and economic demands while fostering continued growth and utility; and the constant drive to better all these attainments both individually and collectively. We converted these objectives into the four chapters of this book.

Milestones of Aviation, we believe, encompasses aviation not just as the mechanics of flight but, moreover, as the development and operation of heavier-than-air craft also. Working closely with our sponsor, the National Air and Space Museum's Department of Aeronautics, we selected our authors for their general knowledge of aviation and for their expertise in the specific field that they covered. Not every reader familiar with aviation history will agree with the milestones—the airplanes, aircraft designers, or events— that our authors selected. Our coverage had to be selective because of limited space; we did not cover helicopters or dirigibles, and we restricted our treatment of naval aviation. Any shortcomings or omissions are the full responsibility of the editor and the authors.

Throughout our work, the staff at the National Air and Space Museum freely shared their world-famous expertise and provided choice criticism of the numerous drafts that they generously reviewed. Their advice allowed the authors and editor to refine the chapters and create a fabric from many disparate threads. Especially helpful were F. Robert Van der Linden, R. E. G. Davies, Howard Wolko, Claudia Oakes, and the acting chairman, Dr. Dominick Pisano, who also wrote the bibliographical essay and selected appropriate quotations for use. Dr. Hardesty deserves further mention, for without his initiative, enthusiasm, and support this book would not have been possible. Ms. Graboske, the indispensable catalyst for this undertaking, was remarkable in persistently shepherding this project from creation to publication.

I extend a special thanks to Martin Levin, who shaped the project. The publisher, Hugh Levin, the authors, and I appreciate his endurance; little did he know what an ordeal awaited him at the hands of these aviation historians! I trust that the final product will repay him for many trying hours. To Hugh Levin and his hard-working assistant Ellin Yassky Silberblatt I express my gratitude, and for their editing and production work, the staff of Harkavy Publishing Service deserves many thanks. The stunning appearance of this volume bespeaks the praises due to its designer, Nai Chang.

To Hugh also goes credit for obtaining the services of Karen Wyatt, photographic researcher without peer, who spent hundreds of hours searching for and securing the book's numerous illustrations. The history of aviation could not have been related intelligibly without the illustrations Karen obtained.

To the following individuals and organizations I offer my sincere thanks for their assistance: Harry Gann of Douglas Aircraft Company; Eric Schulzinger of Lockheed Aeronautical Systems Company; Marilyn Phipps and Elizabeth Reese of Boeing Airplane Company; Tim Calloway of the British Royal Air Force Museum; M. Nicoleau of the French Musée de l'Air; Lt. Col. Darrell C. Hayes of the United States Air Force, Airlift and Contingency Branch, Office of Public Affairs; Werner Bittner of Lufthansa Airlines; Cynthia Reed-Miller of the Henry Ford Museum and Greenfield Village; Larry Wilson, Melissa Keiser, Dana Bell, Brian Nicklaus, and volunteer Bob Dreesen of the National Air and Space Museum's Information Management Division staff; and the United States Air Force, 1361st Photo Squadron.

Finally, I thank my wife, Mary Ann, and our children, Anne and James, for their willingness to share me with this work for months on end. Their understanding and support have been essential to the successful completion of this book.

John T. Greenwood
Annandale, Virginia
May 1989

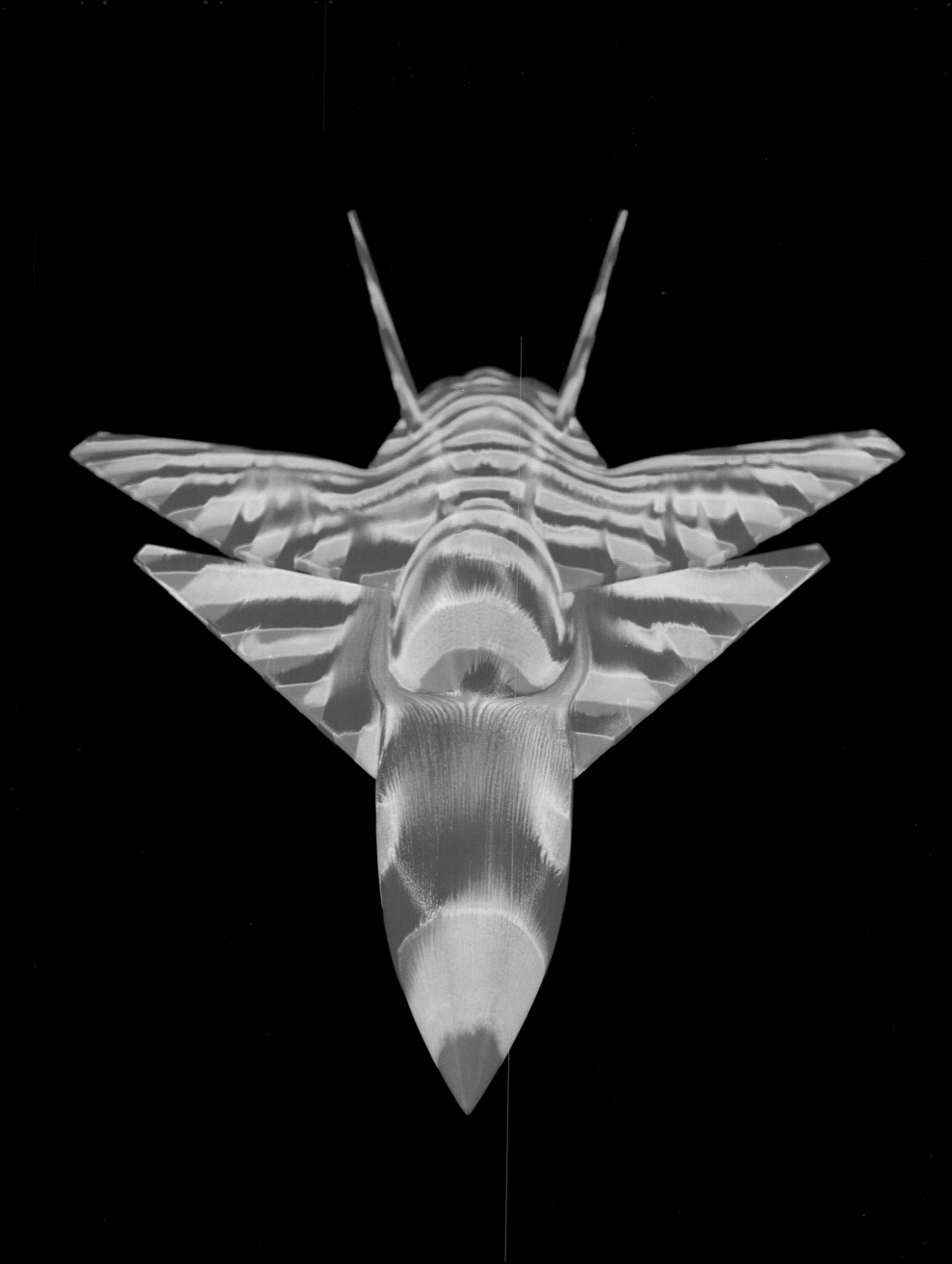

INTRODUCTION

Michael Collins

Astronaut, Gemini-Titan 10 and Apollo-Saturn 11 and
former Director, National Air and Space Museum

One day a young boy named Paul Garber took the trolley from Washington to Fort Myer, Virginia, to watch the Wright brothers demonstrate their first military airplane. The year was 1909, and it had taken the Wrights only six years to find a military application for their new machine. Today Paul Garber is Curator Emeritus at the Smithsonian Institution's National Air and Space Museum in Washington, D.C., and he is now watching spacecraft in addition to aircraft.

In 1924, four biplanes known as Douglas World Cruisers set out to circumnavigate the globe, and two of them made it. General Leigh Wade was one of the pilots on that epic trip, which took 175 days. In 1986 General Wade witnessed the nonstop, round-the-world flight of Dick Rutan and Jeana Yeager in their frail *Voyager*, which took only *nine days*. What a span of achievement, what a dizzying technological pace, that allowed Garber and Wade to witness such changes in their lifetimes!

Yet they are not alone. Aviation touches the daily lives of millions—from the food we eat to the vacations we take. The communications satellite allows us to "see" around the world, and if seeing is not enough, the modern jetliner will take us to the continent of our choice in a matter of hours.

These advances in aviation have been accelerated by competition. The necessity for defense, the challenge of winning an air race, the need to out-perform a commercial rival: competition has driven aviation and will continue to do so. But the traditional parameters of speed, altitude, distance, and size are yielding to a new list: reliability, safety, efficiency, comfort, environmental compatibility. As always, designers will try to maximize lift and thrust, minimize weight and drag. They will be aided in their search for new materials and techniques by the space program, which places an even higher priority on weight-saving than aeronautics has done.

Advances in electronics have changed the world of aviation just as they have the other facets of our lives. Computers are now essential in the design and manufacturing of aircraft, as well as in increasingly sophisticated on-board systems. For example, some military aircraft, such as the F-16 and B-2, are fundamentally unstable, and rely on computers to avoid tumbling out of control. As aircraft speeds increase, it becomes difficult, if not impossible, to duplicate flight conditions using wind tunnels; thus very powerful computers are now being used as sophisticated predictors in lieu of these tunnels. The use of microelectronic devices will accelerate as their capacity grows. Every 18 months or so the number of components that can fit on a microchip doubles.

Facing page:
Wind tunnels provide aircraft designers and builders with an indispensable tool for research and development. Over the years engineers have developed numerous ways of testing the aerodynamic efficiency of aircraft designs, especially for supersonic fighters. In this wind tunnel test, Lockheed Aeronautical Systems Company's engineers coated the model of a generic fighter with fluorescent oil paint and then used a black light to produce stunning images which accurately showed aerodynamic flow over the aircraft structure and revealed potential trouble areas and "hot spots" in the design.

In many respects, the Beechcraft Starship represents the future of aircraft design and construction. Built almost entirely with extremely strong and lightweight composite materials, replacing heavier metallic structural materials, the 14,250-pound aircraft seats 10 passengers and has a maximum speed of 405 mph.

Both military and commercial aircraft have become so expensive that the small entrepreneur is becoming an endangered species. The entire Western market for large transport aircraft is now split by only three companies: Boeing, McDonnell Douglas, and Airbus Industries. Today a decision to build a new plane is preceded by years of study and analysis, a little voodoo, and a lot of corporate handwringing. The new B-2 bombers will cost over *half a billion* dollars each. No longer can two brothers do it all. Their invention has spawned giant corporations. Lindbergh, the lone eagle, has been replaced by a flock of starlings (respectable birds, certainly, but it's not the same). The space program has its astronauts, but they are just the tip of an immense technological iceberg, and they and the public know it. If there is any room left for the small enterprise, it is at the narrow end of the scale—in ultralight aircraft, for example—or in the business of providing aircraft components.

However, if aviation has lost some of its glamour, it has certainly made up for it in increased economic impact. Today the aerospace industry has surpassed agriculture as this nation's greatest contributor to a favorable balance of trade. Having lost most of the electronics market to the nations of the Pacific rim over the past decade, we need to keep exporting airliners, the only major American product that still dominates the world market.

Of course, most people think of the airplane not in relation to the nation's economy but in more personal terms. While millions of Americans have never flown, millions of others think nothing of hopping on a $99 special to Miami at the first sign of snow.

Undeniably, flight has caused our planet to shrink, and in ways that are both good and bad. Flowers flown in from South America grace our tables, but cocaine from South America is undermining the foundations of our society. Our children fly to Europe for a semester's work, but then they perish at 30,000 feet when a terrorist bomb explodes on their return trip. Generally, however, increased mobility and shortened travel times have improved the quality of our lives. During the 1930s Pan American Airways was almost an arm of the State Department and in the forefront of our diplomacy; Pan Am employees were the first, and perhaps only, Americans to be seen in the more remote Asian and South American nations. The airplane really was the instrument that brought about the adoption of Hawaii as the 50th state in the Union and opened communications around the Pacific basin. Now routinely, the airplane sets us down among our global neighbors, whom we usually discover to share our concerns, values, and hopes for the future. This understanding is essential in working out solutions to global problems.

Today's jet airliner is a marvel of grace and efficiency, whistling through the sky at 600 miles per hour while hundreds inside enjoy almost luxurious conditions. I have decided that I even like airline food. What I don't like is walking at four miles per hour through endless caverns, trying to intercept my luggage, riding on a carousel at two miles per hour—then off to a distant parking lot or a long wait for public transportation. A portal-to-portal look at our transportation system is needed to bring the other components up to the same relative level of performance as the airplane itself.

While I have not been privileged to see all that Paul Garber or Leigh Wade have seen, I vividly remember my first plane ride, in a Grumman Widgeon, and my graduation from flying school, where the speaker was Roscoe Turner, the famous barnstormer and air racer. Roscoe flew with jodhpurs, a waxed mustache, and a pet lion. I flew to the moon with rocket motors and sophisticated computers. I like to think about this startling contrast from a window seat, seven miles up, as I watch this beautiful planet slip by at ten miles per minute. I hope you will enjoy the pages of this book, as the milestones slip by, and ponder how aviation has changed the life of our planet.

FARTHER

FARTHER
The Quest for Distance

TERRY GWYNN-JONES

The Wright *Flyer* occupies the central position
of honor in the Main Gallery of the Smithsonian
Institution's National Air and Space Museum.

On December 17, 1903, a glorious 12 seconds of flight over the sands of Kitty Hawk, North Carolina, opened a new era in world history.

The Wright brothers' stuttering 120-foot flight—slightly more than half the wingspan of today's Boeing 747—seems incongruous compared with other distance milestones in aviation. Besides representing the first triumph of powered flight, this flight was the starting point from which the progress of aviation is measured. Indeed, on that remarkable day Wilbur and Orville Wright indulged in the first quest for distance—a minuscule example of the years of competition to follow. Alternating as pilots, they made another three flights, each a little farther, until Wilbur flew for 59 seconds and covered 852 feet.

Such has always been the competitive nature of people, whether driving their bodies to go faster or farther or applying their skills to guiding vehicles. Such competition brings fleeting fame, but in the long run, the real benefit lies in the steady improvement in the performance and reliability of the machines. Such was to be the case of those heroes of aviation who gambled their lives for distance, propelling the Wright brothers' imperfect invention from a curiosity to today's indispensable vehicle.

Stretching the Boundaries

Incredibly, the events of that bitter December day at Kitty Hawk received little attention. Even in the United States, the secretive brothers' refusal to give out pictures or details of the aircraft exacerbated confused newspaper reporting. Thus, many people believed they were as unsuccessful as other would-be aviators of the day. Over the next two years, the Wright brothers refined their design, and by October 4, 1905, their *Flyer* III covered over 24 miles in 38 minutes and 3 seconds. On the occasions when reporters were invited to witness flights, however, poor weather and engine problems grounded the brothers; consequently, the press generally considered the whole business a waste of time.

Awaiting patents and unable to obtain orders for machines from the government, the Wrights stopped flying for two and a half years to prevent industrial spying. During their self-imposed exile, the first European flights took place. At first they paled compared with the Wrights' achievements. On

December 17, 1903: the dawn of modern flight. Orville Wright making the world's first successful manned, powered flight in the Wright *Flyer* at Kitty Hawk, North Carolina. His brother Wilbur, who had stalled attempting to get airborne three days earlier, ran beside the right wing tip in an effort to keep it from dragging in the sand until the *Flyer* was airborne.

Pages 14–15
Jeana Yeager and Dick Rutan reached the last great distance milestone on December 23, 1986, when they landed the Voyager at Edwards Air Force Base, California, thus completing, without refueling, the first nonstop flight around the world.

Wilbur Wright (1867–1912).

Orville Wright (1871–1948). Both portraits by S.E. Malik.

In 1908, Wilbur Wright carried out a series of remarkable demonstration flights in Europe. At Pau in southwest France in January 1909, coachmen steady their horses as the two-seat Wright A skims overhead.

November 12, 1906, the French-based Brazilian Alberto Santos-Dumont had lumbered about 720 feet in his freakish "14-bis" box kite biplane. A year later, only one European machine had managed to stay airborne for nearly a minute when Henry Farman flew 2,530 feet in a Voisin-Farman I in 53 seconds on October 26, 1907. By mid-1908, however, French designers Gabriel and Charles Voisin had produced a modestly more successful biplane that Henry Farman flew 12 miles on July 6.

Just when it appeared that Europe was catching up, the Wright brothers finally signed commercial agreements in the United States and France and began a series of public demonstrations in France in August 1908. On the last day of that year, at Camp d'Auvours, near Le Mans, Wilbur Wright capped a spectacular series of 104 demonstration flights by circling the field in a two-seat Model A until he had covered 77 miles.

This time their achievement made world headlines. A battle of superlatives followed not only among the journalists but also among skeptical European aviators who had scoffed at the Wrights' claims.

"It is a revelation in aeroplane work. Who can now doubt that the Wrights have done all they claimed? We are as children compared with the Wrights," one exclaimed. A London *Times* report spoke of "triumph . . . indescribable enthusiasm . . . mastery." Major B. F. S. Baden-Powell, past president of Britain's (later the Royal) Aeronautical Society, stated, "That Wilbur Wright is in possession of a power which controls the fate of nations, is beyond dispute."

The first great milestone had taken five years to set in place. Painstakingly carved over the sand dunes of Kitty Hawk and cemented in the French skies, it marked the way to the future.

Spurred by the Wrights' demonstrations, European aviation matured in 1909. The French took to the airplane with typical Gallic fervor and were soon in the forefront. Several among their growing band of designer-manufacturers discarded the pusher-biplane configuration for the tractor monoplane. The most successful was Louis Blériot, whose classic No. XI monoplane was the embryo of the modern airplane. In it he was to make aviation's first epochal long-distance flight—across the English Channel.

At dawn on July 25, 1909, on a clifftop near the outskirts of Calais, Blériot

sat in a monoplane gazing thoughtfully at the English Channel. "He just sat there with an expression of tragic intensity on his pale face waiting for a chance to do it," the London *Daily Mail* reported. His gloomy expression could well have resulted from the knowledge that six days earlier an engine failure had forced down another daring pilot, Hubert Latham, in mid-Channel.

Such a flight had seemed an impossible feat the previous year when Alfred, Lord Northcliffe, owner of the *Daily Mail*, had offered a prize of £1,000 to the first aviator to cross the English Channel. Flying was still an overland adventure. Unreliable engines discouraged pilots from straying far from the relative safety of their airfields. Indeed, the first true cross-country flight, a 16-mile hop from Châlons to Reims by France's Henry Farman, did not take place until October 30, 1908.

Nevertheless, Northcliffe deliberately chose the seemingly impossible. He was acutely aware that the British were lagging far behind the United States and France. The first British aviator, J. F. C. Moore-Brabazon, did not learn to fly until December 1908, and even then it was in France on a Voisin-Farman. Northcliffe was certain that the challenge, bolstered by his newspaper coverage, would divert attention from the Wright brothers. In turn, this would stimulate more rapid progress in the growth of European and, he hoped, British aviation. Northcliffe thought an Englishman might take the prize until he was told that there were only a handful of pilots and machines capable of covering the 22 miles, none of them in Britain.

Blériot later recalled the most important 37 minutes of his life: "As soon as I am over the cliff I reduce speed. There is now no need to force my engine. I begin my flight sure and steady towards the coast of England. I have no apprehensions, no sensations *pas de tout*." Approaching Dover, he battled

Louis Blériot's monoplane was erected in a farmyard near Calais. While Blériot (in the brown flying helmet) discusses the impending flight with supporters, Madame Blériot can be seen by the tail plane. Describing the trial-and-error years, she told journalists: "Believe me, the domestic side of an aviator's wife's life is not a bed of roses. I can say that for eight years in our home my husband has never spoken to me except about aeroplanes."

LOUIS BLÉRIOT

Louis Blériot, the father of the modern monoplane and the pilot on the first epochal flight, was born in 1872. His earliest designs progressed from flapping wings to biplanes, then to a canard monoplane—a series of hell-bent, trial-and-error experiments that nearly always ended in crashes. They terrified his long-suffering wife but earned him newspaper praise for "courageous impatience."

"Today I will show the world I can fly," the pioneer exclaimed before making a bold dash across the English Channel. The flight that Wilbur Wright had shortsightedly dismissed as "a useless risk" not only promoted European aviation but brought Blériot orders from around the world. He established France's first aircraft factory, producing classic monoplanes that set an array of records. Ironically, the plane that ended England's "island impregnability" went to its defense in World War I. When these airplanes were used as unarmed scouts by the Royal Flying Corps, their hapless pilots were ordered to ram any Zeppelins caught crossing the Channel.

When Blériot died a forgotten man in 1936, his contribution to aviation had been buried under an avalanche of progress. By that time he had witnessed the truth of his prophetic words, uttered after the most glorious 37 minutes of his life: "The aeroplane will bring the peoples of the world closer together with new paths of commerce."

Blériot and his wife pose at the site of his dramatic landing on a hillside near Dover Castle. Madame Blériot sobbed, declaring: "When I followed my husband across the channel I felt almost brave. And now I think I will never tremble again. I am cured. Do you hear this Louis? *Ah la gloire!*"

wind gusts and, it is reputed, a severely overheating engine. This might have been the reason Blériot made a hurried downhill landing that shattered the propeller and landing gear.

Blériot's flight evoked unprecedented public attention. Northcliffe made sure that his headline story went worldwide, attracting the same reaction as Neil Armstrong's moon flight did 60 years later. Normally reserved Britons cheered the French hero through London, and 100,000 spectators lined the boulevards of Paris. Besides firing the public's imagination, Blériot's flight set governments to worrying about the invincibility of their navies. While overoptimistic journalists proclaimed the age of island air travel, others focused on the future military implications.

"No Englishman can learn of the voyage of Blériot without emoting that the day of Britain's impregnability has passed away," one newspaper editorialized. A French cartoonist depicted the ghost of Napoleon looking at Blériot's plane and asking, "Why not a hundred years earlier?" The London *Daily Telegraph* prophesied: "Air power will become as vital to us as sea power has ever been." Attacking British upper-class complacency and lack of initiative, H. G. Wells wrote:

A contemporary cigar box celebrates Louis Blériot's epochal flight across the English Channel in July 1909. The Blériot XI is shown overtaking its escort, the French destroyer *Escopette*, which also carried Madame Blériot to England.

One meaning I think stands out plainly enough, unpalatable to our national pride. This thing [the aircraft] from first to last was made abroad. Gliding began when our young men of muscle and courage were braving the dangers of the cricket ball. The motor car and its engine was being worked out over there.... Over there, where the prosperous classes have some regard for education ... where people discuss things fearlessly and have a respect for science, this has been achieved. It means I take it, first and foremost for us, that the world cannot wait for the English. It is not the first warning we have had. It's been raining warnings on us—never was a slacking, dull people so liberally served with warnings of what was in store for them.

Although Blériot's flight was a catalyst, it was five years before Britain caught up. During that period, advances in design were slow, but steady progress was made in improving engine reliability. By 1911 cross-country flights were becoming commonplace in Europe, where the French continued to dominate. Pierre Prier flew nonstop from London to Paris in a Blériot in April, Jules Vedrines won a race from Paris to Madrid, and in June Lieutenant

In May 1911, France's Jules Vedrines was the only competitor to finish the cross-country race from Paris to Madrid. After battling across the Pyrenees in his Morane monoplane, he arrived in Madrid to find that the impatient crowd had gone home. An angry Vedrines gave officials a taste of his temper, even criticizing Spain's King Alfonso XII. Tantrums were to become his trademark. Nevertheless, the king forgave Vedrines and invited him to the bullfights.

Jules Vedrines battled his way out of the slums of Paris to become one of France's great early aviators. Besides his success in the long-distance races of 1911 and a series of world speed records, he linked France and Egypt by air in 1913. He was killed in 1919 preparing for a flight around the world via Australia, China, and Alaska.

The cover of *The Aero* magazine honored French naval Lieutenant Jean Conneau, who was the most successful pilot of 1911. Racing his Blériot XI under the pseudonym "Beaumont," he won Europe's three major long-distance races that year: the 1,000-mile Circuit of Europe, the Circuit of Britain, and the Paris-Rome race. His success was largely due to his rare ability to navigate by map and compass.

The Aero magazine featured this montage of some of the 19 flyers entered in the 1911 Circuit of Britain. British contestants included (1) Gustav Hamel, (4) "Colonel" Sam Cody, (6) H. J. D. Astley, (8) James Valentine, and (9) Collyns Pizey. The French contingent included (3) G. Blanchet, (7) O. de Montalent, (2) Jules Vedrines, and (5) Jean Conneau, the eventual winner.

Jean Conneau took another race from Paris to Rome. The next month Conneau in his Blériot defeated 42 other pilots racing in stages around Europe ("the Circuit of Europe") and then won Lord Northcliffe's 1,000-mile race around Great Britain ("the Circuit of Britain"). Air fever struck even in remote Russia as 11 Russian and foreign pilots raced more than 400 miles from Saint Petersburg to Moscow in late July for a $35,000 prize.

American pilots also were making hazardous cross-country flights. Canadian John A. D. McCurdy made a courageous 90-mile over-water crossing from Key West to Havana in a Curtiss. Harry Atwood flew a Wright Model B biplane 1,300 miles from St. Louis to New York in 12 days in August 1911, and on September 29 Walter Brookins set an American record by flying 192 miles from Chicago to Springfield, Illinois, making two stops. But the flyer who captured American hearts was a genial, nearly deaf ex-college football star named Calbraith Perry Rodgers.

Taking off from New York in a Wright EX (Experimental) biplane, the *Vin Fiz*, Cal Rodgers hopped westward across America, battling to capture the $50,000 prize that newspaper tycoon William Randolph Hearst had offered for the first transcontinental flight. Even though he had only reached Springfield, Illinois, when Hearst's 30-day time limit expired on October 10, Rodgers, chomping on his ever-present cigar, proclaimed, "Prize or no prize, I am bound for California."

Egged on by a $5-per-mile sponsorship from the Armour Meat Packing

Company to promote a subsidiary's grape drink, Vin Fiz (the airplane carried the trademark emblazoned across the bottom of its lower wing in a pioneering aerial advertising effort), Rodgers survived 19 crashes, 5 of them serious. Only the rudder and oil drip pan of his original Wright EX remained once his 49-day marathon had ended. Describing his arrival at Pasadena's packed Tournament Park on November 5, the New York *Times* stated: "The enormous throng broke through the police guards and swept over the field almost mobbing the aviator.... The people simply went mad. Thousands of them will be unable to talk above a whisper for several days so loudly did they cheer this man who had set a new mark in aviation."

Cal Rodgers takes off from Sheepshead Bay, New York, on the start of his 49-day coast-to-coast marathon. His Wright EX (Experimental) *Vin Fiz* was a smaller, single-seat version of the Wright Model B. Equipped with wheels and skids, it had a top speed of around 60 mph. Little of the original aircraft remained after Rodgers crashed his way across the country to California.

At the scheduled stops, Rodgers's sponsors ensured that there were crowds and photographers to greet the cheerful giant. Rodgers died in 1912 after hitting a flock of sea gulls and crashing into the Pacific surf at Long Beach, where he had landed *Vin Fiz* on the sand a few months earlier. His tombstone reads: "I endure—I conquer."

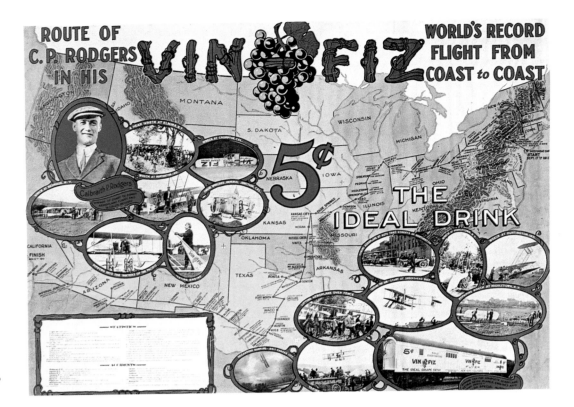

Cal Rodgers's sponsor, Vin Fiz, was one of the first companies to realize the advertising potential of the airplane. His route followed the railway line, and the company provided a special support train emblazoned *Vin Fiz* that carried his wife, his mother, mechanics, spare parts, fuel, and a racing car to rush the flyer, if needed, to the hospital. As Rodgers gamely crashed his way across the continent, the sensational epic became an advertiser's dream. After the flight, Vin Fiz issued this superb promotional poster.

Underlining women's entry into the male-dominated world of aviation, America's first woman pilot, Harriet Quimby, crossed the English Channel in 1912. Moments before take-off, her ground crew held her brakeless Blériot XI while England's Gustav Hamel gave the New York journalist last-minute advice. She died three months later, falling from her air-plane at the Harvard-Boston Aviation Meet.

Over the following years, pilots continued to gain public attention at air shows and speed competitions and by making pioneering cross-country flights. France's Roland Garros captured world attention with the first flight across the Mediterranean, traveling from France to Tunisia on September 23, 1913, and Jules Vedrines flew the 2,500-mile overland route from France to Egypt in November–December 1913. America's Harriet Quimby brought women into the contention with a flight across the English Channel on April 16, 1912, missing world publicity when she was upstaged by the *Titanic* disaster. The flying machine became an international phenomenon as the first barnstormers loaded their machines on liners and sailed to the far corners of the world.

Despite the increasing reliability of these flying machines, the public and most governments still considered airplanes to be dangerous contrap-tions piloted by daring fools. Even so, there was a growing popularity in joy-riding as profligate society thrill seekers frequently paid $1,000 for a brief ride. But only the farsighted saw the airplane as a future method of public transportation.

Its military potential was a different matter. By 1913, even though war was still waged by battleships and cavalry, most developed nations had attached small military aviation wings to their armies and navies. However, the airplane's wartime role was perceived as that of an observation platform for spying on the enemy or directing artillery fire. As early as October 1911, the Italian Air Flotilla had used a Blériot to observe Turkish forces in Libya. Then, on November 1, Lieutenant Giulio Gavatti dropped Cipelli grenades on the Turks; this was the first recorded use of an aircraft for bombing.

Tsarist Russia had founded an Imperial Russian Flying Corps in 1910 and then had held a military design competition. The winner, a young inventor named Igor Sikorsky, became the country's leading aircraft designer. Whereas his counterparts around the world still concentrated on small, single-engine aircraft, the young Russian decided that the future lay with large multiengine passenger machines able to carry heavy loads over long distances.

Many aeronautical experts were still scoffing at Sikorsky's ideas in May 1913, when his first four-engine design, *Le Grand*, also known as the *Russkiy vitaz* (Russian Knight), a four-ton mammoth capable of lifting a 1,625-pound load, flew over Saint Petersburg. Within a year he had built a second machine, called the *Il'ya Muromets* after a legendary Russian warrior, which could carry 16 passengers in the armchairs and sofa of its glazed cabin. Sikorsky made a spectacular long-distance flight to demonstrate the aircraft's potential.

On June 29, 1914, the *Il'ya Muromets* took off from Komendantskiy Field near Saint Petersburg on a 1,590-mile round trip to Kiev. Sikorsky's crew consisted of a second pilot, a navigator, and a flight mechanic. To minimize flying in turbulence, much of the flight was conducted during the cool twilight. After a flight of eight and a half hours, which included the first true

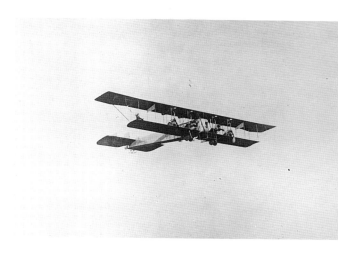

A daring crewman waves from the wingtip of an early *Il'ya Muromets*. The aircraft's lower wing incorporated a plywood walkway, allowing the crew to perform in-flight maintenance on the engines.

Igor Sikorsky's five-ton *Il'ya Muromets* was the genesis of today's airliner. This photo shows its 100-horsepower Argus engines. The revolutionary enclosed fuselage was built for comfort and housed the crew cockpit, a passenger lounge, a bedroom, and a toilet.

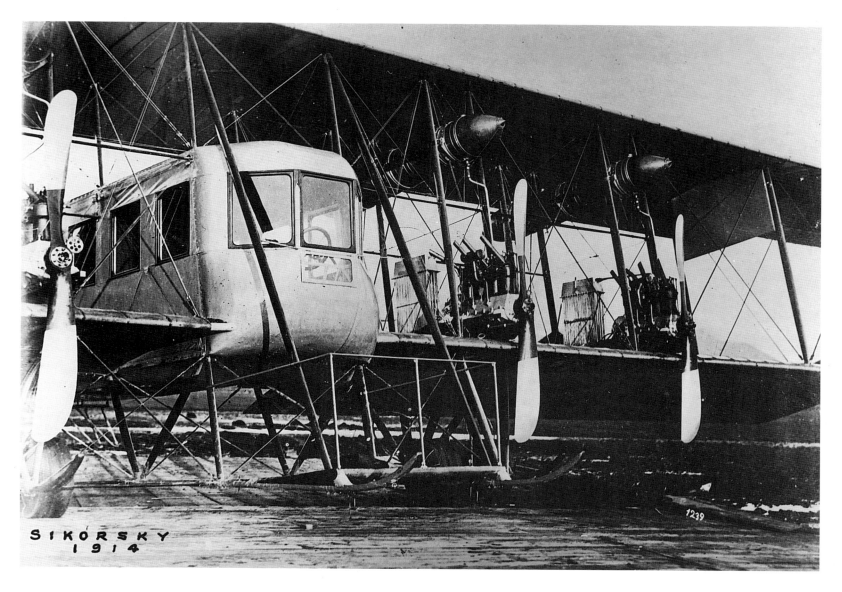

The Story of the Winged S

BY IGOR I. SIKORSKY

Igor Sikorsky was one of the most innovative aircraft designers of the century. In 1913, when many designers were struggling to build small, single-engine airplanes, Sikorsky stretched the limits of the aeronautics of his day when he built and flew the four-engine *Le Grand* and the even larger *Il'ya Muromets* the following year. After the Russian Revolution, he emigrated to the United States and established Sikorsky Aero Engineering Corporation, which pioneered the development of large helicopters.

Tired and somewhat frozen, but well satisfied with my first night flight which had been accomplished in rough weather, I returned to our hangar and there received a message that included an invitation to dinner by the Chairman of the Board of the Russian Baltic Company. I just had time to change my flying suit and start for this dinner party, little realizing at that moment that this evening would have fundamental consequences for my whole life....

It was around eight o'clock on the cold and windy evening of September 17th that I arrived at the home of Mr. Shidlowsky which was located in a good residential section of Petrograd....

There was silence while we drank black coffee which we both liked and, feeling that my chief was not inclined to discuss business, I changed the subject and briefly outlined a few of my general ideas on the subject of the future of aviation. I mentioned that the airplane of the future must be much larger in size, weight and power, must be designed along different lines, and would prove to be much more successful and more reliable than small, single-engined planes. When I stopped my host suggested that I continue my story. I went on describing in more detail the

characteristics of the air giants of the future; the necessity of several motors, one independent of the other, as the only protection from hazards of forced landing in case of engine failure which was so frequent at that time; the importance of a crew of several men who would assist and relieve each other and fulfill the duties of the pilot at the control wheel, the navigator, the mechanic and others. To enable them to perform their duties properly, a large, comfortable closed cabin was necessary, particularly in the severe climate of Russia....

During this discussion I stopped once in a while, but each time Mr. Shidlowsky would urge me to continue with more details. Encouraged, I went more to the point and informed him that for more than one year I had been working on the actual plans of a plane with four motors, a closed cabin and various other new characteristics. I pointed out that no such ship had ever been successfully produced and that the idea was condemned as impossible by many, if not by most, of the authorities on aviation. It was my firm conviction, however, that such an airplane could be produced and that if built and demonstrated, it would open the road to most interesting and encouraging possibilities....

Early in 1913 the fuselage and wings were well under way and produced a substantial impression. The factory personnel started to call the new plane by a short but suitable name, "The Grand"— in the French sense, meaning "large."...

In April the parts of the "Grand" were transported to the military field for general assembly. Soon afterward we had the satisfaction and thrill of seeing the "Grand" fully assembled for the first time....

The "Grand" weighed gross about 9000 pounds. It had a

in-flight meal, Sikorsky landed at Orsha, the midway refueling stop, where the aircraft's tanks were filled to their 2,425-pound capacity. The giant aircraft took off in less than "400 paces"—Sikorsky's measurement of Orsha's improvised airfield.

Soon after leaving Orsha, Sikorsky was forced to shut down one engine when a fuel leak caused a fire. Two crewmen crawled out along the lower wing and extinguished the flames. After flying for a while on three engines —proving his theory of multiengine safety—Sikorsky landed, repaired the fuel line, and continued on to Kiev. During this part of the flight, the *Il'ya Muromets* encountered heavy clouds, persistent rain, and severe turbulence, forcing Sikorsky to fly for long periods by compass. Sikorsky's flight to his hometown of Kiev lasted nearly 13 hours. The return to Saint Petersburg took just over 10 hours of flying time—30 hours total time including the refueling stop—and set an unofficial world distance record. Sikorsky now held nine world records in various duration, distance, and altitude categories.

The flight had confirmed Sikorsky's belief in large multiengine airliners that could carry passengers in comfort and safety over long distances in all span of ninety-two feet and was powered by four 100-horsepower, four-cylinder, water-cooled Argus motors. Besides the size and general arrangement, substantially novel ideas were incorporated in the pilot's and passenger cabins. The front part was occupied by a large balcony; next came the closed pilot's cabin with two seats, double control and all flying instruments. A door in front permitted stepping out on the balcony, while the rear door would open into the main passenger cabin....

Finally, late in the afternoon of May 13, 1913, the "Grand" was ready to fly....

My flight mechanic was at the front balcony ready to give the sign to release the ship to the men who were holding it by the wings. The runway was clear. I gradually opened the throttles....

The plane gradually gained speed along the soft, wet runway. A few seconds later I could feel that the tail went up and the ship continued to gain speed. Inside the pilot's cabin, high above the ground and protected from the air stream, the impression was that the motion was very slow. However, the elevator, and a few seconds later, the ailerons became active, indicating that we were approaching flying speed. I moved the control wheel slowly and slightly backward. The next moment the shocks of the wheels running along the ground disappeared and the earth gradually started to drop away from the plane....

The plane flew extremely smoothly at about sixty miles an hour. It was strange to pilot a ship and not feel a stream of air on the face. Ahead on the front bridge stood the mechanic. Once in a while he would turn his face back with an expression of happiness and triumph. As for myself I had, of course, a feeling of satisfaction, and the huge, steady machine was pleasant to ride, but I was busy with the controls trying to do the important job correctly.

Having reached some four hundred feet, I started to turn to the left. The plane performed nicely. A little later, a second turn at some 600 feet altitude was made, this time passing over the hangars and the point of departure. The mechanic on the front bridge was happily waving his hand to the huge crowd below, the co-pilot behind in the large cabin was looking down through the window. For a short moment a happy realization that this was the long desired achievement flashed through my mind. The next instant, however, I was again busy with the routine test flight....

While still some seven or eight hundred feet high, I tried twice to put the plane in a gliding position, and then by pulling the wheel reproduced a maneuver of normal landing. The plane obeyed so satisfactorily that, contrary to the original program, I decide to make an ordinary landing and not a power stall. About one mile from the field, I turned around and started to come down gradually, aiming at the beginning of the runway. The plane was well under control and having reached the field at an altitude of some fifty feet, I could increase the power slightly and continue to fly over the runway toward the hangars. Having reached the middle of the runway, I cut the engines and easily made an ordinary, reasonably smooth landing. The huge plane came to a stop.

weather conditions. It was a gigantic step forward. Elsewhere, apart from Germany's successful Zeppelin airship airline, passenger carrying still was a matter of thrill seekers joyflighting in the open cockpit of single-engine machines not far removed from the early Wright and Blériot designs. An exception was in the United States, where the St. Petersburg–Tampa Airboat Line started the world's first scheduled airline service on New Year's Day 1914. The company's single-passenger Benoist flying boat carried 1,200 people, at $5 for the 20-mile trip, before the fledgling airline eventually closed at the end of the 1914 tourist season.

The commercial implications of Sikorsky's giant aircraft were not fully appreciated. He received little support in politically troubled tsarist Russia, even though aviation would eventually play a vital role in its vast hinterlands. Elsewhere attention was focused on the military application of the airplane. The day before Sikorsky's remarkable flight, Archduke Francis Ferdinand, heir to the Austro-Hungarian throne, had been assassinated. World War I loomed on the horizon. The *Il'ya Muromets* would become the first long-range heavy bomber—over 70 were produced. In 1920, a demilitarized version briefly

T. O. M. Sopwith founded Sopwith Aviation Company in 1912. His first aircraft was the Sopwith *Tabloid*, which won the 1913 Schneider Cup race. Sopwith was best known for his World War I fighters: the Pup; the Sopwith Triplane; the Camel, of which over 5,000 were built; and the Snipe. Sopwith Aviation closed in 1920, but the Hawker Aircraft Company succeeded it the same year.

constituted Soviet Russia's first airline service, fulfilling Sikorsky's dream. But by then the great designer had fled the Bolshevik Revolution, arriving penniless in the United States to continue his brilliant career.

World War I

The progress of aviation accelerated during the years of World War I. However, the advances were not so much in new design as in improving durability and reliability. Although there was little progress in terms of speed, the need for fighting machines to carry weapons and bombs while patrolling the battlefront had brought great advances in endurance and range. This was particularly evident in the multiengine bombers—mirroring Sikorsky's 1913 giants—that were built in the latter stages of the conflict. More powerful and reliable conventional engines built by companies such as Rolls-Royce, Mercedes, Hispano-Suiza, and Packard and Ford (Liberty engines) steadily replaced the whirling Gnome rotary engines of the early combat days. The best of these engines would carry aviation through the early pioneering postwar years.

The other great advance occurred in the manufacturing process itself. Prior to the war, aircraft were virtually hand-built in small factories and sheds. The unprecedented growth of air power and the horrific attrition rate spawned huge aircraft factories. For example, in 1913 Tom Sopwith's infant company employed six workers and a tea boy casually building a couple of aircraft. By the war's end, Sopwith was employing 3,500 people, 1,000 of them women, and had produced over 16,000 aircraft, with weekly production reaching 90 machines. Britain's total manufacturing capacity peaked at 3,500 airplanes a month. During the four-year conflict, the major combatants built over 160,000 airplanes, including nearly 14,000 built in the United States from April 1917 to November 1918.

After the armistice in 1918, airplane builders and demobilized pilots looked for a different role for their talents. For the new industry to survive, it had to serve the needs of peace. Having outgrown the small prewar market of sporting and socialite flyers, aviation advocates faced the hurdle of changing the public's perception of the airplane as a deadly weapon of war. It was vital that the industry convince hidebound governments and a doubting public that aircraft could have a parallel role as a safe and respectable transportation vehicle. But even the most optimistic among them would not have predicted that aviation would eventually end the era of transcontinental railways and intercontinental ocean liners.

The Atlantic Challenge

Like the English Channel in 1909, the Atlantic Ocean soon became a major challenge to distance flyers. To fly overland was one thing, but to risk one's life for 1,900 miles over water required a much greater faith in aircraft reliability. Britain's crusading newspaperman Lord Northcliffe opened the challenge four days after the armistice when he announced a prize of £10,000 for the first nonstop Atlantic flight. He had made a similar offer in 1913, and although the task was probably beyond the state of the art, several pilots had entered. Supported by department store magnate Rodman Wanamaker, the American Glenn H. Curtiss had even built the H-4 twin-engine flying boat *America*, only to have the outbreak of the war in Europe thwart his challenge. By early 1919, five British crews were preparing for Northcliffe's new challenge. All planned to use converted military aircraft.

World War I ended before the U.S. Navy's new four-engine Navy Curtiss NC flying boats were commissioned. Aware that impending budget cuts could cripple the new naval air arm, the Navy decided to use three of them on a promotional trans-Atlantic flight. With four 400-horsepower Liberty engines and a wingspan of 126 feet, the 14-ton flying boats were the largest seaplanes of their day. The NC-4, captained by Lieutenant Commander Albert C. Read, was the only one to complete the crossing from Newfoundland to Lisbon.

In the United States, with the war ended, there were ominous signs that the budget-conscious government was planning to wind down the Navy's infant air wing. Worried naval officers, wanting to demonstrate the service's capabilities, decided to attempt an Atlantic crossing with three four-engine Navy Curtiss (NC) flying boats, which were derived from the earlier H-4 series. Although not eligible for Northcliffe's prize, Navy airmen believed that with public attention riveted on the Atlantic, the flight would strengthen their position.

By mid-May four British contenders and the U.S. Navy flying boats had arrived in Newfoundland, Canada, the closest landfall to Ireland. The Americans had chosen a longer but marginally safer southern route with a refueling stop in the Azores. As a further precaution and to assist navigation, Navy warships were stationed every 50 miles. On May 16, while the British were waiting for weather to clear along their northern route, the three seaplanes—NC-1, NC-3, and NC-4—took off on the 1,300-mile leg to the Azores.

Provided that their 400-horsepower Liberty engines performed satisfactorily, it should have been a relatively easy task to follow the string of warships, but foul weather hampered the crews. After pulling ahead of the others, Lieutenant Commander A. C. Read's NC-4 encountered dense clouds and a low ceiling. As they were forced to fly out of sight of the ocean, six worrying hours passed before the crew spotted a destroyer. During the night they flew through turbulent rainstorms before sighting one of the western islands of the Azores through a fortuitous break in the clouds. With the weather rapidly worsening, Read elected to land.

The other two aircraft were not so fortunate. Lost and low on fuel, both made emergency ocean landings. A passing Greek ship eventually rescued the seasick crew of NC-1; the men of NC-3 were less fortunate. For 52 hours they drifted eastward through towering seas, battling to keep their crippled seaplane afloat. When they finally came within striking distance of an island in the Azores group, the men started one engine. Using the last dregs of fuel, NC-3 ended a 200-mile drift by taxiing into Ponta Delgada harbor.

On May 27, NC-4 made the 800-mile crossing to Lisbon, becoming the

To the British public, he was "Harry," the cheery little Australian who flew like the devil. To his employer, Sir Thomas Sopwith, Harry Hawker was the greatest of the early test pilots. After his trans-Atlantic failure and miraculous mid-ocean rescue, Hawker's popularity in Britain reached Lindbergh-like proportions. He died testing an aircraft in 1921.

first aircraft to span the Atlantic. The Newfoundland-Portugal crossing had taken just under 27 hours of flight time.

"American ability, American ingenuity, American thoroughness, American nerve have again come into their own," trumpeted the Washington *Evening Star*. Seeing the biggest newspaper headlines since the armistice, Secretary of the Navy Josephus Daniels sent a gleeful message of congratulations to Read that ended, "Now there will be no stopping the Navy."

The intensity of national rivalry was evident in the British press, which devoted a few miserly inches to the American triumph but produced whole columns about an unsuccessful British challenge.

On May 18, when news had reached Newfoundland that Read had reached the Azores, two of the British crews decided to attempt the crossing. Still hoping to beat the Americans to Europe, Sopwith test pilot Harry Hawker and navigator K. Mackenzie-Grieve were first off in their single-engine Sopwith *Atlantic*, a much-modified Sopwith B.1 bomber. When journalists expressed surprise that Hawker had left before the weather cleared properly, the team manager explained, "He is intensely patriotic and wants the honor to go to England." Overloaded with fuel, the second British machine failed to get airborne.

Hawker's gallant attempt ended in a storm in the mid-Atlantic when the Sopwith's radiator boiled. Far off the normal sea routes, with their engine overheating, the airmen sighted a lone freighter and ditched alongside it. The ship was not radio-equipped, and it was a week before news of their rescue became known. During that time all Britain mourned. An American newspaper editorialized: "Hawker and Mackenzie-Grieve have done better than make a sober addition to the science of flying—they have given a lesson in the art of living and dying. . . . They have not only glorified a country, they have enriched mankind."

England rejoiced at the miraculous rescue. Despite their failure, the two airmen became national heroes, exemplifying the adulation the press and public heaped on the pioneering flyers of the era. Win or lose, their exploits would make world headlines, and their names became household words.

Such was to be the case a month later for John Alcock and Arthur Whitten-Brown. Flying a twin-engined Vickers F. B. (Fighting Biplane) 27 Vimy bomber, they finally made the first nonstop Atlantic crossing on June 14 and 15, 1919. Even so, it was touch and go.

An exhaust manifold blew away early in the flight, making conversation impossible. In clouds for most of the flight, Whitten-Brown was unable to get accurate position fixes, and 11 hours out they unexpectedly ran into turbulent cloud. With no blind-flying instruments, Alcock became disoriented. "We lost

Tom Sopwith's B.1 bomber formed the basis of Harry Hawker's specially built Atlantic biplane. Powered by a 360-horsepower Rolls-Royce Eagle engine, it had landing gear that could be jettisoned, and an upturned lifeboat was built into the rear fuselage decking. A problem in the engine's water-cooling system forced Hawker and Mackenzie-Grieve to ditch in mid-Atlantic.

The Vickers Vimy was produced late in World War I as a heavy bomber. Although originally designed to lift 5,400 pounds of fuel and bombs, this special trans-Atlantic Vimy carried 8,650 pounds of fuel as Alcock and Brown staggered off Lester's Field, Newfoundland. Struggling for height, it briefly disappeared behind the low tree-covered rise shown in this photograph. Onlookers thought the Vimy had crashed.

The first nonstop trans-Atlantic flight ended with the crippled Vickers Vimy perched tail-up in an Irish bog. Soldiers from a nearby military installation thought Alcock and Brown were joking when they claimed to have flown the Atlantic. When a local asked about the crash landing, Alcock replied: "Your bog is like the Irish question, not as easy as it looks. . . ."

our instinct of balance. The machine, left to its own devices, swung, flew amok, and began to perform circus tricks," Brown recalled. A violent spin took them to within a few hundred feet of the sea before they broke through the clouds in a nearly vertical turn. Later in the flight, ice threatened to stop one engine and for a time jammed the ailerons.

When they finally crossed the cloud-shrouded coast of Ireland, Alcock decided to play it safe and land on what appeared to be a lush green meadow. The 16½-hour flight ended minutes later with the Vimy ingloriously perched tail up and nose down in an Irish peat bog. It mattered little. They had crossed the ocean nonstop and were heroes. The pair received congratulations from President Woodrow Wilson and knighthoods from King George V. Canadian headlines dubbed the men "Lords of the Air," and the British press wrote of their "imperishable record." American journalists were equally generous in their praise.

"Like Alexander, the record-making aviator will soon weep because he has no more worlds to conquer. . . . For human daring our hats are off to these Englishmen who fought the sun, the stars and Sir Isaac Newton's best theory and beat them all," the New York Times editorialized. Handing them the $50,000 winner's check, the then Secretary of State for War, Winston

Britain's triumphant trans-Atlantic airmen, Sir John Alcock (left) and Sir Arthur Whitten-Brown, photographed by a Vickers Vimy shortly after their flight in 1919. Generously giving the credit to his navigator, Alcock told newsmen: "My part was simple. It's my trade. The navigation was the ticklish part." Six months later Alcock died, crashing in fog while delivering a Vickers Viking amphibian to France.

Churchill, quipped, "I don't really know what we should admire most in our guests: their audacity, their determination, their skill . . . or their good fortune."

Audacious, determined, skilled they were indeed, as had been all the fliers involved in the Atlantic challenge. None would have denied that both the British and American crews had also had their fair share of luck. Nevertheless, the Atlantic victory had confirmed Vickers's faith in the reliability of their Vimy, particularly its 360-horsepower Rolls-Royce Eagle VIII engines. With plans to market a civil version of the bomber, the company entered a sister ship in the second great long-distance contest of 1919—a flight between England and Australia.

On to Australia

Australia's irascible prime minister, Billy Hughes, promoted the marathon flight. The Welsh-born politician had made several passenger flights and was conscious of the role airplanes might play in his sparsely settled and isolated homeland.

"With a view to stimulating aerial activity, the Commonwealth Government has decided to offer £10,000 for the first successful flight to Australia from Great Britain, in a machine manned by Australians," the official announcement proclaimed. The rules stipulated that the flight had to be completed in 30 days.

Equally conscious of the need to arouse interest in commercial flying, Britain's Controller of Civil Aviation, Major General Sir F. H. Sykes, applauded, saying: "I hope all the other Dominions will follow. Then we shall be able to have great prizes hanging out as bait to all ends of the world." However, some Australian newspapers were critical of the government's scheme. The Melbourne Age described it as "A circus flight—a poorly disguised attempt at self-advertisement at the expense of the Australian public."

Though lacking the Atlantic's over-water drama, the 11,340-mile England-to-Australia flight represented a much greater test of endurance for both men and machines. Crews faced the hazards of the European winter, the torrid heat and dust of the Middle East, and severe tropical storms. Of great significance was the fact that the flight was virtually pioneering Europe's future air routes to India, Singapore, the Dutch East Indies, and Australia.

The Vimy was the favorite. The Australian Flying Corps pilots and brothers Captain Ross Smith and Lieutenant Keith Smith were the pilots. Ross Smith's former wartime mechanics, Sergeants Wally Shiers and Jim Bennett, completed the tightly knit crew. Besides the Vimy's Atlantic performance, a major factor in their favor was Ross Smith's wartime experience in desert operations; he had been personal pilot to Lawrence of Arabia. Furthermore, he had already flown the desert route from Cairo to Calcutta.

By early December, four aircraft were spread along the route; a fifth had crashed minutes after takeoff, killing its two crewmen. Across Europe, sleet and snowstorms had slowed all the competitors. On board the Vimy G-EAOU, which the crew joked stood for "God 'Elp All of Us," the windshield iced over and the Smith brothers took turns peering ahead. Each could watch for only a few minutes before their goggles clogged with snow and their faces were covered with icy masks. Even their sandwiches froze solid. In his log, Ross Smith wrote: "This sort of flying is rotten. The cold is hell. I am a silly ass for ever embarking on such a flight."

The crew of a second aircraft was killed when they crashed at night off the coast of Greece. After flying a circuitous route through central Europe to bypass bad weather, another crew was forced down in Yugoslavia and arrested as Bolshevik spies. The remaining contender, the future polar explorer Captain (Sir) Hubert Wilkins, flying a twin-engine Blackburn Kangaroo bomber, force-landed in Crete after an engine failure.

The Vimy kept going. In Egypt, Shiers saved an overheating engine by using chewing gum and friction tape to repair a cracked induction manifold. Resting in the desert near Baghdad, the airmen were caught in a violent sandstorm and, assisted by 50 Bengal Lancers, spent the night holding down the flailing Vimy.

Across Burma and Thailand, down the Malay peninsula to Singapore,

The crew of the Vickers Vimy G-EAOU—with grim humor the airmen said it stood for "God 'elp All Of Us"—stop for a refreshment break in the Australian outback.

violent storms threatened and thrashed the flyers. At Surabaya, bogged in mud, they got away after villagers helped them construct a "runway" of laced bamboo matting: a similar principle employing steel mesh would be used during World War II.

On December 10, days out from London, the Vimy made the 466-mile crossing of the shark-infested Timor Sea and landed at Darwin in northern Australia. They had completed the epic journey in 135 hours of flight time, averaging 75 mph. Australia went aviation-mad. The Smith brothers received knighthoods, and newspapers talked of air services to Europe. Although an international service was still years away, Billy Hughes's grand gesture had paid off by awakening Australians to the possibility of air travel. The following year, Norman Brearley's pioneering West Australian Airways commenced operations; shortly afterward, Queensland and Northern Territory Aerial Service (QANTAS) flew its first outback airline service.

The 1919 successes of the Vimy led to the development of a modified 10-passenger version named the Commercial. Only a few were sold, but they were first in a long line of Vickers airliners. The risks and costs also paid off for Rolls-Royce, which had manufactured the engines for all the British Atlantic challengers and four of the five entrants in the flight to Australia. Their remarkable 360-horsepower Eagle engines earned for the company a reputation for performance and reliability that was to carry them into the future.

Despite the excitement of 1919, the outlook for commercial aviation remained bleak. Worldwide, about a dozen companies were attempting to run profitable airline operations. Likening the problems that faced aviation to those of the early railway engineers, Britain's *Flight* magazine suggested: "It was a very long time before the thinking and conservative public could be brought to discard travel by stage coach and trust themselves to be hustled through the country behind a locomotive. In the matter of aviation there are two things which have to be done. The first is to try out design and construction. The second is to create and maintain public interest and confidence in the aeroplane as a means of travel."

In Great Britain, the short-sighted government did not help the cause, refusing to subsidize commercial aviation. However, in mainland Europe, where the devastation of war had seriously disrupted surface transport in France and Belgium, operators received generous encouragement. In

At Darwin's specially constructed Fanny Bay Airfield, the frontier townsfolk gathered to greet the airmen. Sir Hudson Fysh, who later founded Qantas, recalled the touchdown: "It was one of the most moving sights I can remember. The termination of one of the greatest flights, if not the greatest, in the history of aviation."

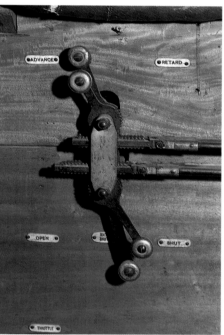

Germany and Holland, this support stimulated the design of a new generation of monoplane airliners that would put them years ahead of other nations. In the United States, both civil and military aviation faced an even greater task gaining acceptance.

The leading edge of heavy aircraft design in 1917, the Vickers Vimy G-EAOU is preserved in a special building at Adelaide Airport, South Australia.

Early Postwar Aviation in the United States

Unlike Europe, the United States did not have available for commercial use a glut of unwanted large military combat aircraft, but plenty of surplus de Havilland DH-4s and DH-9s were available to satisfy the Air Service's needs for years to come. Moreover, the war had not seriously disrupted surface transport. A superb railway service linked most towns and cities, and with aircraft of the day uncomfortable and hard-pressed to average 80 mph, they offered no real advantage over the speed, luxury, and safety of Pullman trains. Moreover, the United States lacked a significant international catalyst, unlike Great Britain and many other European nations, which saw the airplane as a possible future link with far-flung empires. Consequently, the American airlines remained years away.

The struggling U.S. Air Mail Service relied mainly on its Liberty engine powered war-surplus de Havilland DH-4s. In 1920, its airmen flew the first transcontinental airmail. Taking off from Hazelhurst Field, New York, on September 8, an aging DH-4 carried 16,000 letters—some in a suitcase strapped to the wing—on the first leg to Iowa City. Three days later, following a Pony Express—like relay of pilots and planes, the mail reached San Francisco.

For most American surplus military pilots, a career in commercial aviation started with the hand-to-mouth life of an itinerant barnstormer, often in a surplus Curtiss JN-4 Jenny. A handful found work with the struggling air mail service, which, started by the United States Post Office in 1918, had flown 18,806 hours and carried 49 million letters by the end of 1920. In February 1921, as some members of Congress were calling for its disbanding, mail pilots had reduced the coast-to-coast time to 26 hours, prompting the New York *Tribune* to comment: "The feat completed Wednesday was by the very service which certain elements in Congress have just fought desperately to destroy. Can antagonism be continued against such a service with such a record?"

The air mail service was not alone in its battle for survival. With the war over, the government was not interested in the future of military and naval aviation, and appropriations were cut to the bone. There was barely enough to cover the payroll and fuel bills, let alone replace the war-weary de Havilland DH-4s and Curtiss Jenny trainers. This situation had prompted the Navy's trans-Atlantic flight of May 1919.

The plight of U.S. Army aviation was of particular concern to its chief after 1921, Major General Mason M. Patrick. Working behind the scenes, Patrick allowed his outspoken assistant, Brigadier General William "Billy" Mitchell, to be the belligerent advocate of air power, leading the fight for more funds and new aircraft. To demonstrate the versatility of the airplane and keep the service in the public eye, Mitchell encouraged Army pilots to embark on a series of long-distance flights.

The first, a coast-to-coast reliability trial in 1919, had backfired when nine pilots lost their lives. "It proved the necessity of weather reports and other meteorological information for pilots on cross-country flights," the Aircraft Manufacturers Association, Inc., had reported in its 1920 *Aircraft Year Book.* Subsequent Army flights were extremely successful: around the nation's borders; New York to Nome, Alaska; and a series of transcontinental dashes. These flights highlighted the reliability of the Liberty engine that was to be the mainstay of American aviation in the early 1920s. Indeed, it was the Liberty's reliability that in 1923 enabled the Army to achieve the headlines Mitchell had sought.

Given a small appropriation to evaluate new aircraft, Mitchell had purchased two of Anthony Fokker's F. IV high-wing transports, which were modified to take a Liberty 12 engine. The Dutch designer's single-engine monoplanes, along with Hugo Junkers's low-wing F13, were already in airline service in Europe and were swinging the pendulum away from biplanes toward more aerodynamically efficient monoplanes.

The Army Air Service's Fokker F. IVs, called T-2s, were powered by the 400-horsepower Packard Liberty engine, carried eight passengers, and could fly six hours on 130 gallons of fuel. During engineering trials at McCook Field, Ohio, test pilots Lieutenants Oakland G. Kelly and Muir S. Fairchild, who had already begun studying potential aircraft for a nonstop transcontinental flight, determined that a modified T-2 had the load-carrying capacity for such an undertaking. Patrick and Mitchell approved the project in August

Above:
Adapting the Fokker T-2 for transcontinental flight was a masterpiece of ingenious and daring modification. The command seat was jammed beside the Liberty engine. Beneath the fuel tank, a narrow tunnel led to the "off-duty" pilot's seat, which was also equipped with rudimentary controls that were used during crew changeovers.

Above left:
An ardent but abrasive architect of air power, Brigadier General William "Billy" Mitchell (left) got a new boss after his famous 1921 bombing demonstration that upset the Navy. The new Army Air Service Chief, Major General Mason M. Patrick (right), became an equally determined though more tactful supporter of the Air Service and encouraged the Army's pioneering long-distance flights. General Patrick believed strongly that he had to be a flyer himself to understand aviation and establish credibility with his aviators, and so he learned to fly and earned his military aviator's wings in 1923 at the age of 59.

Left:
The Junkers F 13, which first flew in June 1919, was the first all-metal, low-wing monoplane with an enclosed cabin to enter civil airline service. It served in many airlines throughout the world and had an excellent record. The F 13 featured Hugo Junkers's use of duralumin for the airframe and the corrugated metal skin that became a standard feature of Junkers aircraft into the 1930s.

Lieutenants John Macready (left) and Oakley Kelly display their Fokker T-2's transcontinental load of 737 gallons of gasoline and 40 gallons of oil. Calculating that with an 11,000-pound takeoff weight the Fokker's theoretical absolute ceiling would be an inch above ground level, they took off at 10,850 pounds.

1922. Lieutenant John A. Macready, McCook's chief test pilot, was soon appointed copilot when Fairchild was injured in an accident.

The flight was planned with the minute attention to detail that would become the hallmark of NASA's astronaut expeditions a half century later. Besides strengthening the wings and adding extra fuel and oil tanks, they tested various fuels and oils to guarantee the best performance. There was room for only one pilot at the control seat, which was jammed alongside the roaring Liberty engine. An "off-duty" crew position equipped with auxiliary controls was built in the rear of the cabin behind a 450-gallon auxiliary fuel tank. After studying the terrain and weather patterns, the flyers chose a west–east route, starting from Rockwell Field in San Diego, California, and ending at Roosevelt Field on Long Island.

Following two abortive attempts in October and November 1922, one

The route followed by Kelly and Macready on the first nonstop coast-to-coast flight. Proud of their navigation, Macready wrote: "We drew a line across the continent on the map and followed it at night and during the day, with our compass the main reliance a large part of the time. We followed no railroad or established air or mail route and kept our course and exact location throughout, except when high elevations forced us to temporarily deflect from this line."

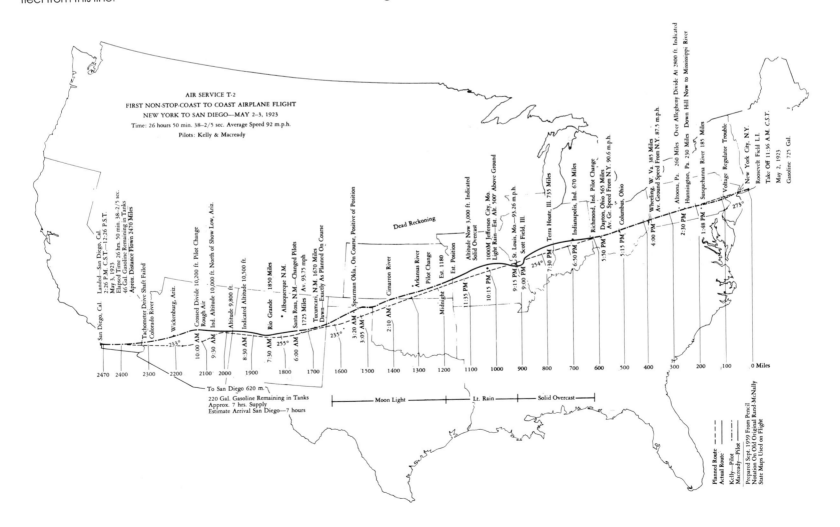

stopped by clouds over the California coastal ranges and the other thwarted by a leaking radiator and cracked cylinder jacket over Indiana, the airmen set off again on May 2, 1923, this time heading west from Roosevelt Field. They needed a push from the ground crew to start the takeoff roll and even then only just got airborne. For the first 20 minutes Kelly flew in ground effect, barely clearing telegraph poles and power lines, waiting for fuel burn-off to reduce the weight. Macready later described their harrowing start: "We scraped along the housetops and hillsides with our Liberty motor running absolutely full power, and for hours we felt as though we could stick out our hands and grab a handful of daisies off the fields."

After they eventually crawled to 1,000 feet and repaired the generator in flight—one advantage of sharing the cabin with the engine—the remainder of the flight was almost an anti-climax of precise, routine operation. Navigation was accomplished by the method of the time: map reading by day and pinpointing the lights of the towns and cities at night. The only surface aid to navigation was a lone searchlight beamed up over Illinois. Exhausted but elated, Kelly and Macready reached San Diego in 26 hours and 50 minutes, averaging 92 mph over 2, 470 miles.

"The greatest significance of this flight is that aviation, given half a chance, will be the greatest factor for progress that has ever existed in the history of civilization," *U.S. Air Service* magazine commented pointedly. A more telling comment came in a fan telegram from 93-year-old Ezra Meeker of New York that read: "Congratulations on your wonderful flight, which beats my time made 71 years ago by ox team at two miles an hour, five months on the way. . . . Ready to go with you next time."

Given reliable engines, the limited fuel-carrying capacity of the aircraft and the endurance of the crew were the primary restrictions on long-distance flying. Even the standard twin-engine bombers of the early 1920s had ranges of only 500 to 600 miles, and so repeated landings and refuelings were necessary to achieve greater distance. If the aircraft could be refueled in flight, only the crew's endurance and mechanical failure would limit the range. Lieutenants Lowell Smith and John Richter completed the first in-flight refueling over Rockwell Field on June 27, 1923. Then, on August 27 and 28, they flew for 37 hours and 15 minutes (3, 291 miles) and were refueled 15 times. The great potential of this technique for extending an aircraft's range was shown in January 1929 when an Air Corps Fokker C-2A, the *Question Mark*, established an air refueling endurance record of 150 hours over

The transcontinental flight of the much modified Fokker T-2 was conducted to promote the U.S. Army Air Service. It generated public uproar when it was announced that as junior officers, Lieutenants Kelly and Macready were barred by red tape from receiving promotion. "The President is only empowered to confer promotions on those officers with ratings of colonel and higher," Secretary of War Weeks told a *Los Angeles Times* reporter, adding lamely, "I will write them a nice letter." The military eventually awarded both men the Distinguished Flying Cross.

AERIAL REFUELING

From the beginning of powered flight, designers and aviators have sought ways to fly farther without stopping to refuel. One obvious solution was larger aircraft that could carry the greater quantities of aviation gasoline required for long-distance flights. Another was more efficient engines that used less fuel. A third was for one aircraft to refuel another in flight so that stopping would be unnecessary until the destination had been reached, the crew was exhausted, or a mechanical failure occurred.

The U.S. Army Air Service took the lead in experimenting with in-flight refueling techniques in the 1920s. Lieutenants Lowell Smith, who later led the around-the-world flight of 1924, and John Richter modified a DH-4B with additional fuel tanks and a hose that could be lowered to transfer fuel to a second modified DH-4B while in flight. They first demonstrated this technique over Rockwell Field, San Diego, California, on June 27, 1923. On August 27 and 28, they flew the DH-4B over San Diego for 37 hours and 16 minutes, with 15 refuelings by the tanker aircraft.

Several years later, the Belgians Crooy and Groenen extended refueled time in the air to 60 hours and 7 minutes. The U.S. Army Air Corps set a world mark in early January 1929 when a Fokker C-2A transport, the *Question Mark*, flew for 150 hours over southern California without landing. The crew, which included future Air Force leaders Carl A. "Tooey" Spaatz, Ira C. Eaker, and Elwood "Pete" Quesada, flew nearly 13,500 miles, and the aircraft was refueled 37 times, receiving 5,600 gallons of gasoline and 245 gallons of oil. In-flight refueling had obvious military implications, as Spaatz reported, because bombers could take off with lighter fuel loads and thus more bombs, be refueled, and have an almost unlimited radius of action.

In September 1934, Alan Cobham outfitted his Airspeed Courier to fly nonstop from London to India, refueled in flight by a Handley Page W.10 aerial tanker. Cobham reached Malta before mechanical difficulties forced him to land. He later formed Flight Refueling, Ltd., that did additional work on aerial refueling techniques and equipment, but the pressures and realities of World War II did little to stimulate further development.

In the early postwar years, the British pushed the "probe-and-drogue," or trailing hose, method of in-flight refueling. Faced with significant range problems in reaching potential Soviet targets with its B-29s, the U.S. Air Force turned to aerial refueling as a way to increase the combat range of its aircraft while awaiting the intercontinental B-36s and B-52s that were in production and development. In November 1947, the Air Force asked Boeing to convert a B-29 to a tanker configuration using the British probe-and-drogue gravity feed system. Experiments with the new KB-29 in May 1948 proved the concept, and the Air Force directed Boeing to convert more B-29s to KB-29 aerial tankers. The KB-29s that refueled the B-50A *Lucky Lady II* on its 94-hour around-the-world flight from February 26 to March 2, 1949, conclusively proved the ability of in-flight refueling to extend the combat radius of the Strategic Air Command's bomber force. With tankers at forward air bases, SAC's medium bombers—B-29s, B-50s, and the new all-jet B-47s—could be based securely in the continental United States and strike any target in the world within hours.

As was typical of Boeing, when the Air Force first directed the new tanker program, the company developed some of its own concepts into important realities. In May 1948, Boeing suggested a new type of refueling apparatus, a "flying boom," to replace the probe-and-drogue system. The Boeing concept was a rigid system of telescoping pipes and pumps that could provide more fuel per minute to the receiver. Fitted to a KB-29, the Boeing system was so successful that the Air Force soon began converting its B-50s to KB-50K tankers with the flying boom system.

Conversion of aging bombers was not the solution to the worldwide refueling requirements of the Air Force, especially with the all-jet B-47s replacing the older piston-engine B-29s and B-50s. In 1950, Boeing and the Air Force converted a C-97A Stratofreighter—the military equivalent of the commercial Model 377 Stratocruiser—to an aerial tanker as the KC-97. By 1953 Boeing had produced 801 KC-97E/F/Gs for the Air Force, primarily to refuel the B-47s.

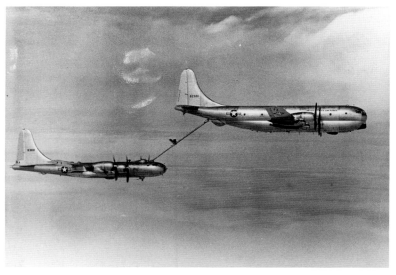

The introduction of the KC-97s allowed the Air Force to deploy its forces rapidly to any trouble spot in the world. When the Korean War began in 1950, SAC deployed some of its strategic fighter units to the Far East, but they had to be crated and shipped on aircraft carriers, and then three weeks were needed to get them into operation. In July 1952, 58 F-84Gs moved from Georgia to Japan in 11 days with air refueling support. By the early 1970s, the use of KC-135s and aerial refueling made the rapid deployment of tactical fighters and strategic bombers from bases in the United States to the war zones in southeast Asia relatively routine. In the spring of 1972, such air refueling support allowed an entire tactical fighter wing of 72 F-4Ds to move from New Mexico to Thailand and to fly combat sorties within a week.

The introduction of the B-52 intercontinental bomber in the mid-1950s led to the development of the KC-135A Stratotanker in tandem with the civilian Model 367-80 (707). The KC-135 could match the B-52 in speed and could carry 31,200 gallons of fuel in its 297,000-pound gross weight. Using the flying

boom system, the KC-135 could transfer up to 1,000 gallons per minute to receivers. The B-52 and KC-135 have remained teamed since the first KC-135s became operational in 1957, but the tankers have also been used on a wide variety of other missions, including refueling fighter deployments, airborne command posts, and transports such as the C-5B. A simple idea to extend an aircraft's range had become an indispensable element of air power.

Facing page (top):
The KC-97 equipped with Boeing's flying boom in-flight refueling system answered many of the U.S. Air Force's immediate needs for aerial refueling in the early 1950s. Usually mated with the Strategic Air Command's B-47 medium bombers at forward bases, the KC-97s provided an important strategic asset well into the 1960s. After the B-47s were retired, the KC-97s continued to serve in the Tactical Air Command, Air National Guard, and Air Force Reserve for a number of years.

Facing page (bottom):
A Strategic Air Command KC-97, its boom extended, locks into the receiver's receptacle to refuel a B-50D.

Top:
This KC-135 is refueling F-16A Fighting Falcon fighters from the 8th Tactical Fighter Wing as they cross the Pacific toward Kunsan Air Base in Korea. In-flight refueling vastly enhances the United States' worldwide air-power effectiveness.

Left (top):
The all-jet KC-135A provided the U.S. Air Force with an aerial refueling capability that did not seriously degrade the speed of the jet fighters and bombers being refueled, as was the case, at 340 mph, with the KC-97. The KC-135As were immediately paired with the B-52s to produce an effective strategic team. Here a KC-135 has refueled a Tactical Air Command F-111.

Left (bottom):
An E-4A airborne command post pulls up to a KC-135A for a lengthy refueling. From the boom operator's position, the telescoping pipe, which can transfer 1,000 gallons of fuel per minute, is visible as is the receptacle in the E-4A's nose section.

March Field, California. Only with bigger aircraft and improved technology did aerial refueling fully mature after World War II.

After the T-2 flight, the Army set its distance sights on the most important pioneering flight of the time in terms of difficulty and international prestige, the circumnavigation of the world. There had already been ill-conceived British and French attempts, and by late 1923 news of further challenges had come from Italy, Argentina, Great Britain, France, and Portugal. World interest heightened at the prospect of an informal race.

The people of Portugal, hoping to promote an aerial heir to Ferdinand Magellan, publicly subscribed to an attempt by Majors Brito Pias and Sarmento Beires. Portugal had burst on the world scene the previous year when two of its naval fliers, Captains Sacadura Cabral and Gago Coutinho, had made an island-hopping first crossing of the south Atlantic. Although the flight took over two months and resulted in the wrecking of two of the Portuguese Navy's three seaplanes, the airmen's courage had fired national pride.

Until the U.S. Army became involved, the British challenge, mounted by Vickers to promote the new Vulture amphibian, seemed the best organized. Pilot A. Stuart MacLaren had even shipped a spare Vulture ahead to Tokyo. But the Vickers preparations paled against Major General Patrick's plan to use four specially constructed biplanes adapted from the Douglas Aircraft Company's DT-2 torpedo bomber. Powered by the trusted Liberty engine, these Douglas World Cruisers could operate on both floats and wheels. The carefully chosen route was divided into seven sections, each with its own support team and advance officer dispatched ahead to make arrangements and establish supply dumps. U.S. Navy vessels were stationed along the route. As with the transcontinental flight, nothing was left to chance. The project was a masterpiece of planning and organization, the key to its eventual success.

Choosing an eastbound route, the British were the first off on March 25, 1924. Sarcastic onlookers suggested that the overladen Vickers took so much water to get airborne that it had been designed to water-taxi around the world. The Portuguese left Lisbon eight days later, also heading east. On April 6, the U.S. Army's four Douglas World Cruisers took off from Seattle, bound for Japan via Alaska and the Aleutians. France's Captain Peltier D'Oisy left Paris on

Douglas World Cruisers depart for Seattle from Clover Field, near the Douglas factory in Santa Monica. At Seattle their wheels were replaced with floats for the flight around the northern rim of the Pacific Ocean. They were reconfigured as land planes to cross Asia and Europe, and floats were reinstalled for the Atlantic crossing.

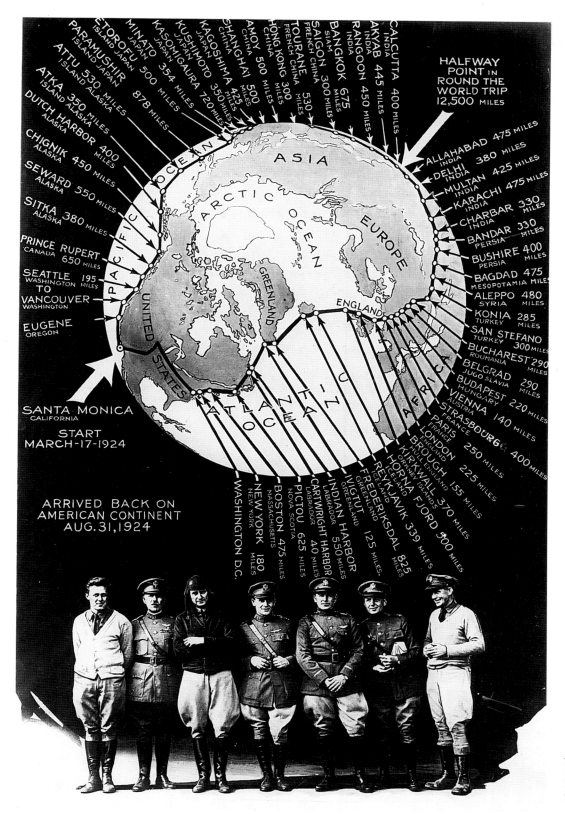

ETOROFU ISLAND JAPAN
PARAMUSHIR ISLAND JAPAN 530 MILES
ATTU ISLAND ALASKA 878 MILES
ATKA ISLAND ALASKA 350 MILES
DUTCH HARBOR ALASKA 400 MILES
CHIGNIK ALASKA 450 MILES
SEWARD ALASKA 550 MILES
SITKA ALASKA 380 MILES
PRINCE RUPERT CANADA 650 MILES
SEATTLE WASHINGTON 195 MILES
TO VANCOUVER WASHINGTON
EUGENE OREGON
SANTA MONICA CALIFORNIA
START MARCH-17-1924
ARRIVED BACK ON AMERICAN CONTINENT AUG.31,1924

MINATO JAPAN 500 MILES
KASUMIGAURA JAPAN 354 MILES
KUSHIMOTO JAPAN 720 MILES
KAGOSHIMA JAPAN 350 MILES
SHANGHAI CHINA 425 MILES
AMOY CHINA 500 MILES
HONG KONG CHINA 500 MILES
TOURANE FRENCH CHINA 300 MILES
SAIGON FRENCH CHINA 530 MILES
BANGKOK SIAM 300 MILES
RANGOON INDIA 675 MILES
AKYAB INDIA 450 MILES
CALCUTTA INDIA 445 MILES 400 MILES

ASIA
ARCTIC OCEAN
PACIFIC OCEAN
EUROPE
GREENLAND
ENGLAND
UNITED STATES
ATLANTIC OCEAN

HALFWAY POINT IN ROUND THE WORLD TRIP 12,500 MILES

ALLAHABAD INDIA 475 MILES
DELHI INDIA 380 MILES
MULTAN INDIA 425 MILES
KARACHI INDIA 475 MILES
CHARBAR INDIA 330 MILES
BANDAR PERSIA 330 MILES
BUSHIRE PERSIA 400 MILES
BAGDAD MESOPOTAMIA 475 MILES
ALEPPO SYRIA 480 MILES
KONIA TURKEY 285 MILES
SAN STEFANO TURKEY 300 MILES
BUCHAREST ROUMANIA 290
BELGRAD JUGO-SLAVIA 290 MILES
BUDAPEST HUNGARY 220 MILES
VIENNA AUSTRIA 140 MILES
STRASBOURG FRANCE 400 MILES
PARIS FRANCE 250 MILES
LONDON ENGLAND 225 MILES
BROUGH HULL ENGLAND 155 MILES
KIRKWALL ORKNEY ISLANDS 370 MILES
REYKJAVIK ICELAND 500 MILES
HORNA FJORD ICELAND 339 MILES
FREDERIKSDAL GREENLAND 300 MILES
IVIGTUT GREENLAND 125 MILES
INDIAN HARBOR LABRADOR 40 MILES
CARTWRIGHT LABRADOR 550 MILES
PICTOU NOVA SCOTIA 625 MILES
BOSTON MASSACHUSETTS 475 MILES
NEW YORK NEW YORK 180 MILES
WASHINGTON D.C.

Although this composite picture has some inaccuracies, it clearly illustrates the land-hugging route required by the Army's world flight.

April 24, supposedly bound for China; he was hoping to circle the world. Three months passed before the Italian and Argentinean crews departed, by which time only the Americans were still airborne.

The American world flight took 175 days to complete. Only two of the original four aircraft completed the 26,345-mile epic in 363 hours and 7 minutes of flying time. One aircraft had crashed in Alaska, and another had force-landed in the north Atlantic. Both crews survived.

"In what is probably the greatest opportunity for future scientific development of transportation your enterprise has made America first. I trust the appreciation of your countrymen will be sufficient so that in this field America will be kept first," said President Calvin Coolidge's official homecoming greeting.

But his words had a hollow ring. Only three months later General Patrick was again pleading for increased funds. Highlighting the plight of American aviation, he stated, "There is today in the United States no commercial aviation deserving of the name, and the aeronautical manufacturing industry is unprepared to meet the demand for quantity production in the event of an emergency."

As an exercise in showing the flag, the U.S. Army undertaking had been an unqualified success. Besides being lionized at home, the American flyers received tumultuous receptions at the cities they visited during their flight. Nevertheless, the team effort and ground support they required (the two victorious World Cruisers wore out 10 engines) highlighted the fact that the aircraft of the day were still too imperfect, and the facilities too sparse, for an unattended machine. Indeed, none of the other challengers completed the flight. D'Oisy shed tears after wrecking his Breguet XIX in Shanghai. The U.S. Navy rescued Italy's Antonio Locatelli after he ditched his Dornier Wal in the north Atlantic. Argentina's Pedro Zanni wrecked his Fokker taking off from Hanoi, and Portugal's hopes ended when the aircraft was severely damaged at Macao.

After wrecking his first Vickers in Burma, MacLaren was able to continue when the World Cruiser team leader, Lieutenant Lowell Smith, arranged for the Navy to ship its rival's spare aircraft from Tokyo. "Hats off to the Stars and Stripes for real sportsmanship," MacLaren cabled. The English challenge ended when the Vickers was forced down by fog near an island in the Bering Sea while heading for the Aleutians.

Pioneering the International Commercial Airways

Despite continuing indifference to commercial aviation in the United States, elsewhere in the world significant airline activity was taking place, with Junkers and Fokker monoplanes playing a major role. The idea of air travel was slowly taking hold in Europe, and 17 nations were operating airlines by the end of 1924. Elsewhere, Australia, Canada, Japan, South America, and Persia had air services.

Nations with colonial ties began to contemplate overseas services. The timesaving possibilities of international air travel were staggering. Besides the development of suitable long-range passenger aircraft, however, the task of persuading the skeptical public to travel such vast distances by air remained. Nevertheless, by 1925 both the British and the Dutch were scouting the route to their Far East possessions.

The eccentric, monocled, aristocratic visionary and director-general of aviation, Sir William Sefton Brancker, who had previously managed Britain's pioneering airline, Aircraft Transport and Travel, Ltd., led the British thrust. To experience a proposed route, Brancker completed an 18,000-mile survey to Rangoon, Burma, and back in a single-engine de Havilland D.H.50 biplane. His pilot, Alan Cobham, was employed to promote the company's aircraft; British designers still clung tenaciously to their slow but safe biplanes. A K.L.M. (Royal Dutch Airlines) Fokker F. VII monoplane surveying the route to Batavia (Jakarta) in the Dutch East Indies (Indonesia) had preceded Cobham and Brancker along the route.

Cobham's flight with Brancker was the first of a series of airline route surveys that were to make him a giant among long-distance pilots. In November 1925, accompanied by mechanic A. B. Elliott and a photographer, he flew from London to Capetown, his D.H.50 emblazoned with the message "Imperial Airways Air Route Survey." Arriving back in London 45 stops and 17,000 miles later, Cobham announced that service to the southern tip of Africa was feasible.

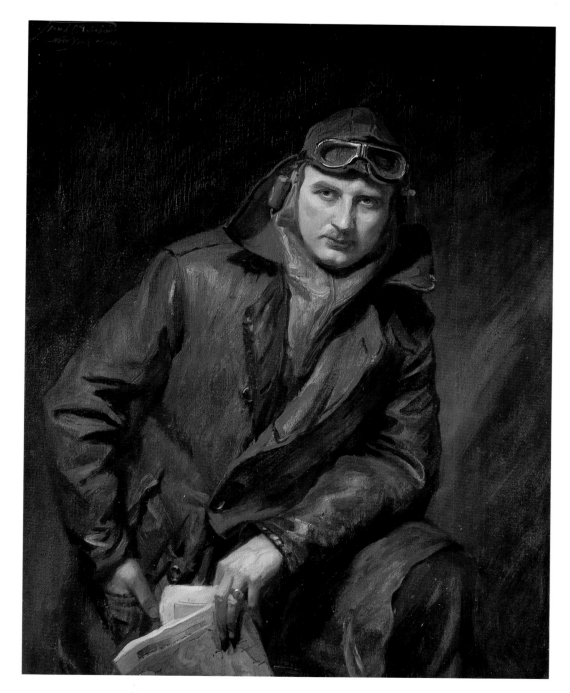

Between the two world wars, Sir Alan Cobham became a household name in Great Britain. The former air force pilot and barnstormer was called "the air ambassador of the Empire." Besides his airline–proving flights, Cobham also brought aviation to Britain's masses. Cobham's Air Display flying circuses put on over 12,000 performances and carried nearly 1 million passengers. His Flight Refuelling company pioneered techniques for extending range by using aerial tankers.

However, Cobham was dissatisfied with his government's unenthusiastic reaction to civil aviation and looked for a new way to generate attention. Someone suggested that he land on the Thames alongside the Houses of Parliament and deliver a petition. Cobham explained his reaction: "I had a brainwave. What if I terminated one of my long-distance flights in that manner, when the eyes of the world—and the press above all—were already on me? What if I flew to Australia with such a return in view?"

Mindful of his Thames destination, Cobham equipped his D.H.50 with floats, and on June 30, 1926, he and Elliott took off for Australia. Cobham later recalled feelings of foreboding crossing Europe and the Middle East. Near Baghdad, they were flying low over an area where the Royal Air Force (RAF) had recently bombed warring Arabs when one took a potshot at the airplane, fatally wounding Elliott. A distraught Cobham almost gave up, but urged by Brancker, he continued with a new mechanic.

Air-minded Australia gave them a riotous reception. In Sydney, a newspaper reported, "They were engulfed in a wave of humanity, who cheered and threw hats and everything movable in the air." In Melbourne, authorities feared for their lives as thousands swept past barriers and surged onto the landing ground as Cobham touched down. Scuffles broke out as the crowd rushed the official enclosure.

Six weeks later, the banks and boats of the Thames were jammed with cheering Londoners as Cobham's D.H.50 flew down over Westminster Bridge onto the water. He had no need to enter the Houses of Parliament to deliver his petition, for waiting on the riverbank stood almost the entire membership of Britain's government. Cobham's monumental 28,000-mile flight, made in 68 stages and 326 hours of flying time, had taken three months to complete.

Cobham's three survey flights linked Britain with the parts of its empire where an airline service was practical and necessary. However, three years passed before Imperial Airways opened its route to India, and nine years before the airline's ponderous biplanes carried passengers to Australia. By then K.L.M., which had been flying to Indonesia for four years, was reequipping with modern Douglas airliners. Nevertheless, more than any other British pilot, Cobham laid the foundations for international air travel, a fact that was recognized when he was knighted by King George V. Justifying his rather "un-British" display of showmanship, Cobham wrote, "I did bring civil aviation right up to the seat of government and the attention of the powerful, physically and in a most dramatic way."

Cobham also played a role in the production of the most famous British light aircraft of the era. When asked the ideal specifications for a small touring biplane, he told Geoffrey de Havilland that it must have a range of 350 miles, cruise at 80 mph, and have a spare seat for the pilot's girlfriend. The company quickly produced the D.H.60 Moth, which Cobham tested by flying a round trip from London to Zurich in one day.

In the 1930s, reengined with de Havilland's remarkably economical and reliable 120-horsepower Gipsy engine, D.H.60s would set an array of records and become one of the world's most successful aerial tourers. Jim Mollison, C. W. A. Scott, and Francis Chichester dashed between England and Australia in the little biplane. In their slipstream followed women record setters: England's Amy Johnson, New Zealand's Jean Batten, and Australia's Lores Bonney.

Just as the Gipsy Moth was to become synonymous with Britain's sporting Empire hoppers, the remarkable Breguet XIX enabled France's globe-trotting pilots to start an international craze for nonstop long-distance flying. Refined from a 1921 military biplane and powered by a rugged and

Alan Cobham was more than a superb pilot. A visionary businessman, he also had a flair for gaining public attention and energizing the government. This was best illustrated by his famous landing in front of London's Houses of Parliament. Cheered by thousands, he approaches over Westminster Bridge before landing on the Thames. After flying to Australia and back on schedule—to the minute—he delivered a petition to waiting British parliamentarians.

The de Havilland D.H.60 Moth established Great Britain's flying club movement at a time when only the rich could afford to fly. Foreseeing that Britain would one day need a pool of trained pilots, the visionary Director of Civil Aviation, Sir Sefton Brancker, was determined to see flying clubs catering to the "man in the street." Attracted by the little biplane's low cost, simplicity, and reliability, he encouraged the Air Ministry to subsidize five flying clubs and equip them with Moths. Within a few years Britain's sporting flyers were empire-hopping in touring versions of the Moth.

THE EMPIRE-HOPPING MOTH BRIGADE

During the early 1930s, more than any other aircraft type, Geoffrey de Havilland's miraculous D.H.60G Gipsy Moth brought British aviation to the world. South Africa, the Soviet Union, India, Japan, Australia, Canada, Iceland, Greenland —there was hardly a corner of the globe where the little two-seat tourer had not flown.

The long reach to Australia became the Moth's favored airway. Beginning in 1930, when Britain's Amy Johnson raced to Darwin in her Moth *Jason*, the next five years brought a succession of solo long-distance flyers. Long before sailing alone around the world, Sir Francis Chichester flew his Moth to Australia and then, on floats, used it on the first solo crossing of the Tasmanian Sea to New Zealand.

In 1931 Charles W. A. Scott flew a Moth to new records (in both directions) between England and Australia. Months later, Jim Mollison's Moth cut the westbound record by two days. The following year, Scott again lowered the eastbound record. Australia's Lores Bonney became the first woman to fly solo to England. New Zealand's Jean Batten broke Amy Johnson's London-Darwin record and set another in the opposite direction. So it went, with records seesawing between members of the Empire-hopping Moth brigade.

Speed had little to do with the D.H.60G's phenomenal success; it was the aircraft's simplicity, economy, and reliability. Burning around six gallons per hour, the 120-horsepower air-cooled Gipsy engine produced a cruising speed of 85 mph and kept on going. Records became a matter of who got the best tail winds and required the shortest rest breaks.

The ubiquitous Gipsy Moth also set the standard in aero club training machines. It was superseded by the world's most successful biplane trainer, the famed D.H.82A Tiger Moth, which was used to train the air forces of the British Commonwealth during World War II.

While working as a typist, Amy Johnson got the flying bug after seeing the 1928 Hollywood epic *Wings*. She used her savings for flying lessons. In her D.H. Gipsy Moth *Jason*, she became the first woman to solo between England and Australia. Taking off from Croydon, near London, on May 5, 1930, she reached Darwin in 19 days. In this photograph of her arrival, a spare propeller is strapped to the fuselage, a common practice on flights across remote lands. Later married to pilot Jim Mollison, Johnson made numerous long-distance flights.

Fearing her husband's disapproval, Australia's pioneer airwoman Lores Bonney learned to fly in secret. In 1933, she arrived at Croydon Airport outside of London in her Gipsy Moth, *My Little Ship*, with a spare propeller strapped to the fuselage. She was the first woman to fly from Australia to England, but her chance to set a record was dashed early in the flight when she crashed in a storm on an island off Burma. In her repaired Moth, Bonney eventually reached England after a number of interesting stops, including one in Turkey. In 1937, flying a Klemm Eagle, she became the first pilot to solo the 18,200 overland miles between Australia and South Africa.

Lores Bonney reaches England.

Bonney in her D.H.60.

Bonney and colleagues.

efficient 500-horsepower Hispano-Suiza engine, the Breguet was a fast and remarkable load carrier.

In 1926, Breguet XIXs broke the nonstop record three times. Successive flights from Paris to Omsk, to Bandar Abbas (Persia), and to Jäsk (Persia) raised the record to 3,353 miles. The pilot on the Jäsk flight was Dieudonné Costes, a Gascon who had learned to fly in 1912 at Louis Blériot's school. Costes and his compatriots also used the wide-ranging Breguets to show the flag in France's African colonies and Manila. When Peltier D'Oisy's Breguet flew the 6,296 miles from Paris to Peking in 63 hours and 30 minutes, Germany quickly responded. Intent on developing a passenger route to Peking, Deutsche Luft Hansa used two of its new trimotor Junkers G24 airliners for the flight, which left Berlin in July and returned in September.

The Atlantic Once Again

In 1919, sparked by Lord Northcliffe's Atlantic prize, French-born hotelier Raymond Orteig had offered a $25,000 prize for a 3,600-mile nonstop flight between New York and Paris. The prize had remained unclaimed as pilots awaited the development of aircraft with the required range and reliability.

In September 1926, French fighter ace René Fonck appeared to have found such a machine. His aircraft, optimistically named *New York–Paris,* had been manufactured by Igor Sikorsky, who since fleeing Russia had established a small factory at Roosevelt Field, New York. Like his 1914 *Il'ya Muromets,* Sikorsky's new S-35 trimotor airliner was large and luxurious. It performed brilliantly during tests but, when loaded with the 2,380 gallons of fuel Fonck required, was nearly 10,000 pounds overweight. On takeoff it failed to clear the runway, cartwheeled, and burned, killing two crewmen. "It is the fortune of the air," the cavalier Fonck said with a shrug.

The *New York–Paris*'s ill-fated attempt marked the beginning of six years of trans-Atlantic flights. Of more than 60 attempted by 1932, less than a third would be successful, and 23 aircraft would crash or vanish. In terms of technical progress, little was gained. Yet from these flights would emerge aviation's greatest public hero, Charles A. Lindbergh. His flight would outshine aviation's two other epochal events: Blériot's 1909 cross-Channel flight and Neil Armstrong's 1969 moon walk.

By May 1927, after another overloaded Atlantic challenger had crashed on takeoff, killing its two pilots, three more aircraft were being prepared to fly from New York to Paris. One was the Wright-Bellanca *Columbia* owned by abrasive war-salvage millionaire Charles Levine. Another was the trimotor Fokker F.VII/3m *America,* sponsored by Rodman Wanamaker and commanded by Rear Admiral Richard Byrd, U.S. Navy, who had flown to the north pole with Floyd Bennett the previous May. While these well-heeled teams had not entered the contest for Orteig's $25,000 prize, such was not the case with the third challenger, a hard-up young mail pilot.

Charles Lindbergh had put his $2,000 life savings toward a specially built Ryan monoplane, which he named *Spirit of St. Louis,* after several of the city's businessmen supplied the balance of its $10,000 price tag. Lindbergh hoped to repay them from Orteig's prize. His decision to make the flight alone in a modest little airplane captured the public's imagination. Indeed, he had no alternative, for there was room for only one in the tiny crew area behind the Ryan's huge cabin fuel tank. Like the other American challengers, Lindbergh had equipped his Ryan NYP (New York–Paris) with the new Wright Whirlwind J-5C engine. Wright's air-cooled radial engine was to prove the most reliable of its time.

AERO DIGEST
CUTAWAY

FUEL TANK VENT
FLAME-PROOF FIREWALL
WELDED STEEL ENGINE MOUNT
OIL TANK - 27 GAL.
SPARK ADVANCE CONTROL
INTAKE MANIFOLD
EXHAUST STACK
WRIGHT J-5-C ENGINE
STANDARD STEEL
PROPELLER

PITOT HEAD
FUEL TANK - 58 GAL.
TANK SUPPORT STRAP
THROTTLE CONTROL ROD
FUEL TANK - 209 GAL.
PLYWOOD LEADING EDGE
WING ROOT FAIRING
FUEL TANK - 86 GAL.

CABLE PULLEY
AILERON CONTROL CABLE
REAR SPAR

N-X-211
RYAN

MAGNETO COOLING LOUVRES
CARBURETOR PRE-HEAT
TIRE VALVE ACCESS

INFLATABLE LIFE RAFT
WICKER SEAT
STOWAGE RACK (MAPS, PENS, ETC)
STABILIZER CONTROL
INSTRUMENT PANEL
THROTTLE
AILERON CONTROL BAR
CONTROL COLUMN
RUDDER PEDAL
ELASTIC SHOCK CHORD

WIND-DRIVEN GENERATOR
FAIRING ASSEMBLY
ELEVATOR CABLE
RUDDER CABLE
PIONEER EARTH INDUCTOR COMPASS
TAIL SKID
ELASTIC SHOCK CHORD
RUDDER POST BUMPER
STABILIZER SCREW JACK
ELEVATOR CONTROL HORN

RYAN NY-P   "Spirit of St. Louis"

As Lindbergh made his final preparations, France's battle-scarred ace, Captain Charles Nungesser, and his one-eyed navigator, Captain Francois Coli, vanished over the Atlantic while attempting an east–west crossing. Wounded 17 times, with a platinum jaw and plates in his leg, Nungesser was the darling of Parisian society. The news that his Levasseur PL-8 biplane *L'Oiseau Blanc* (White Bird) was missing sent France into mourning. In the United States, public sentiment mirrored that across the Atlantic, and a benefit performance at New York's Roxy Theatre raised $35,000 for the airmen's families.

Foul weather delayed Lindbergh for a week, giving journalists time to produce an avalanche of articles about the shy midwesterner. Lindbergh was disturbed by wild and inaccurate reports. "Contacts with the press became increasingly distasteful to me. I felt that interviews and photographs tended to confuse and cheapen life," he recalled. Unused to newspaper ballyhoo, he was offended by sobriquets such as "Lucky Lindy" and "Flying Fool." Nevertheless, the media attention laid the groundwork for the unparalleled world reaction that followed his flight.

By the time the weather had begun to clear over the Atlantic and Lindbergh had headed for the airfield, he was a newsprint hero. The world loves an underdog, and that was how he was portrayed—the young country David was about to meet his Goliath—the Atlantic Ocean.

Lindbergh's takeoff from rain-soaked Roosevelt Field on May 20, 1927,

The Ryan NYP (New York-Paris) was purpose-designed. Lindbergh and the designer, Donald Hall, determined the distance on a globe in the San Diego Public Library and then built an aircraft that was essentially a flying fuel tank. Stability, comfort, and even the pilot's forward vision were sacrificed to the planned 4,000-mile range. The attention given to streamlining and the disproportionate size of the fuel tanks are clearly shown in this *Aero Digest* cutaway.

The Spirit of St. Louis

BY CHARLES A. LINDBERGH

Charles Lindbergh's solo flight from New York to Paris in May 1927 is the greatest single event in aviation history after the Wright brothers' flight of December 17, 1903. His was an achievement of the human spirit as much as of the technical durability of his airplane, *Spirit of St. Louis*.

From Start Point of England to Cape de la Hague of France is eighty-five miles. In the past, I would have approached an eighty-five-mile flight over water, in a land plane, with trepidation. It would have appeared a hazardous undertaking. This evening, it's just part of the downhill glide to Paris. Why, I should be able to paddle halfway across the Channel with my hands if I were forced down. What's eighty-five miles in contrast to an ocean—or to that space above the clouds at night?...

A strip of land, ten miles or so in width, dents the horizon—Cape de la Hague. The coast of France! It comes like an outstretched hand to meet me, glowing in the light of sunset....

The sun almost touches the horizon as I look down on the city of Cherbourg, embracing its little harbor. Here is France, two thousand feet underneath my wing. After three thousand, four hundred miles of flying, I'm over the country of my destination. I've made the first nonstop airplane flight between the continents of America and Europe. There'll not be another night above the clouds. There's no longer any question of turning back across the water. No matter what happens now, I'll land in France. It's only two hundred miles to Paris, and half of that will be in twilight....

As a matter of fact, how will I return home? Why not fly on around the world?...

Flying on around the world would show again what modern airplanes can accomplish. Besides, it's beneath the dignity of the Spirit of St. Louis to return to the United States on board a boat.... It would be great fun to take off from Europe one day and land at home, on Lambert Field, the next. I can see the pilots and mechanics running up to my plane.

"Where did you come from?"

"I came from Ireland."

"From Ireland—when did you leave?"

"I left yesterday."

I would say it all casually, just as though I'd landed on a routine mail flight from Chicago....

The Spirit of St. Louis is a wonderful plane. It's like a living creature, gliding along smoothly, happily, as though a successful flight means as much to it as to me, as though we shared our experiences together, each feeling beauty, life, and death as keenly, each dependent on the other's loyalty. We have made this flight across the ocean, not I or it....

Within the hour I'll land, and strangely enough I'm in no hurry to have it pass. I haven't the slightest desire to sleep. My eyes are no longer salted stones. There's not an ache in my body. The night is cool and safe. I want to sit quietly in this cockpit and let the realization of my completed flight sink in. Europe is below; Paris, just over the earth's curve in the night ahead—a few minutes more of flight. It's like struggling up a mountain after a rare flower, and then, when you have it within arm's reach, realizing that satisfaction and happiness lie more in the finding than the plucking. Plucking and withering are inseparable. I want to prolong this culminating experience of my flight. I almost wish Paris were a few more hours away. It's a shame to land with the night so clear and so much fuel in my tanks.

I'm still flying at four thousand feet when I see it, that scarcely perceptible glow, as though the moon had rushed ahead of schedule. Paris is rising over the edge of the earth. It's almost thirty-three hours from my take-off on Long Island. As minutes pass, myriad pin points of light emerge, a patch of starlit earth under a starlit sky—the lamps of Paris—straight lines of lights, curving lines of lights, squares of lights, black spaces in between. Gradually avenues, parks, and buildings take outline form; and there, far below, a little offset from the center, is a column of lights pointing upward, changing angles as I fly—the Eiffel Tower. I circle once above it, and turn northeastward toward Le Bourget....

It's only a hundred yards to the hangars now—solid forms emerging from the night. I'm too high—too fast. Drop wing—left rudder—sideslip—Careful—mustn't get anywhere near the stall. I've never landed the Spirit of St. Louis at night before. It would be better to come in straight. But if I don't sideslip, I'll be too high over the boundary to touch my wheels in the area of light. That would mean circling again—Still too high. I push the stick over to a steeper slip, leaving the nose well down—Below the hangar roofs now—straighten out—A short burst of the engine—Over the lighted area—Sod coming up to meet me—Deceptive high lights and shadows—Careful—easy to bounce when you're tired—Still too fast—Tail too high—Hold off—Hold off—But the lights are far behind—The surface dims—Texture of sod is gone—Ahead, there's nothing but night—Give her the gun and climb for another try?—The wheels touch gently—off again—No, I'll keep contact—Ease the stick forward—Back on the ground—Off—Back—the tail skid too—Not a bad landing, but I'm beyond the light—can't see anything ahead—Like flying in fog—Ground loop?—No, still rolling too fast—might blow a tire—The field must be clear—Uncomfortable though, jolting into blackness—Wish I had a wing light—but too heavy on the take-off—Slower, now—slow enough to ground loop safely—left rudder—reverse it—stick over the other way—The Spirit of St. Louis swings around and stops rolling, resting on the solidness of earth, in the center of Le Bourget....

CHARLES LINDBERGH

"The life of an aviator seemed to me ideal. It involved skill. It brought adventure. It made use of the latest developments of science. Mechanical engineers were fettered to factories and drafting boards while pilots have the freedom of wind with the expanse of sky. There were times in an aeroplane when it seemed I had escaped mortality to look down on earth like a God," wrote Charles Lindbergh.

The Minnesota boy who had dropped out of college to fly was recalling his boyhood days in 1912 attending his first air show, his first flight in a Lincoln Standard biplane 10 years later, his almost traditional beginnings as a barnstormer and wingwalker, and the lonely night hours flying the mail before he became the world's most famous pilot.

Lindbergh's fame was due to more than his skill and daring in flying the Atlantic in 1927 or his flights around the Pacific and Atlantic rims pioneering air routes for Pan American Airways. Other pilots were equally skilled and adventurous.

Handsome, modest, charming, and courageous, the overnight hero became America's role model. Soon after the epochal Atlantic flight, the Lindbergh miracle was magnified as he and the *Spirit of St. Louis* circled the 48 states,

visiting 82 cities and taking his dream of aviation's future to the people. Overflying communities he could not visit personally, Lindbergh dropped message bags extolling citizens to support his vision of the United States becoming the world leader in commercial aviation.

His enormous popularity grew as he gained world attention surveying Pan Am's future airline network. During World War II, despite initially opposing American involvement, he flew 50 combat missions demonstrating the F4U Corsair's combat potential and taught long-range flying techniques to P-38 pilots. In his later years, Lindbergh turned away from technology and devoted his energy to conservation.

The shy young aviator who became a folk hero remained a public figure until his death in 1974. As noted historian Tom D. Crouch wrote: "Charles Lindbergh was the most photographed figure of his era. As the lean young man with the infectious grin posing beside a silver monoplane; the pathfinding pilot of the thirties; the impassioned spokesman for peace; or the postwar voice of environmental sanity, his face remained familiar to the readers of American newspapers and magazines for almost half a century."

Following his trans-Atlantic triumph, Lindbergh toured the then 48 states in the *Spirit of St. Louis*. More than 30 million Americans saw him and listened as he promoted aviation. He also made a goodwill tour to Mexico and Central and South America where this rare profile photograph was taken by Frank Tuma, a Panama-based U.S. Army Air Corps pilot.

American business capitalized on Lindbergh's popularity. Tin Pan Alley's sheet-music marketers produced numerous instant hits. This revamped edition of "Oh, Charlie Is my Darling" battled with other titles such as "Lucky Lindy," "Lindy, Youth with the Heart of Gold," and "Lindbergh, the Hero of Our Heart."

More than 500 vessels jammed New York Harbor to welcome Lindbergh aboard the mayor's steam yacht (just below and closest to the fireboats). It is estimated that 300,000 spectators jammed the Battery. "Colonel Lindbergh, New York City is yours," declared Mayor James J. Walker.

Facing page (bottom):
This headline from the *St. Paul Daily News* in Minnesota, Lindbergh's home state, epitomized the front pages of the world's press. *The New York Times* devoted its first 16 pages to the flight. Lyndon Baines Johnson, the editor of the student newspaper at San Marcos (Texas) College, wrote: "Do not sigh for Lindbergh's wonderful luck, but determine to emulate Lindy's glorious pluck."

was a cliffhanger. The Ryan dropped back to the ground twice before finally struggling over the telegraph wires at the edge of the field. Once the fuel overload was burned off, the flight was remarkably trouble-free. The greatest hazard proved to be fatigue. Lindbergh resorted to all the airman's tricks: holding his eyelids open, slapping his face, pinching himself, and sticking his face into the icy slipstream. Despite his efforts, he spent periods in a trancelike state, neither awake nor asleep.

Reporting the pandemonium at Paris's Le Bourget airfield at the end of Lindbergh's epic flight of 33 hours and 30 minutes, the New York *Times* reported: "The movement of humanity swept over soldiers and by policemen and there was the sight of thousands of men and women rushing madly across half a mile of not too even ground. Soldiers and police tried for one small moment to stem the tide, then joined it, rushing madly as anyone towards the aviator and his plane."

As if to assuage the loss of its own heroes, France took the American to its heart with an unprecedented national outpouring of emotion for a foreigner. Throughout the world, newspapers were crammed with the news. The New York *Times* devoted 16 pages to Lindbergh. Heads of state cabled congratulations. "A superhuman will has taken space by assault. . . . Glory be to Lindbergh and his people," Italy's dictator Benito Mussolini said in a handwritten note.

The United States and the world had its aviation hero, yet Lindbergh's flight had been more a symbolic triumph than a technical one. True, the *Spirit of St. Louis* crossed the Atlantic, but so could other aircraft, as *Columbia* and *America* proved soon after, and they were commercial machines whereas the Ryan was little more than a flying fuel tank. In terms of technical progress, Lindbergh's conquest of the Atlantic had been a victory for the Wright Aeronautical Corporation's faith in air-cooled engines and to a lesser degree for the Pioneer earth inductor compass that all three machines carried.

But the public, which neither understood nor cared about such matters, rejoiced in the achievement. To them, all previous trailblazing flights, many over greater distances and equally inhospitable terrain, seemed inconsequential. Despite Britain's 1919 crossing, the Atlantic had been perceived as aviation's Achilles' heel. Now, hard on a flurry of failures, a lone flyer in a little airplane had casually linked New York and Paris. By making it look almost

Charles Lindbergh's *Spirit of St. Louis* now permanently hangs in the National Air and Space Museum.

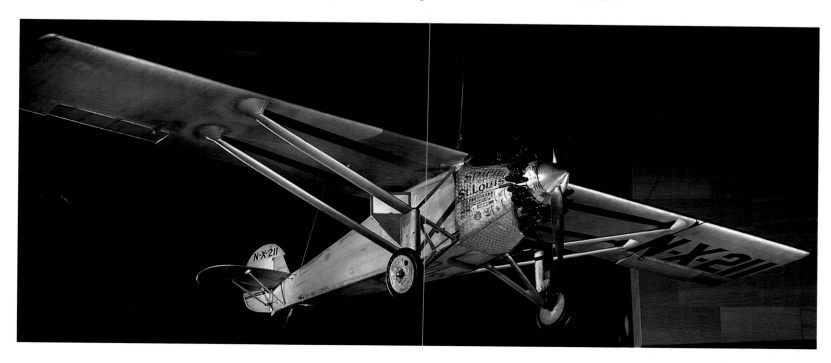

 **EXTRA** ★ St. Paul Daily News ★ **SPORTS** COMPLETE N.Y. STOCKS

VOL. XII   THREE CENTS   SATURDAY, MAY 21, 1927   THREE CENTS   NO. 173

LINDBERGH IS IN PARIS

FLIER COMPLETES AIR DASH FROM NEW YORK

LE BOURGET FIELD, PARIS, MAY 21.—Capt. Charles Lindbergh, the flying mail man, arrived today by air from New York at 10:21 p.m., Paris time, it was officially announced.

Lindbergh completed his journey in 33 1-2 hours, a flight of approximately 3600 miles by way of the New England coast, Nova Scotia and New Foundland.

He is the first man ever to fly from New York to Paris and when the wheels of Lindbergh's monoplane touched the ground the dream of airmen that the North American and European continents had been linked in nonstop airplane flight was realized.

Since 7:51 a.m., eastern daylight time yesterday, Lindbergh had been en route on the great air circle alone in the cabin of his machine with four sandwiches, hot chocolate and a bottle of water to sustain his strength.

He was sighted over Ireland early today, then over Plymouth England; a short time later over Cherbourg, France, and then came the arrival at Paris.

NEW YORK, May 21.—Within 500 miles of his goal, Paris, Capt. Charles A. Lindbergh, America's 25-year old "flying fool," was sailing over St. George channel between Ireland and England shortly after 2 o'clock, New York time, this afternoon.

His remaining route lay over Land's End, the southern tip of England, to either Havre or

Flight Sends Wright Stock Up 5 Points

NEW YORK, May 21.—Interest here in "Lucky" Lindbergh's solo hop for Paris was so great today as to cause "hardboiled" operators on the New York stock exchange to allow their hearts to rule their heads. When it was reported that Lindbergh was sighted off Ireland, professional operators gave vent to their exuberance by buying Wright Aeronautical stock, makers of the engine in "Lucky's" plane. The stock rose five points.

HERE'S PARIS FLIGHT LOG

NEW YORK, May 21.—The log of Lindbergh's flight, by eastern daylight time, follows:

7:51:30 1-5 a.m. Friday—Took off at Roosevelt field.

9:05 a.m.—Passed East Greenwich, R. I.
9:15 a.m.—West Middleboro, Mass.
9:40 a.m.—Halifax, Mass.
12:45 p.m.—Cape St. Mary, N. S.
1:05 p.m.—Springfield, N. S.
1:50 p.m.—Milford, N. S.
3:05 p.m.—Mulgrave, N. S.
4 p.m.—Main Adieu, N. S.
Last time seen on North American Mainland.
4:05 p.m.—Mulgrave, between the mainland and Cape Breton island.

Los Angeles Off On Trial Cruise

LAKEHURST, N. J., MAY 21.—The navy dirigible Los Angeles took off from the air station

SPIRIT OF ADVENTURE

Photo upper left: Captain Charles Lindbergh in the cockpit of his plane before his epochal non-stop flight from New York to Paris today. Middle photo: Lindbergh is shown with B. F. Mahoney, president of Ryan Airlines in California, builders of the monoplane. Upper right: This photo of Lindbergh's plane in flight shows how it looked today when the tiny airship reached Paris, victory and the $25,000 Orteig prize. Alone in "The Spirit of St. Louis," which has conquered the Atlantic skies, rides the spirit of youth and adventure in the person of 25-year old Lindbergh. Photos by International Newsreel.

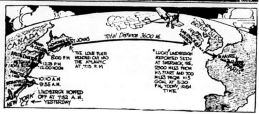

LINDBERGH IS

53

WRIGHT'S OCEAN-CONQUERING WHIRLWIND

No engine had a greater impact on long-distance flying in the 1920s than the Wright Aeronautical Corporation's air-cooled Whirlwind radial. Besides powering Lindbergh and others across the Atlantic, Whirlwinds took Kingsford-Smith across the Pacific, the U.S. Army to Hawaii, Byrd to both poles, and Wilkins across the top of the world.

Charles J. Lawrance designed the first Whirlwind J-1 in 1922. The U.S. Navy was so impressed with its performance and ease of maintenance that it persuaded the huge Wright company to acquire Lawrance's struggling business. By 1927, Lawrance's latest nine-cylinder, 220-horsepower Whirlwind J-5C was in mass production.

Air cooling did away with the complex, cumbersome, and unreliable liquid cooling systems of the period that reputedly caused a third of all forced landings. The Whirlwind was not only more reliable but, being around 25 percent lighter than equivalent liquid-cooled engines, produced a much higher power-to-weight ratio. Furthermore, the superb cooling properties of the J-5C's redesigned cylinders allowed pilots to select a leaner, more economical fuel mixture without overheating.

The more powerful Cyclone had replaced the Whirlwind.

Frederick B. Rentschler.

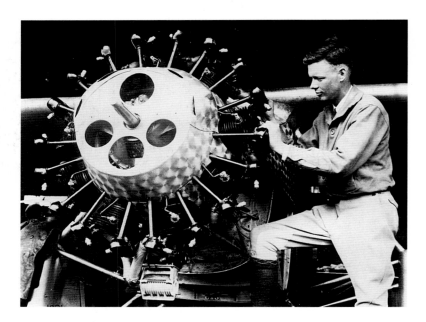

Lindbergh inspects his Wright Whirlwind J-5 engine. Within six weeks of his trans-Atlantic flight two other aircraft, both powered by the Whirlwind, flew from New York to Europe. The engine's reliability and fuel economy made it the choice of most 1920s long-distance flyers.

By then the drag penalty of the bulky radials had been minimized and the cooling had been improved even further by Fred Weick's brilliant NACA engine cowling. In 1939, Pan American's giant Boeing B-314 flying boats serviced the Pacific and Atlantic powered by four 1,500-horsepower Double Cyclones that were descended from the little Whirlwinds that first flew the oceans.

Even Wright's great competitor, Pratt & Whitney, owed its beginnings to the Whirlwind. In 1925, former Wright executive Frederick B. Rentschler used Whirlwind technology when he established Pratt & Whitney to produce Wasp air-cooled radials. Over the next 20 years, Wright and Pratt & Whitney competed for the lion's share of the world market, producing power plants for airliners, transports, and the giant bombers of World War II. The dominance of their roaring radials was not eclipsed until the advent of the jet engine.

simple, Lindbergh gave the world faith in the ultimate dream of intercontinental air travel. Furthermore, the incredible press and public reaction would convince American businessmen to invest in aviation. Philadelphia merchant Ellis A. Gimbel pledged $100,000 worth of business for a Philadelphia–Paris air service. Though still far-fetched, Gimbel's offer was a sign of changing attitudes.

A remarkable and little-known reaction came from Japan, where, intent on a nonstop Pacific flight, a newspaper purchased a second Ryan NYP. Kawasaki built a 50 percent larger version, but it lacked the necessary range.

1944: A MONUMENTAL JAPANESE FLIGHT

One of the most remarkable long-distance flights was completed by a Japanese aircraft during World War II. Its genesis went back to Charles Lindbergh's 1927 conquest of the Atlantic.

Determined to establish its aviation credentials, Japan searched for its own Lindbergh to make the first nonstop Pacific crossing. After an abortive plan involving an overgrown Kawanishi-built copy of Lindbergh's Ryan, two Japanese attempts employing Junkers A-50s failed. The flight became a national obsession. Even after the American *Miss Veedol* completed the crossing in 1931, Japanese airmen made another valiant attempt that ended when their Junkers W.33 vanished.

In 1940, Japan's *Asahi Shimbun* newspaper, which had promoted numerous long-distance flights, proposed a nonstop goodwill flight from Tokyo to New York. Two special twin-engine Tachikawa A-26 (Ki-77) aircraft designed to fly more than 11,185 miles were constructed. Powered by 1,170-horsepower Nakajima Ha-115 radials, the A-26 weighed nearly 37,000 pounds carrying its maximum 3,052-gallon fuel load. However, because of its 96-foot-span high-aspect-ratio wing, the monoplane needed only a 4,500-foot takeoff run.

The flight was scheduled for 1942, but Japan's entry into World War II in December 1941 aborted the project. One Ki-77 was lost on a clandestine flight from Singapore to Berlin in July 1943. In July 1944, to prove that the Ki-77 could have reached New York, the second aircraft circled over Manchuria for an unofficial record of 10,212 miles in 57 hours and 12 minutes. It was the equivalent of flying from Tokyo to New York with nearly 3,500 miles to spare! Had the war not intervened, Japan's long-legged Tachikawa might have pre-empted by 34 years the achievement eventually accomplished by a Boeing 747SP in 1975.

This naive design exercise prompted Japan to develop its own long-distance machine, the Tachikawa A-26 (Ki-77), which eventually set an astonishing distance record during World War II.

In October 1927, attention turned to the south Atlantic, where France's Dieudonné Costes prepared for a nonstop crossing. Since Portugal's dramatic 1923 marathon, Spain's Ramon Franco and Italy's Marchese de Pinedo, both utilizing Dornier Wal flying boats, had also made staged crossings. Mussolini had ordered the Italian effort "for the glory of Fascist Italy."

Costes and his navigator, Joseph Le Brix, planned to restore lost national pride after the crash of *L'Oiseau Blanc*. Honoring their dead comrades, they named their Breguet XIX *Nungesser-Coli*. Their flight from Saint Louis on the Senegalese coast of Africa to Port Natal, Brazil, took 21¼ hours and was followed by a triumphant aerial tour of the United States that ended in San Francisco. Shipping their airplane to Tokyo, they flew home across Asia, arriving back in Paris as France's new aviation heroes. On September 27 to 29, 1929, accompanied by Maurice Bellonte, Costes flew the scarlet Breguet XIX *Point d'Interrogation* (Question Mark) nonstop from Paris to Manchuria—a

France's Dieudonné Costes and his navigator, Joseph Le Brix, made this first nonstop crossing of the south Atlantic on October 14 and 15, 1927. After the crossing, they toured South and North America. Part of the route is emblazoned on the fuselage of their Breguet XIX *Nungesser-Coli*. It was named after two dead comrades who vanished while trying to beat Lindbergh across the north Atlantic in their biplane *L'Oiseau-Blanc*.

Costes and Le Brix over the Canal Zone after their south Atlantic flight. Costes had been chasing records since 1925, when he crashed in Germany trying for a world long-distance record. A year later he finally set a new non-stop mark with a 3,313-mile nonstop flight from Paris to Jask, Iran.

staggering 4,912 miles—and set a new distance record. The following year, the pair achieved France's ultimate aviation goal: a Paris–New York flight.

On April 12 and 13, 1928, Hermann Koehl, James Fitzmaurice, and Baron von Hünefeld in the German Junkers W33 floatplane *Bremen* completed a troubled east–west Atlantic crossing from Ireland, missing New York by 1,000 miles and landing at Greenly Island, Labrador, Canada. The Frenchmen were determined to do better. Setting out from Paris on September 1, 1930, they battled the prevailing winds to New York. When *Point d'Interrogation* arrived 37 hours and 18 minutes later, the scene was reminiscent of Lindbergh's Paris landing. Some 140 policemen held back the crowd as Lindbergh rushed to greet France's greatest long-distance flyers.

Solo to Australia

The public euphoria generated by Lindbergh and Costes during 1927 continued throughout 1928 as Australian and American aviators grabbed world attention. Bert Hinkler fired Australia's opening shot in February 1928 with the first solo England-Australia flight. Unlike Alan Cobham, Hinkler was not concerned with airline pioneering. His interest lay in promoting the light airplane as an economical family tourer of the future. As early as 1920 he had flown nonstop from London to Turin in a tiny Avro Baby. "Let the Zeniths get hold of that," the exhilarated Australian had exclaimed after averaging 32 miles per gallon.

His 1928 dash to Australia was done in Avro's latest sporting biplane, a two-seat Avian powered by a miserly 85-horsepower Cirrus engine. Departing in secret on February 7, he reached India before the press caught up with the news. From then on the world followed his race for home, swept up by the concept of a lone flyer challenging the elements. Flying by day and

Facing page (top left):
The jubilant Costes and Bellonte received a traditional New York ticker-tape parade. The overwhelming reception echoed the emotional greeting France had given Lindbergh three years earlier.

Facing page (top right):
Dieudonné Costes (front cockpit) and Maurice Bellonte prepare for takeoff for New York from Le Bourget airfield, Paris. The weather was not ideal. Costes recalled: "We took off in the face of the mists. Sixty square metres of cloth fabric had to lift 6,300 kilos. Our battle with the elements had begun." The next morning, while her husband was still battling Atlantic storms, Madame Costes told waiting newsmen: "I went to bed last night to dream of him in the great loneliness of the black night over the sea. But how could I sleep?"

Facing page (bottom):
In September 1929, 37 hours after leaving Paris, the scarlet Breguet XIX *Point d'Interrogation* (Question Mark) touched down at New York's Curtiss Field. France's Costes and Bellonte had become the first to link the two cities by flying from east to west against the prevailing wind. Several years earlier globe-trotting French pilots in their long-legged Breguets had started the world craze for nonstop long-distance flying.

Left:
After Bert Hinkler's 1928 solo dash from England to Australia, the folding wings of his Avro Avian enabled it to be towed through the streets of Brisbane. Before his safe arrival, the Australian authorities remained strangely aloof. Wishing to discourage do-or-die flyers who were harming aviation's image, the prime minister had announced that his government would not assist inadequately organized "unofficial" flights.

At the end of his 1928 flight from England, Hinkler toured Australia in his Avro Avian, posing for photographers in the business suit that was his trademark. His modest manner appealed to the average Australian, but he lacked the flair to attract big business backers. Hinkler died in 1933 attempting to set a new England-Australia record.

Hinkler's Avro Avian prototype G-EBOV is displayed in Brisbane's Queensland Museum. Though never achieving the popularity of the de Havilland Moth, Avians made several long-distance record flights from England to Australia and South Africa. In 1930, Sir Charles Kingsford-Smith used his Avian IVA *Southern Cross Junior* to lower Hinkler's England-to-Australia record by nearly six days.

fussing over his engine by night, Hinkler navigated halfway around the world by a *Times* atlas. His 11,005-mile flight took 128 flying hours spread over 15 days, halving the Smith brothers' record that had been set in 1919.

A British newspaper coined the phrase "Hustling Hinkler," and an American composer picked up the theme. Before Hinkler reached home, Tin Pan Alley sheet music pianists were playing "Hustling Hinkler up in the Sky." Australians sported "Hinkler Homburgs" (his favorite headgear), and couples danced the "Hinkler Quickstep." The press called him "the Australian Lindbergh," a title repeated often between October 27 and December 7, 1931, when Hinkler again made world headlines with the first solo flight of a light aircraft from New York to London via the Caribbean, Brazil, western Africa, and Spain.

The Pacific Challenge

The Pacific remained as the last great transoceanic challenge. In June 1927, the U.S. Army galvanized attention with the first flight from the mainland to Hawaii. Having established a chain of Pacific bases stretching to the Philippines, the military wanted to demonstrate the feasibility of flying at least to Hawaii. A Navy effort in 1925 had failed, but that did not deter Army Lieutenants Lester Maitland and Albert Hegenberger from attempting the 2,360-mile flight from Oakland, California.

The Army had recently purchased a Fokker C-2 transport, an American-built version of the F. VIIA/3m trimotor powered by 220-horsepower Wright Whirlwind J-5s. Maitland knew that it could lift the required fuel load. The Army made sure it was fitted with a specially built 71-foot wing and equipped with the latest in blind-flying instruments and navigational and radio equipment. Hegenberger had spent years testing blind-flying instruments and navigation systems and studying the problems of transoceanic operations. He was acutely aware that a small (as little as 3½ degrees) track error could result in their completely missing the tiny island target. Thus he realized the value of the revolutionary new radio navigation system they were to test en route, flying along beams transmitted from radio beacons installed at San Francisco and Hawaii.

The Army Fokker, exotically named *Bird of Paradise*, set off on June 28, 1927. Thirty minutes out, Hegenberger tuned the radio to receive coded signals that indicated whether they were on the beam. The signal kept them on course for about an hour and then stopped because of a receiver problem. From then on, with much of the flight in darkness and cloud, they were forced to rely on Hegenberger's superb dead-reckoning navigation while Maitland flew "blind" on instruments. They reached Wheeler Field, north of Honolulu, safely after 25 hours and 49 minutes.

Hegenberger's prophetic report recommended the establishment of a school of navigation and the provision of more accurate flight instruments. It was a blueprint for American military aviation to move from fair-weather flying to all-weather operations. He wrote: "Without the ability to fly to a distant objective, under adverse conditions if necessary, the vision and striking power means very little. Mobility involves both distance and direction. Under service conditions this means navigation independent of landmarks."

Using superb planning and preparation, the Army airmen had completed the longest nonstop over-water flight to date and proved that Hawaii was a stepping-stone for an island-hopping trans-Pacific flight. Only weeks later, Australian airmen Charles Kingsford-Smith and Charles Ulm arrived in California intent on using the same stepping-stone to bridge aviation's last ocean barrier.

The Australians planned the flight as a prelude to a trans-Pacific air mail service. However, they had trouble finding backers when, shortly after their arrival, the tragic Dole Pineapple Derby race of August from Oakland to Hawaii almost negated the hard-won gains of 1927. Directly and indirectly, the scramble of ill-prepared contestants for the $35,000 prize money accounted for the deaths of 10 flyers. Only two out of eight starters reached Hawaii. Worldwide public revulsion at the needless loss of life almost ended the Australian challenge until a wealthy American shipping magnate, Captain G. Allan Hancock, backed the venture.

Kingsford-Smith and Ulm purchased the Fokker F. VIIB/3m *Detroiter*, previously owned by Arctic explorer Sir Hubert Wilkins. Renamed the *Southern Cross*, it was fitted out with Whirlwind J-5C engines and the best available blind-flying instruments and radios. To ensure the bull's-eye accuracy required

Lieutenants Albert F. Hegenberger (left) and Lester J. Maitland and their Fokker C-2 transport *Bird of Paradise*. Their 1927 flight from Oakland to Honolulu was superbly planned and executed. However, only two months later American aviation suffered a body blow from the disastrous Dole Air Derby. Flown over the same route, it led to the loss of 10 aircraft and 10 lives, including those lost in prerace preparation.

CHARLES KINGSFORD-SMITH

Charles Kingsford-Smith epitomized the popular image of the dashing young flyer. World War I fighter pilot, Hollywood stuntman, barnstormer, record breaker, and airline trailblazer, he pioneered more ocean routes than any other pilot.

Unlike his reserved American counterpart, Charles Lindbergh, "Smithy" was an extrovert. However, behind the wide grin and public pranks was a visionary but cautious pilot. His preparations were characterized by the same meticulous attention to detail that earmarked the U.S. Army's pioneering flights. "We planned and plotted on a fixed policy of trusting for the very best and preparing for the very worst. That was the policy on which we studied transoceanic flying, loading, fuelling and navigation," he wrote.

Whereas most aviators still flew by a visual horizon, Smithy realized that aviation's commercial future hinged on flying by instruments. Echoing Lieutenant Hegenberger's comments

after the U.S. Army's Hawaiian flight, he cautioned: "Until a man can fly in a black void for hours seeing these instruments and nothing else, he is not a safe pilot to fly a plane over long stretches of water. To do so he must have immense faith in his instruments."

In an era of devil-may-care flyers, such professionalism enabled Kingsford-Smith to be first across the Pacific (in both directions), pioneer the Tasmanian Sea, and make the first London–New York crossing as well as numerous flights between England and Australia.

Unfortunately, his commercial acumen did not match his flying skills. His copilot, Charles Ulm, was the business brain; after their partnership ended, Smithy finally allowed financial pressures to override his professional judgment. Ailing and close to bankruptcy, he vanished in 1935 challenging the England–Australia record.

"Just as dawn was breaking at 7:25 A.M. Warner tried continually to pick up a radio bearing from Brisbane. . . . We had finally broken through the storm barrier, and although we were cold and gloomy after our atrocious night, the wind had dropped and the morning's paleness was creeping upon the horizon and we felt happy again." Artist Denys Faithful's evocative painting of the *Southern Cross* recalls Kingsford-Smith's description of dawn shortly before sighting the Australian coast.

to hit their island targets, the aircraft carried a master aperiodic compass, three steering compasses, and two drift meters. Two Americans joined the crew: ship's captain Harry Lyon as navigator and radio operator James Warner. Six flight tests were conducted, gradually increasing the Fokker's fuel load until it carried the 1,300 gallons required for the 3,200-mile leg from Hawaii to Fiji.

Their careful planning paid off on May 31, 1928, when the *Southern Cross* lifted easily into the air from Oakland Airport. Encountering none of the radio problems Maitland and Hegenberger had suffered, they rode the radio beams and reached Hawaii without a hitch. "The importance of radio as an aid to air navigation is growing, and it was our valuable ally," Kingsford-Smith remarked.

From Hawaii on, it was a different story. Clouds, squalls, rain, and turbulence made the 33½-hour leg to Fiji a nightmare. With one engine affected by rain, Warner radioed: "One motor sounds bad. Dropped to 60 miles an hour." Head winds and the attempt to outclimb clouds reduced their fuel margin, and for a short time it appeared they might not reach Fiji. Similar conditions were encountered on the final leg to Australia. "One after another rainstorms charged at us. There was no lull. We flew in a black void. Raking winds jolted the plane. It was a supreme test of engines and blind flying," Kingsford-Smith wrote, recalling that the combined strength of both pilots was needed to keep control.

Fifteen thousand people greeted them at Brisbane Airport on June 9. Deafened by the engines' roar, the aviators stumbled from the aircraft, unable to hear the welcoming speeches. The following day, a quarter of a million people were at Sydney's Mascot Aerodrome to cheer the Pacific flyers.

The first nonstop Pacific crossing came three years later, following six unsuccessful attempts, three Japanese and three American. Former "Flying Circus" pilot Clyde Pangborn and Hugh Herndon, Jr., a playboy with a penchant for flying, left Japan chasing a $25,000 carrot dangled by Tokyo's *Asahi Shimbun* newspaper. Gaining initial momentum from a downhill ramp, Pangborn just managed to get the fuel-bloated Bellanca *Miss Veedol* airborne at the end of its 8,000-foot beach airstrip. He then jettisoned the landing gear, increasing the monoplane's range by about 600 miles. Despite an inattentive Herndon wandering well off course while Pangborn slept, they eventually belly-landed safely at Wenatchee, Washington, after covering 4,883 miles in just over 41 hours.

Ending the first true trans-Pacific flight, Charles Kingsford-Smith and Charles Ulm bring their Fokker F.VIIB/3m *Southern Cross* down over the rooftops of Sydney, Australia. Despite his devil-may-care public image, Smith planned the flight with meticulous attention to detail. "We maintain with some justice that ours was a more efficiently organized flight than those that had failed," he said.

Sir Charles Kingsford-Smith's beloved "old bus," the *Southern Cross*, is displayed at Brisbane's new International Airport. The stately Fokker F.VIIB/3m stands in a special glass hangar under the approach path to the old Eagle Farm Airport, where it ended its trans-Pacific crossing in 1928.

Fulfilling the Dream

Despite the conquest of the oceans, transoceanic flying remained a hit-or-miss affair, too dangerous for the public to contemplate. Moreover, the aircraft of the day were still incapable of carrying a profitable payload over such distances. The slow but steady growth that had occurred in airline travel involved overland routes, in many cases replacing pack animals in remote regions.

The milestone makers of the 1920s, who dreamed of airliners linking the continents, impatiently marked time until design caught up with promise. Many would take part in the next decade of milestones, which were less concerned with trailblazing than with refining aircraft and equipment. They provided a public arena in which designers, manufacturers, and airline builders eventually fulfilled the promise.

In 1933, Italy gave a dramatic illustration of improvements in transoceanic reliability with a formation of 25 Savoia-Marchetti S-55X flying boats. In January 1931, Italy's flamboyant Air Minister, General Italo Balbo, had led 12 Savoia-Marchetti S-55A flying boats in the first formation flight across the South Atlantic from Orbetello, Italy, to Natal and then to Rio de Janeiro, Brazil, a distance of 6,426 miles. Now he commanded the aerial armada that set off on July 1 to visit Chicago's "A Century of Progress" World's Fair. One aircraft capsized on landing at the first refueling stop, Amsterdam, but thereafter the flight continued with machinelike precision. Intensive training paid off as the crews held formation through rain and fog banks to Iceland. Flying in eight flights of three, Balbo's superbly disciplined airmen arrived at Chicago and landed on Lake Michigan. Ten days later, they made the return flight via the Azores. Despite the loss of another aircraft in a takeoff accident at Lisbon, and after 12,300 miles, the remaining 23 airplanes arrived home at Orbetello still holding impeccable formation.

The massed flight had been an unsurpassed example of organization, planning, and airmanship and had illustrated the advanced state of Italy's aircraft industry. In particular it was a triumph for Isotta-Fraschini and its

Some people have unfairly portrayed Air Marshal Italo Balbo as a comic opera character. He not only planned the brilliant Italian trans-Atlantic formation flights in 1931 and 1933 but also piloted the lead aircraft. Back home, Balbo and his men were greeted like returning Roman legions. Promoting him to air marshal in the ancient Forum of Rome, Mussolini stated: "It is a tribute that your country owes you, Balbo." Ironically, when Balbo was shot down by Italian antiaircraft guns over Tobruk in 1940, most people believed his death had been engineered by Mussolini. By then Il Duce considered the popular airman a political threat.

Left to right:
General Italo Balbo's 24 Savoia-Marchetti S-55X seaplanes flying along Chicago's lakefront on July 15, 1933. The first formation flight across the north Atlantic, Balbo's flight provided a dramatic illustration of Italian air power. Though branded as a publicity exercise for Mussolini's fascist state, this 1933 double crossing of the Atlantic was a remarkable achievement.

18-cylinder, 750-horsepower engines, which had carried the formation twice across the Atlantic without a single failure. Mussolini's friendly air invasion was a salutary lesson in air power, as America's Colonel Eddie Rickenbacker pointed out:

> The advent of the Italians will render us a real service if it jogs our national consciousness into the realization that we have now lagged in the air until we are fourth in terms of air strength. This should be a bitter pill for the country that gave heavier-than-air flight to the world—and whose attitude at the moment seems to be let the world do as it darned well pleases with it.

Though lagging in military air power, the United States leapt ahead in the production of commercial aircraft. The day Balbo's formation had taken off from Italy, Donald Douglas's revolutionary twin-engine, all-metal DC-1 airliner made its first flight at Santa Monica, California. Three months earlier, on March 30, 1933, a similarly configured Boeing 247, the first truly modern airliner, was accepted for service by United Air Lines.

Lockheed and Northrop led the world in single-engine transports. A supreme example was Lockheed's Vega, which had been greatly refined since its debut in 1927. The most significant modification had been the installation of a drag-reducing cowling around its radial engine. Designed by the U.S. National Advisory Committee for Aeronautics (NACA), the streamlined cowling increased the Vega's performance by nearly 20 percent. The innovative NACA cowling soon became the standard for America's burgeoning radial-engine fleet.

Since April 1928, when Hubert Wilkins and his pilot, Carl Ben Eielson, had flown a Vega on the first trans-Arctic flight from Point Barrow, Alaska, to Spitsbergen, the Lockheed had been involved in many record flights. Amelia Earhart used one to solo the Atlantic on May 20 and 21, 1932, and then

Captain George H. Wilkins and Lieutenant Carl Ben Eielson completed the first transpolar flight in this Vega 1 in April 1928 and repeated the feat over the south pole in November 1928.

Lockheed's Vega made more headlines than any other aircraft between the two world wars. Designed by Jack Northrop as a fast executive transport, it outperformed most military aircraft of the day. Its superb airframe streamlining was enhanced by the NACA engine cowling, which increased its speed by approximately 20 mph. Powered by a 450-horsepower Pratt & Whitney Wasp, Post's immortal *Winnie Mae* had a top speed of around 180 mph.

Howard Hawks and Roscoe Turner flew Vegas to set a dazzling array of long-distance speed records. The Vega *Winnie Mae*, flown by one-eyed Wiley Post, set another great milestone—an around-the-world solo flight.

The former oilfield roughneck had already flown *Winnie Mae* around the world from June 23 to July 1, 1931, accompanied by his Australian navigator, Harold Gatty. Post had joked that the flight was made "to take the record away from the balloons," referring to the previous record of three weeks that had been set by Germany's airship *Graf Zeppelin* in 1929.

Besides the solo challenge, the importance of Post's 1933 flight lay in its technical achievements. It provided the ultimate test of two new inventions that later became standard equipment for aviation: the Sperry Gyroscope Company's prototype autopilot and the automatic direction finder (ADF), a navigational aid developed by the U.S. Army Air Corps. Post also fitted his 450-horsepower Pratt & Whitney engine with a new Hamilton Standard variable-pitch propeller that increased its speed and range. Finally, Post spent months intensively training himself to combat the fatigue and the physiological problems, known today as "jet lag," that he anticipated during his eight-day cockpit vigil.

Post took off from Roosevelt Field on July 15, 1933. Turning on "Mechanical Mike," his nickname for the autopilot, Post dead-reckoned his way across the Atlantic. Once he was within range of European broadcast stations, he tuned in the ADF for guidance to Berlin's Tempelhof Airport. After 26 hours jammed in the cockpit, Post's crumpled suit prompted a journalist to whimsically report, "One notices that a trouser-press is not a standard fitting even in American aeroplanes."

Despite several unscheduled stops crossing the Soviet Union, Post was well ahead of the record when he refueled at Edmonton, Alberta, Canada. On the last leg, overcome by fatigue, he catnapped across the continent. To keep from dropping into a deep sleep, Post held a wrench tied by a string to one finger. Each time he fell asleep, the wrench dropped from his grasp, jerked the finger, and woke him. Thanks to this novel alarm, Post arrived safely at Roosevelt Field in under eight days, cutting more than 21 hours off his previous time. Although it was nearly midnight, New Yorkers jammed the

In 1931, Wiley Post (right) and his Australian navigator, Harold Gatty, made the first circumnavigation of the world by a lone aircraft. Their Lockheed Vega *Winnie Mae* covered the 15,474-mile route in 8 days, 15 hours, and 51 minutes, with 13 refueling stops.

Wiley Post lost an eye working on an oil rig in 1926. His $1,800 compensation check bought his first aircraft—a beat-up Canuck (Jenny) biplane—and started the career of one of the giants of early aviation. After Post's fatal crash in Alaska with humorist Will Rogers in 1935, a fellow pilot wrote: "He was a tough, scarred, absolutely fearless Oklahoma boy. . . . If ever a man belonged in the cockpit of an airplane, that man was Wiley Post."

The most important technical achievement of Post's solo world flight was the success of this Sperry autopilot. Though it was not yet in production, the Sperry Gyroscope Company agreed to install the prototype in *Winnie Mae*. Primitive compared with today's electronic systems, Elmer Sperry's complex network of hydraulic lines and automatic sensors kept the Vega straight and level for much of the flight. Referring to the autopilot and a radio direction finder the airman also tested, the London *Times* stated: "Post definitely ushers in a new stage of long-distance aviation."

airfield, surging toward the taxiing plane. "Thousands and thousands of excited men and women climbed over and under fences," *Time* magazine reported.

The New York *Times* prophesied: "The days when human skill alone and an almost bird-like sense of direction enabled a flyer to hold his course for long hours through starless night or a fog are over. Commercial flying in the future will be automatic."

Post telegraphed the Sperry factory: "Pilot [autopilot] worked all the time except short time when line broke. Been impossible fly such weather without." With the knowledge gained from the flight, Sperry modified its invention, which was soon standard equipment on American airliners.

Two years later, the farmer's son who had dropped out of school after the eighth grade designed and built the first pressure suit and introduced the world to tropospheric air travel. With *Winnie Mae*'s engine supercharged, on March 5, 1935, Post flew at over 30,000 feet in the jet stream from Burbank, California, to Cleveland, Ohio. His flight was a prelude to jet airline techniques that would become commonplace a quarter of a century later.

Although they were not completed in time for him to enter, Post's high-altitude experiments were intended to gain a competitive edge for his aging *Winnie Mae* against more advanced aircraft in the 1934 England-Australia Air Race.

The MacRobertson Air Race of 1934

"Make it the greatest race yet conducted in the world, make as few conditions as possible consistent with reducing risks to the minimum," sponsor Sir MacPherson Robertson, a self-made Australian chocolate millionaire, told race organizers, never dreaming of the far-reaching effects it would have on commercial aviation.

Flying in the glare of worldwide publicity, Charles W. A. Scott and Tom Campbell Black flew a purpose-designed de Havilland D.H.88 Comet racer to victory in the race from Mildenhall to Melbourne. But second and third places went to America's new generation of airliners, the Douglas DC-2 and the Boeing 247. With an eye to a future Holland—Netherlands East Indies—Australia service, K.L.M. entered a new Douglas DC-2. Flying by strict airline routine—even carrying three adventurous passengers—K.L.M. Captain K. D. Parmentier reached Melbourne in three days and 18 hours. Two and a half hours behind came Roscoe Turner and Clyde Pangborn in a Boeing 247.

"This was just the result I wanted. To show that a transport plane could reach Australia in four days," Sir MacPherson declared, applauding the

The Dutch challenge almost came to grief at Albury, 175 miles from the finish. The KLM Douglas DC-2, caught in a severe electrical storm, force-landed at night on the little town's race course, which was lit by a row of car headlights. The next morning, the townspeople manhandled the bogged airliner onto a makeshift plank runway, and Captain Parmentier was able to finish second.

Roscoe Turner's Boeing 247D took third place in the 1934 MacRobertson race. The world's first modern airliner, the 247 entered service with United Air Lines in early 1933. Turner's race aircraft was sponsored by Hollywood's Warner Brothers and had extra fuel tanks installed in the passenger cabin. Though never achieving the success of its rival Douglas DC-2, Boeing eventually built 75 of these 10-passenger airliners. After the race, Turner's 247 entered service with United Air Lines.

professional precision with which K.L.M.'s experimental service had demonstrated the capabilities of the modern airliner. His race had marked the transition from slow, uncomfortable fabric-covered machines to fast, all-metal passenger aircraft. The airliner had finally come of age.

K.L.M. quickly ordered 12 DC-2s, starting an invasion of Europe by American equipment that ended Fokker's domination. American airlines followed suit. Nowhere was the effect more deeply felt than in Britain, which still relied mainly on ponderous biplanes. London's *Saturday Review* objectively analyzed the facts:

> Britain has won the greatest air race in history; but she has yet to start on an even greater air race; a race in commercial and military supremacy. . . . No British liner, no British service machine in regular use in any Royal Air Force squadron at the present time is fast enough to have finished the race within a thousand miles of the American machines. It is almost incredible, but it is true. . . .

Pan Am Spans the Pacific

In 1935, Pan American Airways (P.A.A.) capped the years of Pacific pioneering and improving aircraft design. Since its first service in 1927, when a cross-hired Fairchild floatplane flew between Key West, Florida, and Havana, P.A.A. had spread through the Caribbean and South America. Unable to negotiate

Facing page (bottom left):
Charles W.A. Scott was the most colorful aviation hero of Britain's Moth brigade. Noted for his urbane charm, wicked wit, and devastating rudeness, he fascinated the media. Besides winning the MacRobertson race with Tom Campbell Black, he won the 1936 England—South Africa race. His 1931 Moth flights sparked a spate of record-breaking on the lonely route to Australia.

Facing page (bottom right):
The winning de Havilland D.H.88 Comet *Grosvenor House* touches down at Melbourne Australia 71 hours after leaving England. Three race-designed Comets were built for the MacRobertson Race. Powered by two 230-horsepower D.H. Gipsy Six engines, the sleek monoplanes met their race design parameters; a cruising speed of 220 mph and a range of 2,800 miles.

One of Pan American's Sikorsky S-42 flying boats of the type that flew Pan Am's Pacific routes in the mid-1930s.

with the British and French over future Atlantic air service rights, Pan Am's visionary founder, Juan Trippe, had concentrated on the Pacific. Trippe had employed Charles Lindbergh as a technical adviser. From late July through mid-September 1931, Lindbergh and his wife surveyed an air route to China via Canada, Alaska, Japan, and the Soviet Union in a Lockheed Sirius floatplane. However, because the United States refused diplomatic recognition of the Soviet government, P.A.A. was denied permission to operate along the Siberian coast.

Unperturbed, Trippe issued specifications for a long-range flying boat to travel a trans-Pacific route using Hawaii, Midway, Wake, and Guam as staging posts to Manila and China. The Sikorsky and Martin companies responded with proposals for four-engine monoplane flying boats. Both bids were accepted, and in 1934 Pan Am took delivery of the first Sikorsky S-42. Late the following year, the first of Martin's elegant M-130s was delivered. Although lacking the range to carry a worthwhile payload over the Pacific, a refitted S-42 conducted route survey flights during the summer of 1935. The airline also undertook the massive task of building bases on Midway, Wake, Guam, and in Manila.

On November 22, 1935, the Martin M-130 *China Clipper*, loaded with 111,000 letters and under the command of Captain Edward Musick, prepared for takeoff from San Francisco Bay. On the docks 125,000 people marveled as all the airline's new Pacific bases reported that they were "standing by for orders" via a special radio link. Over a microphone, Juan Trippe addressed the pilot: "Captain Musick, you have your sailing orders. Cast off and depart for Manila in accordance therewith." As the band played "The Star-Spangled Banner," the *China Clipper* lifted off the water and headed out over the partly completed Golden Gate bridge for Hawaii. In a little under 60 hours of flying time and 8,210 miles later, Musick landed safely in Manila Bay.

Eleven months later, Pan American began flying passengers on this route. Nine passengers paid $1,438 (about $20,000 today) for the round-trip flight to Manila. By previous airline standards, the service was superb. Passengers were pampered in armchair comfort enhanced by silver-service meals. Overnight they slept at Pan Am's island hotels surrounded by tropical luxury: swaying palms, cool verandas, and smiling islanders in immaculate white uniforms. The age of elegant air travel had arrived, albeit only for the very wealthy. By 1937, routes to China and Auckland, New Zealand, had been opened.

Pan American's ultimate goal was the Atlantic, and in 1937 an S-42 conducted a series of survey flights via Newfoundland. Britain's first Short S.23 Empire flying boat also surveyed this route for Imperial Airways, but neither

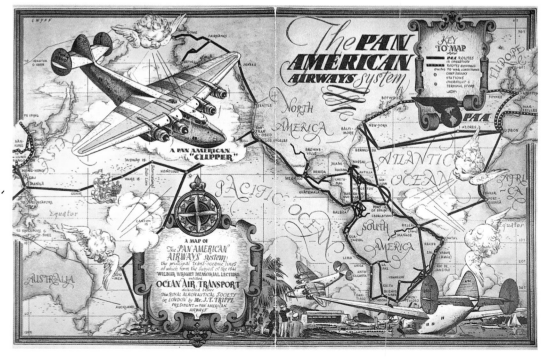

Passengers disembark from a Martin M-130 at Pan Am's Hawaiian Clipper Base at the Ford Island Naval Air Station at Pearl Harbor. After the 18-hour stage from California, trans-Pacific passengers spent the night in a hotel. The procedure was repeated at Midway and Wake islands, where Pan Am constructed its own hotels, and at Guam—the final staging post to Manila.

The extent of the Pan American Airways route system in 1941 is shown by this map produced for Juan Trippe's Wilbur Wright Memorial Lecture. It features the company's Boeing B-314 Clippers. Twelve were built, all subsequently operated as military transport aircraft during World War II.

machine could carry a worthwhile trans-Atlantic payload. This had been the problem as far back as 1930, when the French had run intermittent seaplane mail services across the south Atlantic. France's most famous ocean flyer, Jean Mermoz, had completed 23 crossings before his Latécoère 300 flying-boat vanished in midocean in 1936.

Germany had also made numerous experimental seaplane mail flights in the north and south Atlantic. In August 1938, a German Focke-Wulf Fw 200 Condor flew nonstop from Berlin to New York, signaling that land planes would one day replace the transoceanic seaplanes.

Overnight to Hawaii — $278

During the late 1930's, Pan Am's guidebooks and travel posters evoked the mystery of the Orient, the tropical pleasures of Hawaii, and the heritage of America's swift nineteenth-century clipper ships that plied the China trade. Prominently featuring the Martin M-130 and luxurious new Boeing B-314 Clipper flying boats on its trans-Pacific service, Pan Am pioneered the commercial air routes across the Pacific before World War II. Powered by four 1,550-horsepower Wright Double Cyclone engines, the 84,000-pound Boeing B-314 carried 30 passengers and mail at 184 mph. The largest commercial aircraft of its day, the B-314 enabled Pan Am to begin the first regular trans-Atlantic service.

In August 1938, Germany used the Atlantic to demonstrate the potential of its Focke-Wulf Condor. Commanded by Captain Alfred Henke, Deutsche Lufthansa's Fw 200 *Brandenburg* flew 3,970 miles from Berlin to New York in 24 hours and 56 minutes and made the return journey in just under 20 hours. Discussing the relative safety of the *Brandenburg* versus flying boats and airships, *The Aeroplane* stated: "We still do not approve of depending for one's safety entirely on airscrews and motors." Its commercial future cut short by World War II, the Luftwaffe's long-legged Condors ranged the Atlantic, tracking Allied shipping for Germany's U-boat fleet and attacking merchant ships.

to Carswell Air Force Base at Fort Worth, Texas, after a flight of 23,452 miles in 94 hours and 1 minute. The flight's success was due to four in-flight refuelings by KB-29 aerial tankers. These refuelings verified the concept of aerial refueling for range extension and endurance that Lowell Smith and John Richter had demonstrated in 1923. The first jet flight around the world came on January 15 to 18, 1957, when three of SAC's B-52 intercontinental bombers from Castle Air Force Base, California, flew 24,325 miles in 49 hours and 19 minutes with four in-flight refuelings by KC-97 tankers.

Because of a lack of sufficient commercial motivation and military backing, however, the final milestone of a nonstop, nonrefueled around-the-world flight would not be put in place until Dick Rutan and Jeana Yeager momentarily rekindled the euphoria of Lindbergh's epoch in their purpose-built *Voyager* in December 1986.

Before World War II brought the golden era of aviation to a close, the airline boom was beginning. Ten airline companies were operating intercontinental services. In Europe 30 major airlines operated 819 passenger aircraft, and in the United States 17 companies operated 256 airliners.

On June 28, 1939, Pan American Airways flew the first trans-Atlantic passenger service, closing the final gap in the world's airline network. The Boeing 314 flying boat *Dixie Clipper* carried nine crew members and 22 passengers who paid $675 round trip (the equivalent of about $8,000 today). The gleaming 40-ton Clipper was driven by four 1,500-horsepower Wright

AROUND THE WORLD ON ONE TANK OF GAS

Aviation's last great distance milestone was passed on December 23, 1986, when *Voyager* completed the first nonstop, nonrefueled flight around the world. Pilots Dick Rutan and Jeana Yeager spent nine days, three minutes, and 44 seconds in the airplane's tiny cabin.

Setting out from Edwards Air Force Base in California, they flew westward 26,358 miles, closely hugging the equator to take advantage of the easterly trade winds. This entailed flying in regions notorious for tropical storms. Without pressurization to allow a higher climb, Rutan likened the problem to flying through a forest and dodging the tree trunks.

Voyager was the brainchild of Burt Rutan, famed for his innovative home-built canard designs. Constructed almost entirely of moulded lightweight composite materials, the 110-foot-wingspan aircraft weighed only 2,250 pounds. This enabled its two Teledyne Continental engines (totaling a mere 240 horsepower) to lift the 7,011 pounds of fuel required for the flight. Once the initial fuel load had been reduced, *Voyager* cruised on the 110 horsepower rear engine.

Like Wiley Post during history's most dramatic flight, Rutan and Yeager received extensive media attention until they arrived back safely at Edwards with just 106 pounds of fuel. As with their predecessor, the pair's greatest trial was mental and physical exhaustion, particularly in the late stages, when they had serious fuel feed problems. "There's nothing I hate more than sweating fuel," Rutan reported.

Though a brilliant example of modern technology, the flight of *Voyager* was not about design advancement or future commercial applications. Rather, it exemplified the human spirit challenging history's "Milestone Impossible"—simply to be first.

The end of *Voyager's* milestone flight at Edwards Air Force Base.

Voyager: Around the World Non-Stop

BY JEANA YEAGER AND DICK RUTAN, WITH PHIL PATTON

In December 1986, Jeana Yeager and Dick Rutan flew their specially designed *Voyager* around the world to establish a final milestone in distance flying—around the world without stopping or refueling. Fatigue and weather proved almost as great a challenge to the pilots as the distance.

In the trailer back in Mojave, the Africa crossing was being anticipated with considerable anxiety, and everyone wanted to be on the scene.

Mike Hance of mission control was trying to set up Voyager's passage with air control in Nairobi. The man in the tower, a native named Patrick Oamuyo, had a hard time understanding everything. Mike spelled out our names—"Dick: Delta India Charlie Kilo"—but he could not get the fellow to understand that Voyager was an airplane that was going to fly around the world and—in a few hours—over his head, en route.

"What kind," said Patrick Oamuyo, "what kind rocket this is?"...

It was bright daylight in Africa, but well after dark in Mojave. The wind was beginning to whip around the antenna masts and shake the trailer.

"I think we'd better wake Len up," said Larry Burch to Conway Roberts, who was on duty in mission control. We were about an hour and a half from the lake—in the middle of our rendezvous with Doug, although no one in the trailer knew that—and Burch had already sent a message to be transmitted in the blind: "Thunderstorms over Lake Victoria. Divert to south."...

We got Len's message, saying just to work our way through and not, repeat not, divert north. But we had already worked out our course on our own. The weather looked terrible in front of us, so, whatever the danger, we had decided to fly north—north over the red crosshatched danger zone.

There were three places we had been told never, never, never to fly. One was Somalia; the other two were Uganda and Chad. But now we were about to enter Uganda. We were going to fly right over Entebbe Airport, where the Israelis had staged their famous hostage rescue....

So now we headed for the mountains, running both engines flat out and to hell with the fuel burn figures; the engines screamed as they tried to climb over this stratus layer....

We were crossing much too late in the day. We should have gotten here hours before. Now the heating on the jungle floor was pumping up the storms. We were really in trouble. This was the worst time we could ever be here. But there was nothing we could do except keep going....

The wingtips were scraping the clouds. We couldn't see the ends of them, we didn't want to look at them anyway, but we wanted to know they were there....

Now we pushed the engines for best power, forgetting range. We just kept going, kept hoping and praying, and remembered there was no way we could allow Voyager into one of those clouds. No way.

Right then I realized that Jeana wasn't saying anything. I watched her reflection in the radar screen while I flew, and I could see that her position was very strange. She was lying there just like a cat, on knees and elbows, hands forward, but with her face flat on the floor. I called her on the intercom, but there was no response.

"Jeana, you've got to stay awake."

She'd never slept like this.

She'd been trying to stay awake, help dodge the storms, but she just couldn't.

Double Cyclone engines developed from the pioneering 200-horsepower Whirlwind.

During 1939, American domestic airlines carried nearly 2 million passengers—more than half the world's total—and in the 12-month period ending March 1940, they enjoyed a 100 percent safety record. The introduction of the Douglas DC-3, which then accounted for 80 percent of the American airline fleet, made this possible. Despite its tardy entry into the airline business, the United States had leapfrogged the world.

Though still an expensive alternative to surface transport, air travel had come of age. A major factor had been the great advances in engine design not only in terms of reliability but also in terms of a vastly improved power-to-weight ratio. This allowed aircraft companies to design and build larger and more comfortable aircraft that could carry larger payloads over greater distances. Building on the experience of the long-distance flyers, experienced and highly trained professionals replaced seat-of-the-pants barnstormers. The milestones of distance had tested and refined new aircraft, equipment, and flying techniques. Hand-in-hand had come the instruments, radios, and navigation aids vital to safe all-weather operation.

I reached over and touched her. She was cool to my touch. There was no blinking light on her oxygen! No light on the panel for her oxygen. She wasn't breathing!

Then, flying the airplane with my right hand, I reached over with my left to rub her back and neck. No reaction. I shook hard, rubbed her shoulders and neck, and shook again.

All of a sudden she came back to life, leaping up, almost hitting the roof. "What?"...

She couldn't stay awake, and if you're not careful you don't ever wake up, or you wake up with a headache you have the rest of your life. I worried about this and whether I was in any shape to make sure she was getting oxygen while flying the plane and dodging thunderstorms. If she was dead, what would I do? Land, fly on with a corpse? I wondered, and I felt all alone....

We had underestimated the oxygen. With fatigue and her cold she couldn't absorb enough, so I turned her valve up a little bit. Or did I? I thought. Did I already do that?...

In the trailer there had been nothing to do but wait, nervously, with cups of coffee and jokes. Then a new position was relayed in.

"They're west of the lake already!" Conway Roberts said.

Conway couldn't believe it. He went over to the map and fiddled with the pushpins and then took out his flight computer and went over it....

Then Conway understood what we had done. He suspected it right away: there was a nice curve to the planned course around the south of Lake Victoria on the map, and Conway figured it out. We had just sliced that curve off and gone straight across the north side....

Jeana was stirring now, coming back to life. She had an awful headache, and her stomach was churning. It was still hard for her to stay awake....

I checked the log and pulled out the map. Glancing over at the Omega, I read the coordinates there and plotted them. And then I realized where we were: three quarters of the way past Yaounde to the coast. The mountains! I glanced over at the radar, and they were right there, two big shadows.

The image got me going with a jolt, and I made an immediate left turn of twenty degrees to pull the airplane around Mount Cameroon....

The second mountain, Santa Isabel, was about fifteen miles away on an island, and I made sure we gave it a wide berth as we headed out over the coast, leaving the beautiful small city called Douala behind us, and into the Atlantic.

A few minutes later, at 0030 Z, I radioed for our position and gave a set of coordinates.... Somebody went scrambling to the maps to sort out the locations.

"We have you on the map, Dick," Walt radioed back, wondering if we were lost, if the fatigue was getting to me somehow, but trying to sound as if everything were under control.

"And what does that mean?" I said.

Walt was perplexed. "Say again?"

"What does that mean? It means we've made Africa, baby. We've made Africa, and we're on our way home...."

We had always thought Africa would be the hardest, and it was—up till then. For a moment I thought we were home free, and that flying across the dark continent was the greatest thing we had ever done in our lives...never mind that we still had a third of the world to go.

On the ground, aerodromes, navigation beacons, and air traffic and meteorological services supported the new industry.

In 1919, only the rich and daring had had the nerve to climb aboard the first rickety airliners, trusting to luck and the weather. Two decades later, only a matter of money prevented the world from commuting in fast, sophisticated comfort. The jumbo-jet age evolving from World War II would break that final barrier.

Besides pioneering the world's future air routes, the quest to fly farther created and maintained public interest. By fostering confidence in the capabilities of the airplane, long-distance flights eventually encouraged the public to fly and, more important, enticed business people to invest in aviation.

The pioneering men and women who established milestones around the world were the public relations teams of the airplane's formative years. They captured the limelight, fired the world's imagination, and kept the dream alive until design caught up with promise. Today we climb on board an airliner and cross an ocean as casually as our grandparents boarded a train. That is their legacy.

FASTER

AND HIGHER

FASTER AND
The Quest for Speed and Power

JOHN D. ANDERSON, JR.

HIGHER

Three times a week, a sleek white dart blasts into the heavens over metropolitan Washington, D.C. The sound is unmistakable—a powerful roar distinctly stronger than that of the more conventional airliners that routinely fly into and out of the three major airports in the area. This is the sight and sound of the British Airways supersonic transport (SST), the Concorde, as it takes off from Dulles International Airport in suburban Virginia on its way to Heathrow Airport outside London—a trip that will take the aircraft to 2.2 times the speed of sound at altitudes between 50,000 and 60,000 feet.

The Concorde is the epitome of a major driving force in aviation since its beginning: the quest to fly *faster* and *higher*. This ceaseless search has been marked by stunning successes as well as abject failures, massive efforts to advance technology toward a seemingly endless progression of new and better airplanes, and the intense mental and physical courage of the men and women who designed and flew these aircraft.

This chapter is the story of the people and flying machines that established the milestones of faster and higher flight—one of the most spectacular intellectual and practical successes of the twentieth century. It is a story that is still evolving as you read these words.

The key to faster and higher flight is a simple technical concept: *thrust minus drag*, or

$$T - D$$

When the thrust from one or more engines, T, is greater than the drag of the airframe, D, the airplane can accelerate to higher speeds. However, D increases as velocity increases—drag essentially increases as the square of velocity, V^2. Finally, when a velocity is reached at which D equals the maximum thrust, $T - D$ is zero; the airplane can no longer accelerate in level flight and has reached its maximum velocity. Hence, in the design of an airplane, *the higher the thrust and the lower the drag, the faster an airplane can fly*.

The concept of $T - D$ also pertains to maximum altitude. When an airplane is climbing to a higher altitude, thrust is always greater than drag. Indeed, as altitude increases, both maximum thrust and drag decrease as the air density becomes lower, air being much thinner at high altitudes. However, at high altitudes the thrust decreases faster than the drag, and when an altitude is reached at which $T - D$ is zero, the airplane can no

Pages 78–79:
A Soviet Tupolev Tu-144 supersonic transport prepares for takeoff with its hinged nose in the dropped position and its flaps down. The sleek 290,000-pound Soviet SST first flew in December 1969, two months before the Anglo-French Concorde. The leading edge of the ogival wing planform sweeps smoothly from the needle-shaped nose to the trailing wing tip. The underwing engine nacelles house four NK-144 engines, each with 43,000 pounds of thrust. Although capable of speeds over 1,500 mph (Mach 2+), the Tu-144 had significant technical problems that were compounded by a crash at the 1973 Paris Air Show. After several years with *Aeroflot*, the Tu-144 was finally withdrawn from service in June 1978.

Facing page:
This British Airways model of the Anglo-French Concorde supersonic transport (SST) is the epitome of the quest for speed and altitude in a commercial transport. Powered by four Rolls-Royce/SNECMA Olympus turbojet engines with 38,050 pounds of thrust, it cruises at Mach 2.2 at altitudes above 50,000 feet. The ogival delta-shaped wing has an extremely thin airfoil section that reduces supersonic wave drag. The joint Anglo-French agreement to develop a supersonic transport was signed on November 29, 1962, and the first prototype flew on March 2, 1969. By the late 1970s, both British Airways and Air France had the Concorde in regular service.

longer climb. Thus, again, T − D is the key: *the higher the thrust and the lower the drag, the higher an airplane can fly.* The quest for speed and altitude has always involved the combined drives of more thrust (better, more powerful engines and fuels) and less drag (better aerodynamics).

The Dawn of Manned, Powered Flight

The dream of human flight can be traced as far back as ancient mythology. Witness the early Greek myth of Daedalus and his son Icarus. Imprisoned on the island of Crete in the Mediterranean Sea, Daedalus made wings to which feathers were fastened with wax. With these wings on their arms, they both flew off. Against his father's warnings, Icarus flew too close to the sun. The wax melted, and Icarus fell to his death in the sea.

Through the ensuing centuries, the human desire to soar like a bird was an ever-present dream. But not until the development of rational science, beginning with Isaac Newton in the later seventeenth century, and of the Industrial Revolution in the eighteenth and nineteenth centuries did the necessary theoretical and mechanical tools become available for serious first attempts at human flight. The development of flight was accomplished only through the dedicated efforts of such people as Sir George Cayley in England, inventor of the concept of the fixed-wing aircraft in 1799; Otto Lilienthal in Germany, who developed and flew the first successful human-carrying gliders from 1890 to 1896; and Samuel P. Langley in the United States, builder of the *Aerodrome* and secretary of the Smithsonian Institution at the turn of the century. Around the year 1500, Leonardo da Vinci had developed a concept similar to Cayley's, but his notes were misplaced and were unavailable to aeronautical designers until the late nineteenth century.

After achieving the first sustained powered flight with his unmanned heavier-than-air *Aerodrome* in 1896, Langley came close to achieving the first sustained person-carrying powered flight of his full-size *Aerodrome* in October and December 1903. Structural failure ended Langley's second and last attempt on December 8, 1903, just nine days before the historic first flight of Wilbur and Orville Wright on December 17. Today, the invention of the first *practical* aircraft is attributed to the Wright brothers, who inherited an already large fund of aeronautical data as well as an obsession for flight from their many predecessors of the previous four centuries.

THE WRIGHT BROTHERS

The quest for faster and higher flight began on that cold and windy Thursday—at Kill Devil Hills, four miles south of Kitty Hawk, North Carolina—when Wilbur and Orville Wright accomplished the first successful flight of a manned, heavier-than-air flying machine. The Wright brothers were at the fine edge of the T − D equation. In regard to drag, the Wrights' earlier glider designs of 1900 and 1901 had not been aerodynamically efficient. These gliders had been designed on the basis of the best aerodynamic data then available, especially the work of Lilienthal and Langley. However, the ratio of lift to drag was low. The Wright brothers had felt so dissatisfied with the aerodynamic performance of their 1901 glider that on the train ride back to their native Dayton, Ohio, after their trials at Kill Devil Hills, Wilbur was quoted as saying, "Nobody will fly for a thousand years." Shortly thereafter, the Wrights made a decision of tremendous intellectual courage that was to be the primary reason for their success.

Wilbur and Orville Wright reasoned that the aeronautical data used for designing their earlier gliders must have been flawed. Wilbur wrote: "Having set out with absolute faith in the existing scientific data, we were driven to

doubt one thing after another, until finally, after two years of experiment, we cast it all aside, and decided to rely entirely upon our own investigations." And investigate they did.

Between September 1901 and August 1902, the Wrights undertook a major program of aerodynamic research. They built a wind tunnel in their bicycle shop in Dayton and tested over 200 different airfoil shapes and wing configurations. One result of this wind tunnel work was that the Wrights increased the *aspect ratio*—the ratio of wingspan to chord length for a rectangular-shaped wing—from about 3½ to 6. Although they did not realize it at the time, the theoretical significance of this increase in aspect ratio was that they were, in reality, reducing the induced drag caused by the presence of flow vortices at the wing tips by a factor of 2. The true theoretical significance of the aspect ratio, wing tip vortices, and induced drag was not known until 15 years later, when Ludwig Prandtl, perhaps the most famous aerodynamicist in history, developed his wing theory at the University of Göttingen in Germany.

The aerodynamic experiments carried out by the Wright brothers in 1901 and 1902 were the first practical wind tunnel tests in the history of flight. Francis Wenham designed and operated the first wind tunnel in history at Greenwich, England, in 1871. Horatio Phillips followed Wenham with fledgling wind tunnel experiments on airfoils in 1874, while Nikolai Zhukovsky in Russia in 1891, Ludwig Mach in Austria in 1893, Alfred Wells in the U.S. (at the Massachusetts Institute of Technology) in 1896, and A. H. Zahm (at the Catholic

In the fall of 1901, the Wright brothers built a wind tunnel similar to this version exhibited in the Wrights' cycle shop reconstructed in 1938 at the Henry Ford Museum and Greenfield Village at Dearborn, Michigan. The Wrights tested hundreds of different wing and airfoil shapes in the wind tunnel during the fall and winter of 1901–1902. They used the wind tunnel data to design their successful 1902 glider and then the 1903 Wright *Flyer*. This was the first practical use of wind tunnel data in the design of an airplane.

University of America) in 1901 all worked on basic aerodynamic flow. The Wrights were thus not the first to design and use a wind tunnel, but they were certainly the first to produce aerodynamic data that directly affected successful airplane design. Fully incorporating the new aerodynamic design guidelines that markedly reduced drag, the Wrights' 1902 glider flew spectacularly well compared with the 1900 and 1901 models.

In the fall of 1902, the Wrights returned to Dayton from Kitty Hawk to work on the other part of the T − D relationship—the engine and propeller that generated thrust. At that time, the internal combustion engine was in a state of active but crude development. In 1860, the Frenchman Etienne Lenoir built the first practical gas engine, a single-cylinder device burning ordinary street-lighting coal gas for fuel. In 1876, N.A. Otto and Eugen Langen of Germany developed the four-cycle engine, the ancestor of modern automobile engines, which also used gas as a fuel. Then, in 1885, Gottlieb Daimler and Karl Benz in Germany designed the first gasoline-burning engine, giving birth to the automobile industry.

Against this background, the Wright brothers had no trouble choosing the gasoline-powered internal combustion engine as their power source. However, they had trouble obtaining a suitable engine. In their quest for thrust, the Wrights had divided the responsibilities: Wilbur handled the propeller, and Orville took charge of the engine. Orville initially believed that the automotive industry could supply a proper engine, although it would take special development. From their calculations, the Wrights knew they needed at least an 8-horsepower engine that was as small as possible, weighing, preferably, only 150 pounds. Unfortunately, their specifications were far beyond those of existing automobile engines. After contacting numerous companies, Orville could find nobody willing to fund the research and development necessary to build such an engine. So, as in the case of their aerodynamics, the Wrights took the do-it-yourself approach.

With the help of Charles Taylor, a machinist in the Wrights' bicycle shop, Orville designed and built from scratch a four-cylinder gasoline engine. When finished, the engine weighed 180 pounds. It developed 12 horsepower during the first 15 seconds of operation, dropping slightly below that thereafter—but still above the minimum of 8 required, according to their calculations. Once again, they were at the fine edge of the T − D relationship. Wilbur's responsibility was thus all the more critical because a propeller had to convert the engine's limited horsepower into thrust in the most efficient manner possible.

Wilbur expected this step to be rather straightforward. Marine propellers had been in use for almost a century, and he expected to find an appropriate theory or data upon which to base the design of an aircraft propeller. Such was not the case. After spending days in Dayton libraries,

THE MANLY ENGINE: TIED TO THE WRONG MACHINE

When they first flew on December 17, 1903, the Wright brothers did not have the best aircraft engine available. That honor goes to Charles Manly, the able assistant to Samuel P. Langley at the Smithsonian Institution, who in 1901 designed and built a five-cylinder radial engine that produced 53 horsepower but weighed only 200 pounds. This gasoline-powered engine was designed for the Langley Aerodrome, which was a dismal failure in 1903, though not because of its engine. If anything, the engine might have been too powerful for the frail Aerodrome.

Possibly tainted by Langley's failure, the Manly engine was never used in its original form in any other aircraft. It became a museum piece, except for one period in 1914 when Glenn H. Curtiss modified and again mated it with the Langley Aerodrome. After Curtiss made 93 separate technical modifications the Aerodrome finally flew over Keuka Lake, New York, on May 28, 1914, with Curtiss at the controls. One of the ironies of aviation history is that Manly's engine, which was by far the best aircraft engine until the beginning of World War I, never saw service in a practical airplane.

Orville Wright and his assistant Charlie Taylor designed and built the Wright *Flyer's* 12-horsepower engine shown in this photograph.

Wilbur discovered that no general propeller theory existed and that even an appreciation of their true aerodynamic function was lacking. So, as before, the Wrights relied upon self-initiative. Throughout the winter of 1902–1903, they wrestled with and debated various propeller designs. By early 1903, they were the first to recognize that a propeller is basically a rotating wing made up of airfoil sections that generate an aerodynamic force normal to the propeller's plane of rotation. They made use of their wind tunnel data on different airfoil shapes and chose a suitably cambered shape for the propeller section.

Carrying the do-it-yourself philosophy to the extreme, in March 1903 Wilbur, using a hatchet and drawknife, hacked two propellers out of laminated spruce and then surfaced the propellers with aluminum paint. Orville later wrote:

> We had been unable to find anything of value in any of the works to which we had access, so we worked out a theory of our own on the subject, and soon discovered, as we usually do, that all the propellers built heretofore are *all wrong*, and then built a pair . . . based on our theory, which are *all right*.

They were indeed "all right." The Wright propeller was so efficient that it and the wing-warping approach used to achieve lateral control were the two main technical features that the Europeans copied and developed further after Wilbur's first public flight demonstrations in France in 1908.

In September 1903, the Wrights transported their new machine to Kill Devil Hills in North Carolina. They called the new machine the *Flyer* because,

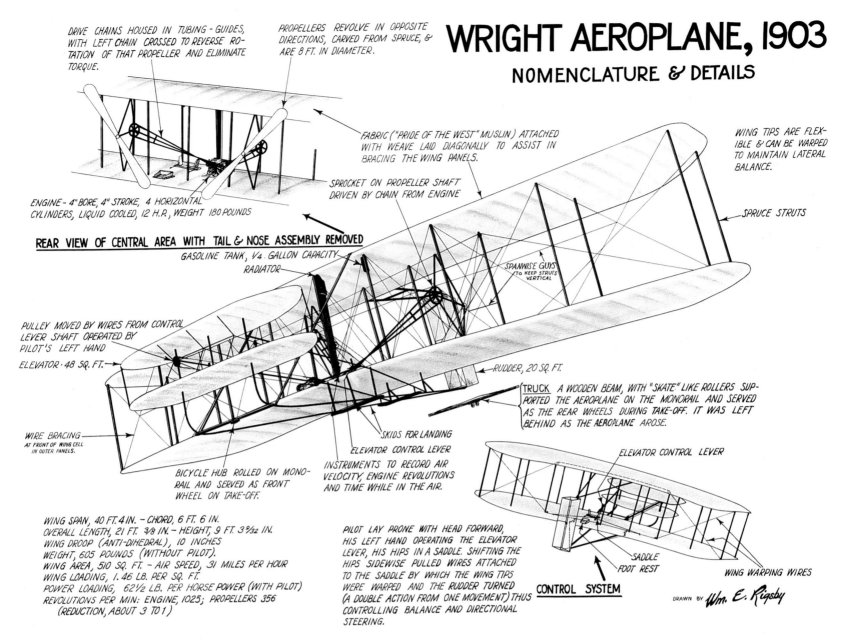

WRIGHT AEROPLANE, 1903
NOMENCLATURE & DETAILS

DRIVE CHAINS HOUSED IN TUBING - GUIDES, WITH LEFT CHAIN CROSSED TO REVERSE ROTATION OF THAT PROPELLER AND ELIMINATE TORQUE.

PROPELLERS REVOLVE IN OPPOSITE DIRECTIONS, CARVED FROM SPRUCE, & ARE 8 FT. IN DIAMETER.

FABRIC ("PRIDE OF THE WEST" MUSLIN) ATTACHED WITH WEAVE LAID DIAGONALLY TO ASSIST IN BRACING THE WING PANELS.

WING TIPS ARE FLEXIBLE & CAN BE WARPED TO MAINTAIN LATERAL BALANCE.

SPROCKET ON PROPELLER SHAFT DRIVEN BY CHAIN FROM ENGINE

ENGINE - 4" BORE, 4" STROKE, 4 HORIZONTAL CYLINDERS, LIQUID COOLED, 12 H.P., WEIGHT 180 POUNDS

SPRUCE STRUTS

REAR VIEW OF CENTRAL AREA WITH TAIL & NOSE ASSEMBLY REMOVED

GASOLINE TANK, ¼ GALLON CAPACITY
RADIATOR

SPANWISE GUYS TO KEEP STRUTS VERTICAL

PULLEY MOVED BY WIRES FROM CONTROL LEVER SHAFT OPERATED BY PILOT'S LEFT HAND

ELEVATOR - 48 SQ. FT.

RUDDER, 20 SQ. FT.

TRUCK A WOODEN BEAM, WITH "SKATE" LIKE ROLLERS SUPPORTED THE AEROPLANE ON THE MONORAIL AND SERVED AS THE REAR WHEELS DURING TAKE-OFF. IT WAS LEFT BEHIND AS THE AEROPLANE AROSE.

WIRE BRACING AT FRONT OF WING CELL IN OUTER PANELS.

SKIDS FOR LANDING

ELEVATOR CONTROL LEVER

ELEVATOR CONTROL LEVER

BICYCLE HUB ROLLED ON MONORAIL AND SERVED AS FRONT WHEEL ON TAKE-OFF.

INSTRUMENTS TO RECORD AIR VELOCITY, ENGINE REVOLUTIONS AND TIME WHILE IN THE AIR.

WING SPAN, 40 FT. 4 IN. – CHORD, 6 FT. 6 IN.
OVERALL LENGTH, 21 FT. ⅜ IN. – HEIGHT, 9 FT. 3 5⁄32 IN.
WING DROOP (ANTI-DIHEDRAL), 10 INCHES
WEIGHT, 605 POUNDS (WITHOUT PILOT).
WING AREA, 510 SQ. FT. – AIR SPEED, 31 MILES PER HOUR
WING LOADING, 1.46 LB. PER SQ. FT.
POWER LOADING, 62½ LB. PER HORSE POWER (WITH PILOT)
REVOLUTIONS PER MIN: ENGINE, 1025; PROPELLERS 356
(REDUCTION, ABOUT 3 TO 1)

PILOT LAY PRONE WITH HEAD FORWARD, HIS LEFT HAND OPERATING THE ELEVATOR LEVER, HIS HIPS IN A SADDLE. SHIFTING THE HIPS SIDEWISE PULLED WIRES ATTACHED TO THE SADDLE BY WHICH THE WING TIPS WERE WARPED AND THE RUDDER TURNED (A DOUBLE ACTION FROM ONE MOVEMENT) THUS CONTROLLING BALANCE AND DIRECTIONAL STEERING.

SADDLE
FOOT REST

CONTROL SYSTEM

WING WARPING WIRES

DRAWN BY *Wm. E. Rigsby*

Wright airplane 1903: nomenclature and details.

totally unlike previous gliders, it was a "flying machine" that featured two large propellers driven with a chain-link mechanism by one engine. After numerous frustrating delays caused by mechanical problems with the propeller shafts and unusually severe weather, the Wrights were ready on December 17, 1903. At 10:35 on that cold and windy morning, the Wright *Flyer* lifted from the sand and flew for 12 seconds, covering 120 feet over the ground. This was the first of four separate flights that day, with the last flight remaining in the air for 59 seconds and covering 852 feet. Unfortunately, a few minutes after this fourth flight, a gust of wind caught the Wright *Flyer* as it stood on the ground, tumbling it over and over and damaging it beyond repair. The first Wright *Flyer* would never fly again. Years later, Orville repaired and reconstructed the original *Flyer*. After residing in the Science Museum in London until 1948, it now "flies" permanently at the National Air and Space Museum of the Smithsonian Institution.

With the 1903 Wright *Flyer*, the T – D relationship was sufficiently, but just barely, satisfied. As reported by Orville, the average airspeed was 30 mph and the altitude was a scant few feet off the ground. But the great quest for speed and altitude had begun.

GLENN H. CURTISS

After the Wright brothers' 1903 success, the next major milestone in faster and higher flight involved Glenn Curtiss. From his youth in Hammondsport, New

York, Curtiss was obsessed with *speed*. He became active in bicycle racing and quickly earned a reputation as a winner. In 1901, he added an engine to his bicycle and became an avid motorcycle racer. By 1902, his fame was spreading and he was receiving numerous orders for motorcycles of his own design. When the Wrights flew at Kitty Hawk, Curtiss already had a motorcycle factory in Hammondsport and was building the best motorcycle engines available. In January 1904, at Ormond Beach, Florida, Curtiss established a new world record for speed for a ground vehicle—67 mph over a 10-mile straightaway. This was more than twice the airspeed of the Wright *Flyer*.

It was only a matter of time before Curtiss would try flying. The seeds were sown in 1904 when he first provided motors for dirigibles designed and flown by Thomas Baldwin, a California balloonist. Baldwin later moved his manufacturing facilities to Hammondsport to be close to the supply of Curtiss engines, beginning a lifelong friendship with Curtiss. In 1906, Baldwin and Curtiss went to the Dayton Fair in Ohio, where they met and held lengthy discussions with the Wright brothers. Years later, these conversations became the crux of the Wrights' lawsuits against Curtiss, in which they accused him of having stolen some of their ideas on powered flight and using them for financial gain.

Within a year, Curtiss became a member of the Aerial Experiment Association (AEA), formed by Alexander Graham Bell, also a close friend of Samuel Langley and an extremely enthusiastic follower of the development of powered flight. Curtiss' main contribution to the AEA consisted of his efficient engine designs. Moreover, under the auspices of the AEA, Curtiss designed and built an airplane, the *June Bug*, with which he won the

Glenn H. Curtiss designed, built, and often flew the Curtiss Model D "Headless" pusher biplane that was a standard airplane in the years immediately following 1910. Easily assembled, disassembled, and repaired, the Headless was a favorite of exhibition flyers, including C. S. "Casey" Jones, Eugene Ely, and J. A. D. McCurdy. Outfitted with a central float and outriggers, the D Hydro became the first Curtiss seaplane to takeoff successfully when it lifted off the water at San Diego, California, on January 26, 1911. The subsequent flight of a Curtiss D-III Tractor Hydro at San Diego in February 1911 convinced the U.S. Navy to buy two Curtiss E seaplanes, designated the A-1 and A-2. These were the first of many Curtiss seaplanes to serve the Navy in peace and war.

After 1908, Glenn Curtiss was a strong competitor of the Wright brothers. He became well known and his airplanes were very popular after Curtiss won the inaugural Gordon Bennett Trophy speed race on August 28, 1909, during the first *Grande Semaine de l'Aviation de la Champagne* (International Air Meet) for heavier-than-air flying machines at Reims, France. Curtiss flew his *Reims Racer*, a larger version of his earlier *Golden Flyer*, to a record-setting speed of 47.65 mph but barely beat Louis Blériot. The *Reims Racer* was powered by an eight-cylinder, 60-horsepower Curtiss V-8 engine and had wingspan 11 feet shorter than that of the Wright *Flyer*. Ailerons placed between the wings at the wing tips provided lateral control, in contrast to the Wrights' use of wing warping. The left aileron can be seen just behind the front wheel; the right aileron is almost completely concealed by the upper wing.

U.S. Navy observers at the Reims Air Meet were so impressed with Glenn Curtiss's flying machines that they began discussions with him immediately afterward. Eugene Ely, a Curtiss test pilot, became the first man to takeoff from the deck of a ship when he flew this Curtiss Model D from the U.S.S. *Birmingham* at Hampton Roads, Virginia, on November 14, 1910. On January 18, 1911, again flying a Curtiss, Ely recorded the first airplane landing on a ship, the U.S.S. *Pennsylvania*, in San Francisco Bay, using grappling hooks to catch arresting wires strung across a special wooden deck. After Ely's landing and subsequent takeoff, Captain C. F. Pond, skipper of the *Pennsylvania*, prophetically reported to Navy headquarters: "I desire to place myself on record as positively assured of the importance of the aeroplane in future naval warfare." Eventually, the aircraft carrier, which revolutionized naval warfare in the coming years, was developed in the 1920s so that fleets could take their aircraft to sea for protection and attack.

Scientific American trophy for making the first straight-line flight of one kilometer (3,281 feet) in public on July 4, 1908. Of course, the Wrights had achieved many more spectacular successes by then, but because they had not carried out their flights in public view, their records were not officially recognized at that time.

Glenn Curtiss set a speed milestone in 1909. During the famous air races held in Reims, France, from August 22 to 29, he won the first Gordon Bennett Cup with an average speed of 47.65 mph over a 20-kilometer course. His airplane, of his own design, was the *Reims Racer.* Now an international success, Curtiss went on to a distinguished career in aviation both as a pilot trying to satisfy his personal obsession with speed and as a designer and manufacturer of airplanes.

For all practical purposes, the two leading aircraft manufacturers in the United States until the late 1920s were the Wright Aeronautical Corporation and the Curtiss Airplane Company. In 1929, after Orville Wright and Glenn Curtiss had sold their respective companies to New York business interests, the two companies were combined into the Curtiss-Wright Corporation, which later produced many well-known aircraft, including the P-36 and the P-40 Warhawk of World War II. However, the company did not survive the lean postwar years and ceased to manufacture aircraft after 1948. A great irony of aviation is that even though the foundations of powered flight rest on the work of Orville and Wilbur Wright and Glenn Curtiss, no airplane today bears the name of either the Wrights or Curtiss.

PORTENT OF THINGS TO COME: THE DEPERDUSSIN RACER

The end of the beginning of the quest for high-speed flight occurred three years later with the design of the Deperdussin racer in 1912. Designed by Frenchman Louis Béchereau for the small company of Armand Deperdussin, the Société pour les Appareils Deperdussin (SPAD), this aircraft worked both sides of the T − D equation. Its aerodynamically clean lines reflected a conscious effort to reduce drag. Unlike most of its predecessors, the Deperdussin had a smooth, rounded *monocoque* fuselage, and a large spinner at the propeller hub faired into the front of the fuselage. The monoplane design utilized a thin wing with bracing wires but did not have massive support struts. Béchereau paid careful attention to minute details to reduce drag and in the process produced the most aesthetically pleasing aircraft to that date.

The Deperdussin used a Gnome rotary engine to achieve thrust. In later

On September 29, 1913, Marcel Prévost flew this refined model of the Deperdussin racer to victory in the 1913 Gordon Bennett Trophy race at Reims, France, with a record-breaking speed of 124.5 mph. The best World War I fighters could not equal that speed until four years later. In terms of aerodynamic drag reduction, the streamlined monoplane Deperdussin was well ahead of the boxy airplanes of its time. The French engineer Louis Béchereau, who designed the Deperdussin and later the famous SPAD XIII of World War I, became the first designer to use monocoque construction successfully when he built the Deperdussin's airframe. Monocoque, or "single-shell," construction was quite different from the conventional, boxlike stringer and former construction method used in other contemporary aircraft. The Deperdussin fuselage was formed around a solid mold and was then built up from thin strips of tulip wood glued together in layers.

The rotary engine was a unique phenomenon of many, mostly French, aircraft of World War I vintage. The propeller was rigidly attached to the engine, and the whole assembly—engine and propeller—rotated around a stationary crankshaft securely bolted to the airframe. This design had the advantage of lightness because of efficient air cooling of the cylinders resulting from its rotary motion. However, the centrifugal force (torque) of the spinning engine caused handling problems and affected the fuel-air mixture supply to the cylinders. This meant the engine had essentially two speeds: off and full power. The seven-cylinder, 50-horsepower Gnome rotary engine shown here was fitted on Louis Paulhan's Voisin-Farman I pusher that Paulhan flew unsuccessfully at the 1909 Reims Air Meet. The rudimentary propeller blades can be seen forward of the engine cylinders.

versions of the racer, a twin-row 14-cylinder Gnome engine producing 160 horsepower was incorporated. The rotary engine was as daring a design as the Deperdussin. First designed by the French engineer Laurent Seguin in 1907, the rotary was a radial engine in which the propeller was fixed to the engine and the entire propeller-engine assembly rotated about a crankshaft securely bolted to the aircraft. With this combination of high thrust provided by the Gnome rotary and low drag associated with the streamlined airframe, the Deperdussin left other aircraft in the dust. Just four years after Glenn Curtiss had set the world speed record of 47.65 mph at Reims, Maurice Prévost won the same Gordon Bennett Cup at Reims in a Deperdussin with a phenomenal speed of 124.5 mph—the first aircraft to fly faster than 200 kilometers per hour. The exponential increase in aircraft performance had begun.

The Strut and Wire Biplanes

The Deperdussin was a special-purpose racing aircraft that was totally unsuited to the practical rigors of aerial warfare. When the Great War began in August 1914, the combatants adhered to the more conventional scheme of strut and wire biplanes. In fact, the basic configuration of most aircraft through 1920 differed little from that of the Wright *Flyer*, except that they were more powerful and sturdy. In terms of the T − D relationship, increases in engine power, that is, increases in thrust, rather than any marked decrease in drag produced most of the improvement.

WORLD WAR I

The pivotal advances in aerodynamic theory that led to a significant understanding of the sources of drag were not made until the pioneering work of Prandtl in Germany during 1914–1918, and these advances were only very slowly applied to the design process. Therefore, aircraft design during World War I was an intuitive "seat-of-the-pants" process. Some designs were almost literally marked off in chalk on the concrete floor of a factory, and the completed machines rolled out the front door two weeks later. These designs suffered from the high drag associated with multiple bracing struts between the wings, innumerable bracing wires that produced drag far beyond what might have been expected from a simple wire, and low-aspect-ratio wings that produced high induced drag from the strong wing tip vortices trailing downstream of the wing.

On the other hand, this was also a period of practical design experimentation. A wide variety of aircraft appeared: some monoplanes, many biplanes, and a few triplanes. Pusher (propeller behind) and tractor (propeller ahead) engine configurations were employed. Single-engine pursuit aircraft flew alongside large multiengine bombers. During the war, several types of military airplanes were thoroughly explored, ranging from light unarmed reconnaissance aircraft to heavy long-range bombers.

In the quest for speed and altitude, four aircraft typify the design accomplishments of that day: the French Nieuport 17 and SPAD XIII, the German Fokker D.VII, and the British Royal Aircraft Factory S.E.5a.

The Nieuport 17 was one of the best fighter aircraft of the middle war years. Introduced into combat by the French in March 1916, it was powered by a Le Rhône 9J rotary engine that produced 110 horsepower. The airframe was typical of the day, a biplane with external bracing wires and struts. Hence, the drag resulting from skin friction over the aircraft surface and the pressure drag caused by flow separation over the blunt-nosed fuselage and especially over the rounded struts and wires produced a relatively high

With a top speed of 107 mph at an altitude of 6,500 feet, the French Nieuport 17 typified the fast fighter aircraft during the middle stages of World War I. The Allies liked the Nieuport 17 so much that British, Belgian, Russian, Italian, American, and numerous French fighter squadrons were equipped with it. Probably the best known French air unit to use Nieuport 17s was the American-manned N124 squadron, the *Escadrille Lafayette*. French aces such as René Fonck (75 victories), Georges Guynemer (54 victories), and Charles Nungesser (45 victories) flew it, and British ace Albert Ball (47 victories) preferred the Nieuport 17 to the S.E.5.

Designed by Louis Béchereau, the SPAD XIII entered squadron service in the spring of 1917 and soon became one of the best fighters of World War I. It had a top speed of nearly 140 mph and was a very high performance machine primarily as a result of its powerful Hispano-Suiza engine. The SPAD had low-aspect-ratio wings that generated high induced drag; the relatively clean aerodynamic lines compensated somewhat for this deficiency. A total of 8,440 SPAD XIIIs were built during the war. These aircraft equipped 81 French fighter squadrons as well as British, Belgian, and American units. Among the many Americans who flew the SPAD XIIIs in the Air Service of the American Expeditionary Forces (AEF) in France were Captain Eddie Ricken-backer, commander of the 94th Aero "Hat in the Ring" Squadron. Rickenbacker ended the war as the leading American ace, with 22 aircraft and 4 balloon "kills."

Facing page:
Built by the Royal Aircraft Factory in England, the S.E.5a was one of the fastest operational fighters of World War I, with a top speed of 138 mph. Many of the leading British aces, including Albert Ball, Canadian William "Billy" Bishop (72 victories), South African A.W. Beauchamp-Proctor (54 victories), Edward "Mick" Mannock (73 victories), and James McCudden (57 victories), won numerous aerial victories flying S.E.5s or S.E.5as. This rebuilt S.E.5a is exhibited at the Royal Air Force Museum at Hendon.

"zero-lift" drag. In contrast, the induced drag, or "drag due to lift," associated with the wing tip vortices was reduced by the rather high aspect ratio of 5.51 for the wing. The net result was a top speed of 107 mph at 6,500 feet.

The Nieuport 17 was later upstaged by the introduction of the SPAD XIII in the spring of 1917. The SPAD traced its roots back to the Deperdussin of 1912. Louis Béchereau, designer of the Deperdussin, also designed the SPAD XIII. When the company fell on hard times in 1913 because its owner, Armand Deperdussin, had obtained 28 million francs in illegal funding, the famous French aviator and the first man to fly the English Channel, Louis Blériot, took over and reorganized it. In the process, the company's name was changed from the Société pour les Appareils Deperdussin to the Société pour Aviation et ses Dérivés, thus retaining the acronym SPAD.

In contrast to the Deperdussin racing airplane, in which the designer Béchereau worked on both aspects of the T − D relationship, the SPAD XIII was an example of brute thrust. Béchereau was aware of the new water-cooled Hispano-Suiza V-8 engine designed by the Swiss engineer Marc Birgikt, who was working in Spain. Throwing aside the rotary engine of the Deperdussin, Béchereau installed a 235-horsepower Hispano-Suiza in the SPAD XIII, achieving a power increase of nearly 50 percent over the older Deperdussin. However, the SPAD was not as streamlined as the Deperdussin but adopted the boxy, biplane strut and wire configuration of the traditional aircraft of the day. Compared with the Nieuport 17, the SPAD's zero-lift drag was 6 percent higher; this was compounded by the low aspect ratio of 3.69 for the wings, creating an inordinately high induced drag (drag due to lift). However, what counts in the quest for speed and altitude is not the individual values of thrust or drag but the difference— T − D—and the SPAD had plenty of T − D because of its high thrust. The net result was one of the best operational fighters of World War I, with a top speed of 138 mph.

As fast was the British S.E.5a, designed and produced by the Royal Aircraft Factory at Farnborough. Also powered by a Hispano-Suiza engine, the S.E.5a was one of the fastest operational fighters of the war, also with a

top speed of 138 mph. Introduced in 1917, the S.E.5a was superior to both the Nieuport 17 and the SPAD XIII, and it epitomized the high-speed airplane of World War I. Indeed, the British ace of aces, Edward "Mick" Mannock, was flying S.E.5as when he downed 50 of his 73 enemy airplanes.

In marked contrast to the other three fighters, the Fokker D.VII was selected for production only after winning an exhaustive flyoff competition in January 1918. The D.VII entered combat in April 1918 and soon established itself as one of the finest fighters of the war. Its internally braced cantilever wings with thick airfoil sections were largely responsible for its excellent performance. Powered by a BMW 185-horsepower engine, the D.VII was one of the war's heavier fighters but still had a maximum speed of 124 mph. Although it had wing and power loadings greater than those of the SPAD XIII and Sopwith Camel, it could outclimb and outfight them both.

In the design of high performance fighters, the *rate of climb* to a certain altitude is usually a more important characteristic than is the altitude itself. An interceptor must reach altitude as quickly as possible, and hence the time rate of climb, or the increase in altitude per minute, is a vital factor. Therefore, the *maximum* altitude is not always an important design factor. In spite of this, the maximum altitude, or *absolute ceiling*, of airplanes increased at the same rate as did maximum speed, and for the same reason—large increases in $T - D$. Hence, in comparison with the altitude record of 508 feet set by Hubert Latham in an Antoinette machine at the 1909 Reims Air Meet, the Nieuport 17, SPAD XIII, S.E.5a, and Fokker D.VII achieved altitudes of 17,400, 23,000, 19,500, and 19,700 feet, respectively.

Despite these developments, it took almost the duration of the war for the speed of fighter airplanes to catch up with that of the prize-winning Deperdussin racer, which set a record of 124.5 mph during the Gordon Bennett Cup competition of 1913. During the first 50 years of manned, powered flight, air races provided the raw incentive for speed. Airplanes were especially designed for this purpose—to squeeze the very last ounce of $T - D$ out of the engine-airframe combination toward the single goal of winning air races. These aircraft were usually single-purpose designs, stripped down to the bare mechanical necessities, with engines designed to operate at the edge of their structural endurance at temperatures that imposed a year's worth of wear and tear in just 10 minutes of full-throttle operation. Aerodynamics became more important in the effort to reduce drag. In short, these racers were special-purpose aircraft that in themselves were not practical everyday flying machines. However, they paced the aeronautical technology that later translated into improved conventional aircraft.

SCHNEIDER CUP RACES

A classic example of air racing was the Schneider Cup competition, which began in 1913 and, after a pause for World War I, continued until the British retired the Schneider Cup in 1931. It was a series of air races with a quirk: the competing aircraft had to be seaplanes. However, the technology that emerged was so important that the Schneider Cup races require special attention. These races began early in the era of the strut and wire biplanes, and they were eventually partly responsible for the demise of the biplane in the early 1930s.

The Schneider Cup races were born on December 5, 1912, when the French industrialist Jacques Schneider announced a competition to promote the development of seaplanes. He offered an impressive trophy to the first nation that could win the race three times out of a series of five successive yearly events. The first competition was held in Monaco in 1913, and Maurice Prévost won with a Deperdussin equipped with pontoons. The winning

A special two-seater Fokker D.VII being tested by the Allies after the Armistice of November 11, 1918.

speed was only 45.75 mph, considerably less than the record of 124.5 mph that Prévost set flying a Deperdussin in the Gordon Bennett Cup race that year. There were two reasons for the difference. First, the pontoons added a considerable drag, greatly reducing the $T - D$ value; second, Prévost crossed the finish line in a manner that did not satisfy the judges and was required to take off again and repeat the final lap. But for this repeat lap, the float-equipped Deperdussin would have averaged 61 mph over the 28-lap, 10-kilometer course. One year later, the winning Sopwith Tabloid biplane greatly exceeded the 1913 record with a speed of 86.75 mph. The winning pilot, Howard Pixton, celebrated his victory by flying two extra laps that set a new world seaplane record of 92 mph.

After being suspended during World War I, the Schneider Cup races were resumed in 1919 in England, where Italian pilot Guido Janello won with a Savoia S.13 biplane flying boat. However, this race was never considered official because of irregularities associated with fog. In 1920, the Italians won again, this time at Venice, with Luigi Bologna flying a Savoia S.12. The Italian winning streak continued in 1921 with Giovanni de Briganti flying a Macchi M.7 flying boat. By this time, the winning speed had reached 117.86 mph.

Italy would have permanently retired the Schneider Cup trophy with a win in Naples in 1922, but the British prevented that with a win in a Supermarine Sea Lion II piloted by Henry C. Baird at 145.7 mph. The designer of the Sea Lion II, Reginald J. Mitchell, won aeronautical engineering fame for his famous Supermarine Spitfire of World War II.

A Navy Curtiss CR-3 (1923). Lieutenant David Rittenhouse, U.S. Navy, is shown standing on the float of the plane he flew to victory at Cowes, England.

Engine power is an essential ingredient in the quest for speed and altitude. The Curtiss Aeroplane and Motor Corporation built some of the best early aircraft engines in the United States. Among them was the powerful D-12 (V-1150) engine, which powered the Curtiss racers and the Army's front-line PW-8 and P-1 Hawk (pictured here) pursuit planes of the 1920s. The D-12 produced 465 horsepower; in combination with an excellent propeller designed after Dr. S. A. Reed, it led Curtiss racers to many victories in the Pulitzer races in the United States and two consecutive wins in the Schneider Cup races of 1923 and 1925.

By the early 1920s, the Schneider competition had become a well-publicized event involving national pride, and the entries had begun to obtain government support for airplane design and construction. The United States won the next two races using Curtiss racers that changed the whole complexion of the Schneider competition. The American entry in the 1923 race was a sleek Navy Curtiss CR-3 whose smooth lines and power spelled *speed*. The slender, streamlined fuselage contained a powerful 500-horsepower Curtiss D-12 engine with 12 cylinders in a V-shaped bank. The engine drove a solid aluminum alloy propeller that incorporated thin airfoil sections based on the designs of Dr. S. A. Reed. David Rittenhouse easily won the 1923 Schneider Cup race at Crowes, England, in a Navy CR-3 at a speed of 177.38 mph.

The following year, the race was scheduled for Baltimore, Maryland. However, the Curtiss racer's competitive edge prompted the British and Italians to design new seaplanes which were not ready in time for the October 1924 races. That left the United States Navy as the sole competitor. In the spirit of good sportsmanship, the Navy chose not to fly the course alone and take the victory, and so the 1924 Schneider Cup race had no official winner.

The 1925 race in Baltimore was a different story. Flying a U.S. Army Curtiss R3C-2, an improved version of the CR-3 with a 619-horsepower Curtiss V-1400 engine, James H. "Jimmy" Doolittle blew away the competition with a speed of 232.57 mph. Doolittle later left the Army and obtained a doctorate in aeronautical engineering from the Massachusetts Institute of Technology. He took part in numerous air races and pioneering aeronautical flights in the 1920s and 1930s before gaining fame during World War II as the leader of the first American bombing attack against Tokyo in April 1942 and then of American strategic bombers against Germany.

In 1926, the United States could have retired the Schneider Cup. However, the lessons of the streamlined Curtiss airplanes had not gone unheeded, and in 1926, Italy beat the U.S. at its own game. Under orders from Benito Mussolini to win the trophy, the Italians placed their bets on Mario Castoldi, who designed his Macchi M.39 specifically for the race. They were not disappointed, for the M.39 became the first monoplane to win since the Deperdussin in 1913. The Macchi's wing had an unusually thin airfoil section, and the plane was equipped with a Fiat AS2 engine that produced 850 horsepower. With Mario de Bernardi at the controls, the Macchi M.39 sped to victory over Chesapeake Bay at 246.49 mph. The Curtiss racers had changed the complexion of the Schneider Cup competition in 1923, and the Macchi M.39 monoplane created a similar revolution in 1926.

Howard Chandler Christy's portrait of Lieutenant General Jimmy Doolittle, commander of the U.S. Army Air Forces' Eighth Air Force in 1944–1945.

An Army Curtiss R3C-2 (1925). Lieutenant Jimmy Doolittle, U.S. Army Air Service, is shown standing on the float of his winning racer at Baltimore, Maryland.

Mario de Bernardi and the Macchi M.39 (1926).

Schneider Cup Winners
(1913—1931)

Date	Aircraft	Pilot	Speed (mph)
April 16, 1913	Deperdussin	Maurice Prévost	45.75
April 20, 1914	Sopwith Tabloid	Howard Pixton	86.75
September 19, 1919	Savoia S.13	Guido Janello	109.77
(1919 result voided)			
September 21, 1920	Savoia S.12	Luigi Bologna	107.22
August 7, 1921	Macchi M.7	Giovanni de Brigante	117.86
August 12, 1922	Supermarine Sea Lion II	Henry Baird	145.70
September 28, 1923	Navy Curtiss CR-3	David Rittenhouse	177.38
No race			
October 26, 1925	Army Curtiss R3C-2	James Doolittle	232.57
November 13, 1926	Macchi M. 39	Mario de Bernardi	246.49
September 27, 1927	Supermarine S.5	S. N. Webster	281.65
September 7, 1929	Supermarine S.6	H. R. Waghorn	328.63
September 13, 1931	Supermarine S.6B	J. N. Boothman	340.08

Neither Italy nor the United States could capitalize on these advances, however, because in England R. J. Mitchell was quietly designing the airplanes that would finally win the trophy. Working for Supermarine, Mitchell had designed the S.4, which was unveiled in 1925. It too was a monoplane with an exceptionally streamlined aerodynamic shape. There were no drag-producing bracing struts and wires, and the thin wing was cantilever-mounted in the midwing position on the fuselage. The engine was a 700-horsepower Napier Lion. Entered in the 1925 race at Baltimore, the S.4 crashed during practice; structural weakness of the wing was blamed.

The British did not participate in 1926, but by 1927 Mitchell had fielded a new model, the Supermarine S.5. Following the design features of the Macchi M.39, Mitchell switched to a low-wing, wire-braced monoplane configuration. Piloted by Sidney Webster, the Supermarine S.5 won the 1927 Schneider Cup race over the waters at Venice at a speed of 281.65 mph. In so doing, the S.5 became the world's fastest airplane, including land planes, quite a feat considering the handicap of the pontoons. With Mitchell's design success, England was soon to win the Schneider Cup outright.

After 1927, the Schneider Cup was contested every two years. In

September 1929, H.R. Waghorn won in a Supermarine S.6 at 328.63 mph, and in September 1931, John N. Boothman, flying a Supermarine S.6B, permanently retired the cup to England after reaching 340.08 mph. Jacques Schneider's challenge had been fulfilled. In less than 20 years, the winner's speed had increased by nearly 300 mph because of better aerodynamic designs and vastly more powerful engines. A 160-horsepower Gnome rotary had powered the Deperdussin of 1913, but a 2,350-horsepower Rolls-Royce "R" was fitted in the Supermarine S.6B. But one more record remained for Mitchell's S.6B. Within weeks of the trophy win, on September 29, the second of two S.6Bs built for the 1931 Schneider competition, its engine boosted to 2,600 horsepower, became the first aircraft to exceed 400 mph when G. H. Stainforth captured the world speed record at 407.5 mph.

A Supermarine S.6 (1929). Flying Officer H. R. Waghorn flew N247 to victory at Spithead on September 7, 1929.

A Supermarine S.6B (1931).

The quest for speed and altitude required airplanes with low aerodynamic drag. In the 1920s, wind tunnels were used for drag reduction experiments. An important wind tunnel was the NACA variable-density tunnel, which was designed by the German aerodynamicist Max Munk and put into operation in March 1923. In this tunnel, models of airplane wings and airfoils could be tested at conditions that simulated real atmospheric flight.

The British victory in 1931 brought to an end a series of air races that ultimately involved well-prepared national teams and spurred the rapid development of aeronautical technology in two directions: toward more engine power and also major drag reduction to increase T − D as much as possible. This experience was particularly useful to Great Britain. The aeronautical lessons that R. J. Mitchell learned with the S.4, S.5, S.6, and S.6B were translated directly into the Supermarine Spitfire, which, together with the Hawker Hurricane, gave the RAF Fighter Command the "narrow margin" over the Luftwaffe in the Battle of Britain in 1940–1941.

AERODYNAMIC DEVELOPMENTS

When the Schneider Cup races ended in 1931, the quest for speed made strut and wire biplanes obsolete. Thereafter, speed was obtained with aerodynamically smooth airplanes, and drag-producing struts and wires were eliminated. Moreover, while men and machines were competing for the Schneider Cup during the 1920s, a quieter revolution was taking place in aerodynamic technology. First, Prandtl's aerodynamic boundary layer theory of 1904 achieved general acceptance, and its application allowed designers to reduce skin-friction drag on airplanes. This theory also provided an understanding of flow separation and thus pointed the way to reduce the so-called form drag caused by flow separation over an aerodynamic surface. Second, the construction of new wind tunnel facilities in the United

States and Europe greatly enhanced the use of wind tunnels in the airplane design process.

In the United States, the National Advisory Committee for Aeronautics (NACA) was established in 1915 to promote aeronautical research and development. By 1917, it had begun construction of the Langley Memorial Aeronautical Laboratory in Hampton, Virginia, where NACA's first wind tunnel became operational in 1920. Of particular importance was the unique variable-density tunnel (VDT) built in 1923 to test wings and airplane models at flow conditions close to those encountered in actual flight. In 1931, NACA built the "full-scale" tunnel with a 30- by 60-foot oval test section in which a full-size airplane could be mounted. During the 1920s and early 1930s, the development of aerodynamic theory and the results of experimental tools, such as NACA'S wind tunnels, helped create the next generation of aircraft, contributing as much as if not more than the international air race competitions.

Fred Weick of NACA's Langley Laboratory concluded tests that led to the development of the NACA cowling for radial engines.

The Era of Mature Propeller-Driven Airplanes

On May 24, 1927, a group of aircraft manufacturers met at Langley Field in Hampton, Virginia; they were concerned about the challenge to the American aeronautical industry posed by the rapid pace of technical developments in Europe. This group formally urged NACA to investigate how to reduce total aircraft drag so that American airplanes would be more efficient and competitive. Subsequently, Fred E. Weick, Langley's leading aeronautical engineer, directed the NACA attack on one of the largest drag-producing features of airplanes equipped with radial engines. The cylinders of these engines were usually exposed to the incoming airflow to promote cooling, but this exposure also created drag, sometimes a very substantial drag.

Fred Weick conducted an extensive series of tests in a wind tunnel at the Langley laboratory, using a Wright Whirlwind radial engine mounted on a conventional fuselage. Various types of aerodynamic surfaces, or cowlings, were used to cover the engine cylinders, partly or completely, directly guiding part of the airflow over the cylinders for cooling purposes but at the same time permitting a smooth primary aerodynamic flow over the fuselage. The best cowling covered the engine completely, and the results were dramatic. Compared with an uncowled fuselage, full cowling reduced the drag by 60 percent. The resultant increase in performance was equally dramatic. When tested on an Army Curtiss AT-5A in 1928, the new NACA cowling increased the maximum airspeed from 118 to 137 mph. So important was this aeronautical engineering innovation to American aviation that NACA was later awarded the 1929 Robert J. Collier Trophy, which was presented annually for the most significant achievement in American aviation. Airplane designers rapidly adopted the NACA cowling, beginning the era of the mature, propeller-driven airplane.

THE LOCKHEED VEGA

The Lockheed Vega perhaps best illustrated the new breed. When the wooden Vega 1 first appeared in 1927 without an NACA cowling on its 225-horsepower Wright Whirlwind J-5, its top speed was 135 mph. Within two years, the new model Vega 5 was equipped with an NACA cowling and the 450-horsepower Pratt & Whitney Wasp engine that increased its top speed from 165 to 185 mph. Designed jointly by Allan Loughead and Jack Northrop, the Vega was a high-wing monoplane crafted to reduce drag.

The first Lockheed Vega produced.

The Lockheed Vega is a good example of mature propeller-driven airplanes at the end of the 1920s and the beginning of the 1930s. One of the first commercial airplanes to incorporate the new NACA engine cowling, the Vega was a high-wing monoplane whose later models had a top speed of 185 mph, as fast as the Army's best biplane pursuits of the day. The Lockheed Vega 5 (NC 625E, Lockheed serial number 63) shown here without aerodynamically faired wheel pants was built in 1929 and served mainly as a corporate aircraft until it was destroyed by fire in Mexico in May 1940.

In addition to the engine cowling, Vegas appearing in 1929–1930 had fixed landing gear covered with aerodynamically faired covers called wheel pants. These features, along with the absence of struts and wires, gave the Vega exceptionally low drag.

In combination with the more powerful Wasp engine, this made the commercial Vega much faster than even some of the contemporary Army and Navy biplanes. Indeed, in 1928, Robert Cantwell flew a Lockheed Vega to victory in the transcontinental race to the National Air Races in Los Angeles and then won the civilian free-for-all speed race at 140.3 mph. With the addition of the NACA cowling in 1929, a number of Vegas did well in various

races. Roscoe Turner won third place in a Vega in the free-for-all, losing only to Douglas Davis in the Travel-Air "R" Mystery and an Army Curtiss Hawk P-3A pursuit airplane but beating a Navy XF6C-6 fighter. Once again, T − D made the difference; with the Vega, it was primarily a low D that resulted in a large T − D.

Although it carried only six passengers, the Vega saw airline service in the late 1920s and early 1930s. Its main public fame, however, was gained in a number of record-setting speed and distance flights between 1928 and 1935, including those of Amelia Earhart, Ruth Nichols, and Arthur Goebel. Wiley Post logged two of these distance records in his Vega *Winnie Mae* when he and Harry Gatty flew around the world in the summer of 1931; he accomplished the same feat solo in 7½ days in the summer of 1933. Today, the *Winnie Mae* stands proudly in the National Air and Space Museum in Washington, D.C.

AERODYNAMIC AND TECHNOLOGICAL ADVANCES

The next step in drag reduction was to eliminate the drag-producing fixed landing gear altogether by retracting it into the wing or fuselage after takeoff. The first aircraft to incorporate an all-metal structure with a smooth

The Lockheed Vega was used extensively in passenger and corporate service but was best known for its numerous speed and distance records. In addition to Amelia Earhart, Wiley Post flew to fame in a Vega, the *Winnie Mae* (NR-105W), shown here. Post flew this plane solo around the world in 7 ½ days during the summer of 1933.

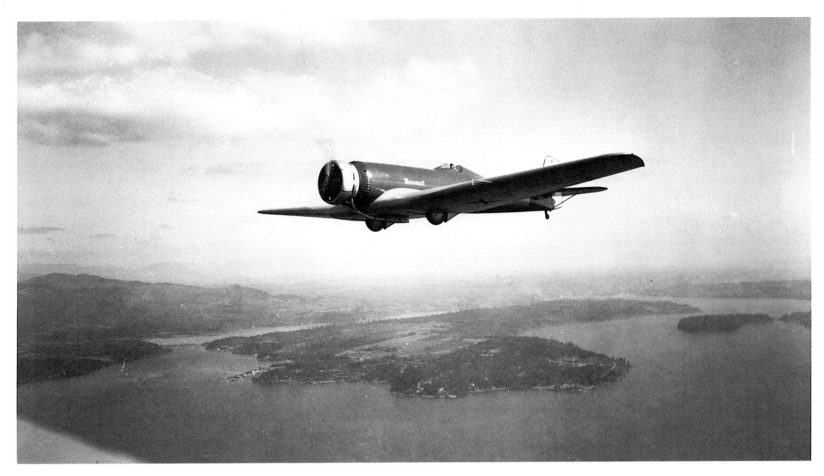

After the Lockheed Vega, the next step was the development of all-metal, stressed-skin construction and the retractable landing gear. The first American commercial airplanes to incorporate these features were the Northrop Alpha and the Boeing Monomail, which first flew in May 1930. The first (Model 200) of only two Boeing Monomails built did not have the more efficient Townend ring cowling, but the later Model 221 shown here was equipped with it. The Monomail reached a top speed of only 158 mph because a fixed-pitch propeller reduced thrust and partly negated the drag improvement resulting from the retracted landing gear. The Monomails used many of the technological innovations later designed into the twin-engine B-9 bomber and its follow-up, the 247 airliner. The Monomail never entered serial production because of its propeller problems and Boeing's decision to gamble with the design and production of the B-9 and then the 247.

The Lockheed Orion's top speed was 225 mph, which in 1931 made it one of the fastest land planes. The retracted landing gear gave the Orion a drag coefficient 25 percent lower than that of the Vega. The Orion 9D2 (NC 799W, Lockheed serial number 208) pictured here was one of the last to come off the production line and was specially built for the Evening News Association of Detroit, Michigan. Appropriately called the Early Bird and carrying the words "Detroit News" on its fuselage, this Orion sported a special wing pod camera and often originated broadcasts that were heard over station WWJ. After serving as a UC-85 in the Army Air Forces during the war, it was scrapped at Los Angeles in November 1947.

stressed skin, a cantilevered monoplane, Townend ring cowling, and retractable landing gear was the Boeing Monomail, which was first flown in May 1930. In spite of the low drag, the Monomail suffered from low $T - D$ because a propeller problem resulted in low propeller efficiency and hence a low T.

A more successful airplane with retractable landing gear was the Lockheed Orion, an outgrowth of the Vega. The Orion was a low-wing monoplane primarily of stressed-plywood construction; the low wing was particularly advantageous for retractable landing gear. The reduced drag

FIXED AND CONTROLLABLE: HOW THE PROPELLER WORKS

As the Wright brothers discovered in 1902–1903, the propeller of a flying machine is a very critical yet complex part of flying. The plane surface of any propeller is twisted so that the rotary motion of the propeller and the forward motion of the airplane cause each section of the propeller to strike the air at an efficient angle of attack to the local airflow direction. When the forward motion of the airplane changes, however, the local airflow direction experienced by the propeller also changes. For a propeller of fixed orientation—one made out of wood like Wilbur Wright's or those for any World War I aircraft—this means that for all speeds other than the design speed, the airfoil sections of the propeller are not using the optimum angle of attack; thus the efficiency of the propeller decreases.

Before the 1930s, all propellers were fixed-pitch propellers and demonstrated a lower efficiency when the aircraft was flying at a speed other than the design speed. This was neither efficient nor economical as the speeds of airplanes increased rapidly in the 1930s. The aerodynamic advantage of varying the propeller pitch during flight was appreciated as far back as World War I, and Dr. H. S. Hele-Shaw and T. E. Beacham patented such a device in England in 1924. Frank Caldwell of Hamilton Standard in the United States produced the first practical design for a reliable mechanism that would vary or control a propeller's pitch in 1926, but it became available in numbers only in the early 1930s. With this variable- or controllable-pitch propeller, the maximum propeller efficiency could be achieved at all flight speeds from takeoff to cruising, and thus the thrust was higher than it would have been with the older, fixed-pitch designs.

The Hamilton Standard Hydromatic variable-pitch propeller came into standard use in 1936 and allowed much greater control of the blades through bevel gears turned by a drumcam in the propeller hub. Later, another refinement, the *constant-speed unit* (CSU), automatically controlled the propeller to permit any desired engine speed. Further improvements were made, and in 1944 a reversible-pitch setting was added that helped slow an aircraft after landing. The progressive improvement of the large three- and four-bladed constant speed, controllable-pitch propellers on the B-29s, B-50s, Lockheed Constellations and C-130 Hercules, Douglas DC-6s and DC-7s, and other piston-engined and turboprop aircraft has been critical in achieving the best possible performance from these aircraft designs and more powerful engines.

A fixed-pitch Hamilton Standard propeller is mounted here on a Wright J-5 Whirlwind on the Fokker F.VII.

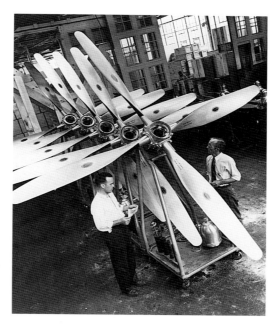

Four-bladed Hamilton Standard Hydromatic variable-pitch propellers undergoing a check at the factory.

A three-bladed constant speed unit propeller being adjusted prior to a flight test.

associated with retracted landing gear gave the Orion a maximum speed of 226 mph, which in 1931, the year of its first flight, made it one of the fastest production land planes. This was also the year of the last Schneider Cup race, in which the top speed of the S.6B was 340 mph, exemplifying the wide gap between special-purpose racers and conventional aircraft.

The NACA cowling, retractable landing gear, all-metal stressed-skin monocoque structures, and flush riveting were major aeronautical engineering breakthroughs of the early 1930s that affected drag reduction. At the same time, two parallel breakthroughs—the variable-pitch propeller and higher octane aviation fuels—greatly increased thrust. Before the 1930s, all propellers were "fixed pitch" and suffered from lower efficiency when the aircraft was flying at a speed other than the design speed. As airplane speeds increased rapidly in the 1930s, this became increasingly unacceptable. Frank Caldwell of Hamilton Standard in the United States produced the first practical design of a reliable mechanical mechanism for varying the pitch (angle of attack) of the propeller in the early 1930s. With this variable-pitch or controllable-pitch propeller, the maximum propeller efficiency could be achieved at all flight speeds, and thus the thrust was higher. The importance of this development was clearly seen in the performance of the Boeing 247. By simply adding variable-pitch propellers to standard 247s after June 1933, Boeing reduced the takeoff run 20 percent, increased the rate of climb 22 percent and the cruising speed 5.5 percent.

Another important advance that increased thrust was the development of high-octane aviation fuel, although the more visibly obvious breakthroughs in the 1930s such as the NACA cowling, retractable landing gear, and variable-pitch propeller often eclipsed it. As far back as 1911, premature ignition had been observed in automobile engines, causing a local detonation and an audible "pinging" that reduced engine power. C. F. Kettering at the General Motors Delco subsidiary identified an additive, tetraethyl lead, that reduced engine knocking considerably. In turn, General Motors and Standard Oil formed a new company, the Ethyl Gasoline Corporation, to produce "ethyl" gasoline with a lead additive.

The Ethyl Gasoline Corporation later identified a hydrocarbon compound, octane, as being very effective in preventing engine knocking. By March 1930, the Army Air Corps had adopted gasoline rated at 87 octane as its standard fuel. The improved fuel allowed the design of engines with larger compression ratios, which meant more horsepower. Higher compression ratios demanded more octane. By 1935 the Army Air Corps had adopted 100 octane as its standard aviation fuel, and this fuel soon became the standard for all high-performance piston-engine airplanes. This apparently simple change had profound impacts on engine and aircraft design and performance; for example, the introduction of 100-octane fuel and technological improvements allowed Wright to increase the R-1820 Cyclone engine from 500 to 1,200 horsepower in the 1930s. In distinct contrast and owing to its own fuel preferences and oil situation, the German Luftwaffe used 87-octane fuel through World War II. This created a problem with engine knocking that significantly compromised the performance of some German aircraft designs.

In the 1930s, the variable-pitch propeller and high-octane fuel were combined with the development of larger piston engines with a growing ratio of horsepower to weight. In the United States, the radial engine reigned supreme. Two of the most important engines in the mid-1930s were the Wright R-1820 Cyclone, which produced 1,100 horsepower, and the Pratt & Whitney R-1830 Twin Wasp, which produced 1,000 horsepower; both were significantly more powerful than the World War I engines of 200 to 400 horsepower. Even more stunning were the liquid-cooled, in-line engines that Rolls-Royce developed in England. The epitome of these engines was the special-purpose "R" V-12 racing engine developed for the Supermarine S.6B of Schneider Cup fame, which generated 2,600 horsepower. Such work eventually paved the way for the development of a wide variety of Rolls-Royce Merlin engines, which powered a number of great aircraft, including the British Supermarine Spitfire and the Hawker Hurricane fighters, the Avro Lancaster and Handley Page Halifax heavy bombers, and the de Havilland Mosquito fighter and bomber variants, and transformed the North American Aviation's P-51 Mustang into, arguably, the finest fighter of the war.

THE DOUGLAS DC-3

The NACA cowling, all-metal structure and stressed skin, cantilever wing, retractable landing gear, variable-pitch propeller, high-octane fuel, and reliable piston engines were combined in one of the most famous aircraft of the 1930s, the Douglas DC-3 airliner. The DC-3 was a further refinement of the DC-2, which had grown out of competition with the Model 247 airliner that Boeing designed for its sister company, United Air Lines. When it first flew and then entered airline service early in 1933, the Boeing 247 represented a large step forward in airplane design—a low-wing monoplane with retractable landing gear, Townend rings on its twin supercharged 525-horsepower Pratt & Whitney Wasp radial engines, cantilever wings, and all-metal stressed-skin construction. It was truly the first modern airliner. With the 247, United

A United Air Lines Boeing 247D wings over New York City. The performance of the basic 247 was greatly improved by the addition of variable-pitch propellers.

The Douglas DC-3 is a good example of the mature propeller-driven airplane of the 1930s. It contained all the essential elements: NACA cowling, retractable landing gear, variable-pitch propellers, and engines rated above 1,000 horsepower.

Air Lines threatened to leapfrog over the other commercial airlines with a revolutionary piece of equipment.

Once it realized the advantage the Boeing 247 would give United, Transcontinental and Western Air (now Trans World Airlines, or TWA) immediately contracted with Douglas for a better aircraft in August 1932. It has been said that Douglas management put a massive picture of the Boeing 247 on the wall of the design department with the statement "Like this, only better." The Douglas engineers did just that and designed a far superior series of airplanes, starting with the single DC-1 in 1933, then the DC-2 in 1934, and finally the DC-3, which propitiously first flew on December 17, 1935. Powered by either twin 1,000-horsepower Pratt & Whitney R-1830 Wasps or Wright R-1820-G2 Cyclones, the DC-3 was fast for a commercial airliner of that day, with a cruising speed of 185 mph and a maximum speed of 229 mph, and could seat 21 passengers. The Boeing 247 was totally outclassed as a commercial airliner, and only 75 were built. In contrast, 10,654 DC-3s and C-47 Skytrains (the military transport version) eventually rolled off American production lines, and approximately 2,500 were built under license as PS-84s (Lisunov Li-2s) in the Soviet Union or L2Ds in Japan. Perhaps the greatest measure of the DC-3's greatness is that some are still in regular service today, more than 50 years after the introduction of the design.

The DC-3 could achieve an altitude of 23,000 feet. If it flew at that altitude for any length of time, however, the passengers and flight crew would be gasping for breath and would soon become disoriented or pass out from lack of oxygen (hypoxia). Indeed, 18,000 feet is about as high as a human being can survive for an extended period of time without an auxiliary oxygen source. For this reason, the quest for altitude in the early

Originally designed and built to meet a requirement established by C. R. Smith, president of American Airlines, the Douglas Sleeper Transport (DST) first flew on December 17, 1935, the thirty-second anniversary of Orville Wright's first flight. The DST entered service with American Airlines in June 1936, followed by the DC-3 in August. The DC-3 and its military transport version, the C-47, became the world's most popular and reliable propeller-driven airliner and air transport; some are still in active service.

The U.S. Army Air Service's LUSAC-11 was fitted with Dr. Sanford A. Moss's experimental turbo-super charger (1919).

days of commercial aviation was physiologically restricted. Another limitation was mechanical. Piston engines also became starved for oxygen above 20,000 feet, and power production greatly suffered at higher altitudes without an auxiliary source.

THE PROBLEMS OF HIGH-ALTITUDE FLYING

The maximum altitude of aircraft increased very rapidly through the World War I years, from Hubert Latham's 508-foot prizewinning altitude in an Antoinette at Reims in August 1909, to 10,168 feet achieved by George Legagneux flying a Blériot in France on December 10, 1910, Harry Oelerich's 25,725 feet in a D. F. W. at Leipzig on July 14, 1914, and the 23,000-foot altitude capability of the SPAD XIII in 1917. As a result of the limitations mentioned earlier, the maximum altitude for aircraft reached a plateau during the 1920s and early 1930s. The altitude ceilings of the SPAD and the DC-3 were the same.

The constraints on high-altitude flight could be overcome by providing auxiliary sources of oxygen. This meant carrying an on-board oxygen supply in the form of a pressurized oxygen tank, with oxygen being supplied to the crews through a hose. Major Rudolph "Shorty" Schroeder, the chief test pilot of the Air Service's Engineering Division, who had flown a Bristol F.2B fighter to a record 28,897 feet on September 18, 1918, made one of the first oxygen-assisted high-altitude flights in an experimental Packard-Le Pere LUSAC-11 from McCook Field in Dayton, Ohio. Designed by the French Captain G. Le Pere for the U.S. Army, the LUSAC-11 was a two-seat fighter powered by a 400-horsepower Liberty engine fitted with Dr. Sanford A. Moss's experimental turbosupercharger.

On September 6, 1919, with some difficulty, Schroeder set a two-man altitude record of 28,500 feet, sucking oxygen from an auxiliary supply and coping with frost on his goggles. The record would have been even higher, but the Liberty engine became oxygen-starved and shut down. Schroeder glided all the way down and made a dead-stick landing at McCook Field. On October 4, Schroeder pushed the record to 31,821 feet. From this time through the 1930s, auxiliary oxygen supplies removed the altitude limitation on crews, especially on military aircraft.

Lieutenant John Macready, Dr. Sanford Moss, Major George Hallett, and Mr. Adolph Berger of General Electric and the Army Air Service's Engineering Division stand beside the record-setting LUSAC-11 used for high-altitude flights.

The altitude constraint on engines was another matter. The solution was to provide a supercharger, basically an air compressor designed to increase the density of the air entering the engine. Thus, even though the airplane was flying through very thin air at high altitudes, the supercharger forced enough high-density air through the engine to provide sufficient oxygen for combustion. Power to run the supercharger came from the main engine either by direct mechanical gearing or from a turbine, a "turbosupercharger," mounted in the exhaust stream of the engine.

The Frenchman Auguste Rateau bench-tested a supercharger for aircraft during World War I. His work was transferred to the General Electric Company in the United States via NACA. There, the G.E. engineer Sanford Moss developed a turbosupercharger for the Liberty engine.

The G.E. supercharger was installed on the LUSAC-11 at McCook Field in 1919. After a number of record-setting efforts, Shorty Schroeder again flew the supercharged aircraft to a new world record of 33,134 feet on February 27, 1920. Schroeder could have gone even higher, but he experienced a main oxygen supply failure and lost consciousness. The LUSAC-11 went into a nearly vertical dive and hurtled earthward over 30,000 feet before the airplane, of its own accord, nosed up and pulled out of the dive, giving Schroeder time to recover consciousness and land safely. Lieutenant John A. Macready, who became the chief test pilot when Schroeder left the Air Service, and who later flew nonstop across the continent with Oakley Kelly, broke the altitude record in the LUSAC on September 18, 1921, when he reached 34,508 feet. Subsequently, during the 1920s and 1930s, supercharger development was pursued vigorously on both sides of the Atlantic Ocean.

Successful high-altitude flight required both an auxiliary oxygen supply for those on board and a supercharger for the engine. In practice, this was almost too much to ask, especially for commercial airliners. Therefore, the practical absolute altitude ceiling for most aircraft into the 1930s remained in the range of 23,000 feet, as mentioned earlier. Experiments, however, continued. On September 28, 1934, the Italian Renato Donati flew to an altitude of 47, 358 feet in an open-cockpit Caproni CA114, but after landing he was immediately hospitalized in a near coma caused by acute oxygen starvation. Another Italian test pilot, Mario Pezzi, in a Caproni CA161b pushed

Wiley Post speculated that jet-stream winds at a high altitude could significantly increase an aircraft's speed in transcontinental flights from west to east. He designed a rubberized pressure suit that looked quite similar to that of a deep-sea diver to allow sustained flights at high altitude. Wearing a suit made by the Goodrich Rubber Company, Post flew to a record of over 50,000 feet in a Lockheed Vega in December 1934. He then attempted several cross-country flights from Los Angeles, getting as far as Cleveland, Ohio, on March 15, 1935, before a loss of oxygen forced him to land. His Vega *Winnie Mae*, which had a normal top speed of 190 mph, covered the 2,035 miles in eight hours and four minutes; its average speed was over 250 mph, and speeds as high as 340 mph were recorded.

After Wiley Post's high-altitude flights, the next step was to pressurize the entire crew and passenger compartment. The Army Air Corps' Lockheed XC-35, a specially modified and strengthened Lockheed 10E Electra, was the first pressurized airplane. It had a service ceiling of 32,000 feet, with a shirt-sleeve environment for the crew.

the altitude record to 51,364 feet on May 8, 1937, and then to 56,049 feet on October 22, 1938.

A solution to the problem of the very low atmospheric pressure encountered at high altitude occurred to Wiley Post. In April 1934, Post asked the B. F. Goodrich Rubber plant in Los Angeles to develop a rubberized pressure suit that would keep the wearer at an effective pressure equivalent to the pressure at 5,500 feet at any altitude. Wearing this suit, Post flew his Lockheed Vega, the *Winnie Mae*, to over 50,000 feet and later to an unofficial 55,000 feet in December 1934. As noted in Chapter 1, Post's pioneering flights early in 1935 confirmed the presence of a strong jetstream at higher altitudes, with significant tailwinds that could cut west-to-east flying times.

From Post's success it was only a short technological leap to pressurizing the entire crew and passenger compartment of the airplane. The Army Air Corps achieved this in the Lockheed XC-35, a modified version of the popular twin-engine, twin-tail Lockheed Electra. After Major Carl F. Greene modified the structural design for the pressurized compartment and two supercharged engines were fitted, the airplane had a service ceiling of 32,000 feet with a shirt-sleeve environment for the occupants. The XC-35 flew as designed in 1937 and was the first fully pressurized airplane. This achievement earned the Air Corps and its test crew the prestigious Collier Trophy for 1937. The technology was quickly incorporated in the initial design of a new airliner, the Boeing 307 Stratoliner, which became the first airliner with a pressurized cabin when it entered service with TWA in July 1940. The pressurization work on the Stratoliner formed the basis for the pressurized cabin of Boeing's B-29 Superfortress. In this period of the mature, propeller-driven airplane, the increase in flight altitude had begun anew.

THE NATIONAL AIR RACES OF THE 1930s

In terms of the quest for brute speed, air races in the 1930s did not stop with the end of the Schneider Cup competition. To the contrary, in the United States, the National Air Races that were usually held in September in Cleveland, Ohio (Chicago in 1930 and Los Angeles in 1933 and 1936), were enormously popular, drawing large crowds, generating national media coverage, and producing great publicity for aviation. The two major speed events of the races attracted the most attention—the Thompson Trophy

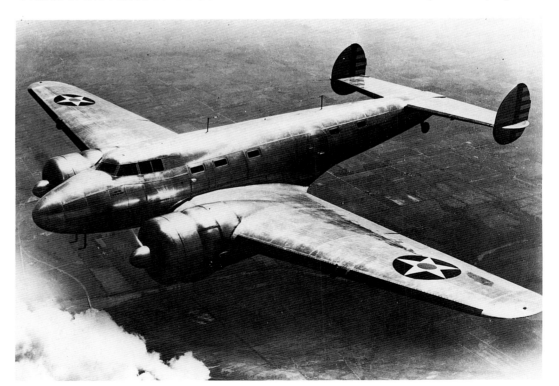

competition (a closed-course speed contest varying in distance from 100 to 300 miles, usually in a 10-mile circuit) and the Bendix Transcontinental Speed Dash (Trophy) race, which terminated at the race site and kicked off the yearly National Air Races.

These races fostered the design of new special-purpose racing aircraft such as the sleek Wedell-Williams racers and the fat, stubby airplane built around an engine, the Gee Bee series of sportsters. Named for their builders, the Granville Brothers, the Gee Bees were unforgiving aircraft, all of which crashed and took an inordinate toll of lives: five racing pilots and the designer himself, Zantford Granville. Jimmy Doolittle, who flew the Gee Bee Super Sportster R-1 to victory in the 1931 Thompson Trophy races, said, "It was the 'touchiest' plane I had ever been in . . . [flying it was] like balancing a pencil on the tip of your finger." Safer aircraft, such as the Laird-Turner Racer (L-RT) and Wedell-Williams designs, dominated the racing scene in the middle and late 1930s, with the winning speeds climbing from 248 mph in 1934 to 282 mph in 1939. These speeds were still considerably lower than the 340 mph of the S.6B of Schneider Cup fame in 1931 and not that much faster than the DC-3 commercial airliner of 1936.

Bendix and Thompson Trophy Winners of the 1930s

Date	Race	Aircraft	Pilot	Speed (mph)
1930	Thompson	Laird Solution	C.W. Holman	201.9
1931	Thompson	Gee Bee Super Sportster	Lowell Bayles	236.2
1931	Bendix	Laird Super-Solution	James Doolittle	223.0
1932	Thompson	Gee Bee Super Sportster R-1	James Doolittle	252.7
1932	Bendix	Wedell-Williams	James Haizlip	245
1933	Thompson	Wedell-Williams	Jimmy Wedell	237.9
1933	Bendix	Wedell-Williams	Roscoe Turner	214.8
1934	Thompson	Wedell-Williams	Roscoe Turner	248.1
1934	Bendix	Wedell-Williams	Douglas Davis	216.2
1935	Thompson	Mr. Mulligan	Harold Neumann	220.2
1935	Bendix	Mr. Mulligan	Benny Howard	238.7
1936	Thompson	Caudron C. 460	Michel Detroyat	264.3
1936	Bendix	Beechcraft C-17R Staggerwing	Louise Thadens	165.3
1937	Thompson	Folkerts KF-1 Jupiter	Rudy Kling	256.9
1937	Bendix	Seversky SEV-S2	Frank Fuller	258.2
1938	Thompson	Laird-Turner Racer	Roscoe Turner	283.4
1938	Bendix	Seversky SEV-S2	Jackie Cochran	249.7
1939	Thompson	Laird-Turner Racer	Roscoe Turner	282.5
1939	Bendix	Seversky SEV-S2	Frank Fuller	282.1

Jimmy Doolittle's Number 11 Gee Bee Super Sportster R-1, which he flew to victory in the 1932 Thompson Trophy race. "S.A.R.A." between the 7 and the 11 on the cowling stands for "Springfield Air Race Association." Gee Bee racers were built at Springfield Airport by the Granville brothers.

F. Warren's painting shows Jimmy Doolittle pulling in to receive the Thompson Trophy after his victory during the 1932 National Air Races at Cleveland, Ohio.

Wedell-Williams with Jimmy Wedell in the cockpit of his red number "44" preparing to leave Floyd Bennett Field, New York, on November 10, 1933. After placing second in the 1932 Thompson Trophy race at Cleveland in NR278V, Wedell flew it to victory in the 1933 race at Los Angeles on July 4, 1933, and then set a world land plane speed record of 305.33 mph in Chicago on September 3, 1933, during the Chicago World's Fair. Wedell died in an air crash in June 1934, and Doug Davis then won the 1934 Bendix Trophy race in NR278V.

The Wedell-Williams *Ring-Free Comet* and the Laird-Turner Racer (L-RT) *Ring-Free Meteor.* "Colonel" Roscoe Turner, possibly the all-time greatest air race pilot, stands in front of two of his greatest air racers: the Number 25 Wedell-Williams NR61Y (rebuilt after a 1936 accident) *Ring-Free Comet* and his Number 29 Laird-Turner Racer (L-RT) (NR263Y), the *Ring-Free Meteor.* Turner had an outstanding record in both the Thompson and Bendix Trophy competitions during the 1930s. He was a three-time winner of the Thompson Trophy, in the Wedell-Williams NR61Y in 1934 and in the *Ring-Free Meteor* in 1938 and 1939; twice finished third in the Thompson competition in NR61Y (1932) and NR263Y (1937); and finished third, first, and second in the 1932, 1933, and 1935 Bendix races in the NR61Y. Turner also teamed with Clyde Pangborn to place third in the 1934 MacRobertson Air Race from England to Australia, flying a Boeing 247 commercial airliner. Turner retired from air racing in 1939 and died in 1970.

A Beechcraft C-17R Staggerwing, winner of the Bendix Trophy race in 1936. The winning pilot, Louise Thadens, is shown leaning on the wing.

MacROBERTSON AIR RACE OF 1934

A unique air race, considered by some the greatest single sporting event in the history of aviation, was the 11,300-mile MacRobertson race between England and Australia held in 1934. The race was organized as part of the Melbourne centenary celebration and was funded by Sir MacPherson Robertson. The contestants were to take off at Mildenhall in Suffolk, England, make stops at prescribed intermediate locations, and land at Melbourne. The de Havilland Aircraft Company in England designed a unique airplane with the single purpose of winning the MacRobertson Race. The D.H.88 Comet was a sleek, aerodynamically refined twin-engine design powered by two de Havilland Gipsy Six R air-cooled in-line engines of 240 horsepower each. The maximum speed of 237 mph was combined with an exceptionally long range of nearly 3,000 miles, an extremely important asset for this race.

Flying a Comet, Charles W. A. Scott and Tom Campbell Black won the race, starting in England on October 20, 1934, and arriving in Melbourne 70 hours and 59 minutes later. In this case, however, the winner was not nearly

The de Havilland D.H.88 was a special-purpose, long-range racer designed specifically to win the England-to-Australia air race in 1934. The Comet's maximum speed was 237 mph, and the winning Comet covered the distance in 70 hours and 59 minutes with intermediate stops. The Comet subsequently influenced the design of de Havilland's D.H. 91 Albatross four-engine airliner and D.H. 98 Mosquito of World War II. The restored Comet flies again over England.

117

as significant as the second and third place finishers—the K.L.M. DC-2 *Uiver* and a Boeing 247, both standard production commercial airliners (see Chapter 1).

The importance of the D.H.88 Comet also reached far beyond the MacRobertson Air Race, because from its design came four-engine D.H. 91 Albatross airliner, whose production was cut short by the war, and the famous de Havilland Mosquito, one of the most versatile and unusual aircraft of World War II. Dubbed the "wooden wonder" because of its molded wooden fuselage and wings, the twin-engine "Mossy" came in a wide variety of bomber, fighter, and reconnaissance versions. It flew so high (over 30,000 feet) and so fast (415, and 425 mph in later MK XVI bomber and P.R. 34 reconnaissance versions fitted with two 1,710-horsepower Merlin 76 engines) that it required no defensive armament and packed a terrific punch as a fighter (four 20-mm cannon and four .303-caliber machine guns). Despite its achievements, the Mosquito's wooden construction made it a dead-end aircraft with no postwar future.

DEVELOPING MATURITY: THE LATE 1930s

In the late 1930s, the maturity of the propeller-driven airplane increased rapidly. Just before World War II, airplanes took on a new, more sophisticated look, typified by the Seversky P-35 and the Hughes H-1 racer. The former was a low-wing monoplane with a full engine cowling and retractable landing gear and was powered by a 950-horsepower Pratt & Whitney R-1830-9 radial engine equipped with a geared supercharger and a variable-pitch propeller. Redesigned in 1936 by Alexander Kartveli, Seversky's chief designer, and produced from July 1937 to August 1938, the P-35 had all the features of the fully mature, propeller-driven fighter airplane. Its top speed was very close to 300 mph, obtained more by a low-drag airframe than by high thrust. Even by contemporary standards the P-35 was underpowered, and for this reason the Army Air Corps ordered only 77. Nonetheless, a civilian version, the SEV-S2, won three consecutive Bendix Trophy races from 1937 through 1939.

In 1939, the Seversky Aircraft Company became Republic Aviation

Facing page:
In 1939, the Seversky Aircraft Company became Republic Aviation, Incorporated, which went on to produce the P-47 Thunderbolt. Note the similarity of the P-47s shown here with the earlier Seversky P-35 and P-43 Lancer. During World War II, the P-47 became a first-line fighter and fighter-bomber with a top speed of 433 mph in the P-47C/D/G models and 473 and 467 mph in the P-47M and N versions. Everything about the Thunderbolt was large. The powerful Pratt & Whitney R-2800 engine in the later variants (M and N models) produced 2,800 horsepower, it weighed from 15,000 pounds in the C/D/G models up to 20,700 pounds in the long-range N that escorted B-29s to Japan in 1945, its armament was eight .50-caliber machine guns plus rockets and bombs in the fighter-bomber versions, and its sheer size and rugged construction allowed it to sustain heavy battle damage and still return safely. In comparison, the P-51D Mustang had a 1,490-horsepower engine and a gross weight of 11,600 pounds.

Below:
The Republic XP-43 Lancer was derived from the XP-41, the final production model P-35, which was fitted with a turbosupercharged engine and was tested extensively at Langley Field in 1939. The Army Air Corps ordered 54 P-43s in 1940 and another 125 in 1941 before switching to the vastly superior XP-47 Thunderbolt in 1941.

Incorporated. Again under the direction of Kartveli, the design features of the P-35 grew through the intermediate XP-43 Lancer into a new airplane, the Republic P-47 Thunderbolt of World War II. Outfitted with advanced versions of the Pratt & Whitney R-2800 engine that could deliver 2,800 horsepower in its later models, the Thunderbolt became one of the largest, fastest, most rugged, and most heavily armed fighters of the war. A highly advanced experimental version, the XP-47J, set the highest unofficial speed ever recorded for a propeller-driven World War II airplane, achieving 504 mph at 34,450 feet in August 1944.

Contemporary with the P-35, Howard Hughes designed and built the H-1 special-purpose racing aircraft. In the middle 1930s, Hughes aspired to three aviation goals: to break the world's speed record for land planes, to set a transcontinental speed record, and to win a Thompson Trophy air race. To accomplish this, Hughes designed and built a new airplane, the H-1, that had all the elements of the mature, propeller-driven aircraft.

Great attention was given to drag reduction during the design and manufacture of the H-1, including a highly polished surface and screw heads slotted to align with the airflow. Two sets of wings were built for the H-1: a short, 25-foot wing for the high-speed attempt and a longer 32-foot wing for the transcontinental flight. At high speed, induced drag is low, and so the lower aspect-ratio wing had an advantage as a result of lower skin friction drag. On the other hand, for the transcontinental flight, the combined effect of lower average speed and high altitudes accentuated the induced drag; thus, a higher aspect-ratio wing was a better compromise.

With the H-1 racer, Hughes accomplished two of his three goals. On September 14, 1935, he set the world speed record of 352 mph for a land plane, and on January 20, 1937, he set a record by averaging 332 mph in a flight lasting 7 hours and 28 minutes from Burbank, California, to New York City. However, Hughes never won the Thompson Trophy. There were complaints that the H-1 racer represented unfair competition, and Hughes never entered the race. Hughes then returned the H-1 to California, where it sat in storage until 1975, when it was given to the Smithsonian's National Air and Space Museum.

During the late 1930s the respected British aviation periodicals *The Aeroplane* and *Flight* carried numerous articles and technical reports on the multitude of new military and civilian aircraft, engines, propellers, and other equipment that was appearing worldwide. The tremendous development detailed in these pages and a final German contest for the world's speed record were perhaps the best indicators of the maturity of the propeller-driven airplanes of the late 1930s.

Among military fighter, bomber, reconnaissance, and trainer aircraft, as well as commercial aircraft, biplanes had practically faded out. Fast, highly maneuverable fighters, such as the Hawker Hurricane, Supermarine Spitfire, and Messerschmitt Bf 109, and equally fast bombers such as the Boeing B-17, Vickers Wellington, Loiré et Olivier LeO 451, Dornier Do 17, and Junkers Ju 88 were conspicuously present. Possibly most significant were the number of large, reliable, multiengine commercial transports covered, among them the Douglas DC-3, Bloch 220, de Havilland D.H.91 Albatross, Armstrong Whitworth A.W. 27 Ensign, Dewoitine D.338, Savoia Marchetti S.M.75, Focke-Wulf Fw 200A, Heinkel He 116, and Junkers Ju 90B.

In an article on the Paris Air Show of 1938, speed was a dominating aspect, with most of the airplanes flying at 310 mph or faster. Within months, Hans Dieterle confirmed this point when he pushed a Heinkel He 100V-8 to

Facing page (top):
A fighter aircraft of World War II was the Supermarine Spitfire, which was the direct descendent of Reginald J. Mitchell's distinguished line of the S.4, S.5, S.6, and S.6B Schneider Cup racers of the late 1920s and early 1930s. The Spitfire was Mitchell's greatest design, one that he personally pushed to completion. Mitchell had originally designed a Supermarine fighter to meet the Air Ministry's Specification F.7/30, but he was dissatisfied with the aircraft and initiated a private undertaking that resulted in the Spitfire. The final design version had a new Rolls-Royce PV-12, later Merlin, engine. When the new fighter [prototype K5054] first flew on March 5, 1936, its performance was astonishing, with a top speed of 355 mph and great handling ability. The Spitfire MK.I with a two-bladed propeller was ordered into production in 1937 and first appeared in Royal Air Force Fighter Command squadrons in the summer of 1938. The Spitfire MK.IAs pictured here preparing to take off in 1939 were assigned to the No. 19 Squadron at Duxford, the first unit to receive Spitfires. While more Hawker Hurricanes than Spitfires were operational at the height of the Battle of Britain from August to October 1940, the Spitfire was the highest-performance British fighter engaged in aerial combat over England.

Facing page (bottom):
This Spitfire MK.VB of the RAF Fighter Command's No. 92 "East India" Squadron shows the Spitfire's elliptically shaped wings, which helped reduce induced drag in accordance with Ludwig Prandtl's famous lifting-line theory. Prandtl's experiments conducted in Germany during 1915–1918 determined that the elliptical wing planform had the least induced drag of any planform tested.

Lufthansa introduced the Junkers Ju90 into its airline in the late 1930s.

In the late 1930s, Air France used the trimotor deWoitine D.338 (foreground) and the Bloch 220 (background), in regular airline service.

Ernst Heinkel intended the Heinkel He 100V-8 to put his company back into the Luftwaffe fighter picture that Rudy Messerschmitt dominated with the Bf 109. Hans Dieterle flew the Heinkel 100V-8 to a record speed of 463.92 mph on April 21, 1939, but five days later a Bf 209 V1 set a new world's record of 469.224 mph. The Luftwaffe soon terminated the contest between Heinkel and Messerschmitt on the eve of Germany's attack on Poland. It had long since decided on Messerschmitt's Bf 109 as its first-line fighter and used it for the remainder of the war.

463.92 mph to capture the world's speed record. Just five days later, Fritz Wendel flew a special Messerschmitt Bf 209 V1, called a Bf 109R for obvious propaganda purposes, to a new world's speed record of 469.224 mph on April 26, 1939. With war looming and the strong impression already given that the world record setter was a production version of Germany's frontline Bf 109 fighter, Ernst Udet, the Luftwaffe's development chief, in July 1939, dismissed all further Heinkel record attempts with the curt comment: "It would be embarrassing if another fighter proves to be faster!" Wendel's record for a piston-engine aircraft stood for 30 years before Darryl Greenamyer finally broke it with 482.46 mph in a modified Grumman F8F-2 Bearcat on August 16, 1969.

WORLD WAR II

During World War II, the propeller-driven, reciprocating engine airplane reached its peak. These wartime aircraft had no new dominant design features; they were only bigger and more powerful. In terms of the $T - D$ relationship, drag reduction began to level off, and hence large increases in engine power primarily drove the $T - D$ difference upward during the war, increasing maximum speeds and altitudes. The following statistics for some famous World War II aircraft are indicative of these trends.

Aircraft	Speed (mph)	Engine Power (horsepower)
Supermarine Spitfire Mk.I	364	1,030
Lockheed P-38F Lightning	395	1,325 (two)
de Havilland Mosquito B.IV	380	1,460 (two)
North American P-51D	437	1,490
Republic P-47N	467	2,800

With these higher speeds came a new aerodynamic problem: compressibility of the air. As air speeds increase, the variations in air density in the flow around the airplane also increase. Moreover, when local pockets of supersonic flow occur on an airplane, shock waves are formed that create large increases in drag. These pockets of supersonic flow can exist even though the velocity of the airplane through the atmosphere is below the speed of sound. When the speed (flight Mach number) is subsonic but high enough so that sonic flow (the flow precisely equal to the local speed of sound) first occurs somewhere on the surface of the airplane, that particular flight Mach number is called the *critical Mach number*. At speeds above the critical Mach number, drag increases rapidly as a result of the presence of shock waves on the airplane. These shock waves with their attendant very high drag gave rise to the myth of the "sound barrier" in the late 1930s and 1940s—the idea that it would be very difficult, perhaps even impossible, for airplanes to fly faster than the speed of sound.

All these effects, which begin to occur at high subsonic speeds, are called *compressibility effects*, and they appeared with some regularity during World War II. The first production-line aircraft to encounter major compressibility problems was the twin-boomed Lockheed P-38 Lightning. In numerous flights during 1941 and 1942, P-38s went into sudden dives from which recovery was extremely difficult. Indeed, several pilots were killed. After extensive wind tunnel tests, NACA proved that the problem was due to compressibility effects: shock waves on the wings were destroying the flow over the tail, causing it to create a diving tendency on the airplane. After considerable investigation, the addition of flaps on the lower wing surface

Airplanes during World War II flew faster and higher than their 1930s ancestors primarily as a result of massive increases in engine power. Speeds became so high that compressibility effects began to pose problems. These problems were overcome in the P-38 only after much attention by aeronautical engineers, including numerous wind tunnel tests in NACA facilities. This YP-38 prototype is shown on a test flight over Southern California.

Lightnings were used as fighters, fighter-bombers, and reconnaissance aircraft in all theaters during World War II. They were the first American fighters of the Eighth AirForce's 8th Fighter Command to see action against the Luftwaffe in Europe, notched the first American victory over a Luftwaffe Focke-Wulf Fw 200K off Iceland on August 14, 1942, and shot down more Japanese aircraft in the Pacific than did any other U.S. fighter. P-38s had a number of other notable achievements: They shot down Admiral Isoroku Yamamoto, Japan's master naval strategist, on April 18, 1943 in the southwest Pacific; when fitted with auxiliary fuel tanks, they were the first fighters to escort the Eighth Air Force's bombers round trip to Berlin from England; and they were the favorites of the two top-scoring U.S. fighter pilots, Richard Bong (40 victories) and Thomas McGuire (38 victories). The P-38L had a maximum speed of 414 mph and a range of 450 miles and weighed more than the P-47—21,600 pounds gross weight. The P-38 Lightning was one of the most famous American fighters of World War II and was in production throughout the entire war; a total of 10,047 were built.

corrected the airflow over the tail when shock waves occurred and fixed the problem. After this experience with the P-38, all high-performance propeller-driven airplanes were designed with compressibility effects in mind.

Another technical development during World War II that affected compressibility effects but that was designed with something completely different in mind was the laminar-flow wing. The nature of the flow inside the thin "boundary layer" adjacent to the surface dramatically affects skin friction drag on an aerodynamic surface. If the boundary layer flow is smooth, it is called *laminar flow*, and the skin friction is relatively low. On the other hand, if the boundary layer flow is irregular, mixed-up, and tortuous, it is called *turbulent flow*, and the skin friction is greatly increased. Given its choice, nature will always prefer turbulent flow, and for all airplanes starting with the Wright *Flyer*, the flow was mostly turbulent, with attendant high skin-friction drag.

In the late 1930s, by means of proper design of the airfoil shape, NACA developed a series of "laminar-flow airfoils" that encouraged large regions of laminar flow and reduced airfoil drag by almost 50 percent. Such a laminar-flow wing was quickly adopted for the P-51 Mustang. However, in practice, these wings did not generate the expected large areas of laminar flow. The NACA wind tunnel experiments were conducted under controlled conditions using models with highly polished surfaces. In contrast, P-51 wings were manufactured with standard surface finishes that were rougher than the almost jewel-like wind tunnel models. Moreover, these wings were further scored and scratched in service. Roughened surfaces encouraged turbulent

THE P-51 MUSTANG

North American Aviation originally designed the NA-73 in a mere 117 days in 1940 to meet an urgent need of the British Purchasing Commission and the Royal Air Force for a fighter for use in Europe. Fitted with an 1,100-horsepower Allison V-1710-F3R engine, the Mustang I first flew in October 1940; the British ordered 150 of the fighters in 1941. The U.S. Army Air Forces at first showed little interest, despite the excellent performance of the XP-51 test aircraft provided by North American. But after Pearl Harbor, the AAF quickly ordered 500 A-36As, a ground-attack version, and then 310 P-51As, while the RAF's Mustang I and IAs went into action in April 1942.

The production-version Mustang I, IAs, and P-51s were equipped with a 12-cylinder, 1,150-horsepower in-line Allison V-1710-39 engine, which performed poorly at higher altitudes, thus greatly restricting their use as fighters. Their top speed was about 387 mph with a range of 350 miles. The P-51A added the 1,200-horsepower Allison V-1710-81 engine, which gave it somewhat better performance.

To improve the inadequate high-altitude performance of the Mustang I, the RAF converted four of them to Rolls-Royce Merlin engines and called them Mustang IIIs. Equipped with Rolls Royce/Packard Merlin V-1650-3 engines of 1,380 horsepower and some minor design refinements, the Mustang III (equivalent to the P-51B/C) pushed its top speed from 387 to 440 mph, had a normal operating range of 400 miles, and increased its service ceiling from 31,800 to 41,800 feet. Additional internal fuel tankage raised the range to 1,300 miles, and external fuel tanks gave the P-51Bs a range of 2,080 miles —enough to reach any target in Germany, and most of occupied Europe, and return to England. In December 1943, large numbers of P-51Bs began arriving in the Eighth Air Force's fighter units, and in March for the first time Mustangs escorted B-17s and B-24s all the way to Berlin and back. The Mustang had the range, speed, agility, and firepower to seize and hold air superiority over the continent. The Luftwaffe's doom was sealed.

With its clear, teardrop-shaped canopy and natural aluminum finish, the P-51D had a 1,490-horsepower V-1650-7 engine, a top speed of 437 mph, and a range of 950 miles and became the most numerous Mustang model; there were 7,956 built during the war. The later model P-51H increased the maximum speed to 487 mph, but only a few of them were completed and saw action before the war in the Pacific ended. The P-51D's performance in Europe in 1944 and 1945 and in the Pacific in 1945 confirmed the Mustang's greatness as a long-range fighter, fighter-bomber, and reconnaissance aircraft. In Europe, the P-51s established the best kill-to-loss ratio (3.6:1) of any U.S. fighter. They claimed 4,950 enemy aircraft in the air and 4,131 on the ground for the loss of 2,520.

The later Mustangs, now redesignated F-51, served in the Air National Guard and Air Force Reserve after the war and then as a ground-attack aircraft in Korea. F-51s remained in the Guard and Reserve for many years thereafter and have also been found around the world as air racers and combat

aircraft in small countries. The Mustang was truly a special breed of fighter.

The early production models of the P-51 fighter in the U.S. Army Air Forces service were armed with four 20-mm cannons that distinguished it from the RAF Mustang I, which had machine guns.

Over 900 P-51B/Cs and almost 900 P-51Ds served in RAF fighter squadrons as Mustang IIIs and IVs during World War II. In February 1944, No. 19 Squadron exchanged its Spitfires for Mustang IIIs and soon thereafter escorted daylight raids by heavy bombers against targets in Germany.

flow; even insect smears on the wing could cause the flow to change from laminar to turbulent. Hence, in practice, the laminar-flow wing never created enough regions of laminar flow to produce the desired level of low skin-friction drag.

The laminar-flow wing did accomplish something totally beyond the original intention of the NACA aerodynamicists. Such a wing had a much higher critical Mach number than did a conventional wing and hence tended to delay the onset of compressibility and its resultant problems. As a result, almost all high-performance airplanes, propeller-driven and jet-propelled, used NACA laminar-flow airfoils from the end of World War II to the present, not for skin-friction reduction caused by hoped-for laminar flow but for drag reduction because of compressibility effects at high subsonic flight speeds.

Today, the propeller-driven airplane powered by a reciprocating engine stands at essentially the same level as it did at the end of World War II. Relentless attention to drag reduction on the one hand and ever-increasing engine power on the other hand have brought about a progressive increase in the $T - D$ relationship. In respect to drag, the drag coefficient gives the aerodynamic quality of an airplane; everything else being equal, the lower the drag coefficient, the lower the drag. Over the years, the zero-lift drag coefficient has decreased progressively.

This Hans Groenhoff photograph shows the three great United States Army Air Forces fighters of World War II. From top to bottom are a Republic P-47D Thunderbolt, a North American P-51A Mustang, and a Lockheed P-38H Lightning.

The Heinkel He 178 became the first jet-propelled aircraft when it flew on August 27, 1939. Heinkel's initial success faded as troubles with the Von Ohain turbojet engines hampered the development of the twin-jet He 280 fighter. Messerschmitt again stepped in, using Anselm Franz's axial flow Junkers Jumo 004 turbojet in his Me 262, which first flew in 1942 and became the first operational jet fighter in 1944.

The Gloster E.28/39 first flew on May 15, 1941, using Whittle's W1X Turbojet engine.

Evolution of Drag Coefficients

Aircraft	Drag	Aircraft	Drag
Nieuport 17	0.0491	Seversky P-35	0.0251
SPAD XIII	0.0367	Douglas DC-3	0.0249
Lockheed Vega	0.0278	North American P-51	0.0163

Perhaps the best of these planes was the P-51 Mustang, for which the drag coefficient was a very low 0.0163, a factor of 3 less than that of the Nieuport 17—an accomplishment that reflected 30 years of aerodynamic refinement. In regard to thrust, engine power increased from 110 horsepower in the Nieuport 17 to a mammoth 3,250 horsepower in the Wright R-3350 engines that powered the Lockheed Constellation airliners of the early 1950s. Piston-engine aircraft have now largely given way to new generations of sleek, fast, large airplanes powered by a new, revolutionary invention—the jet engine.

Arrival of the Jet Airplane

On September 30, 1935, leading aerodynamicists from all corners of the world converged on Rome, Italy. Some of them arrived in commercial airplanes, which in those days lumbered along at speeds of 130 mph. Ironically, these people were gathering to discuss airplane aerodynamics not at 130 mph but rather at the unbelievable speeds of 500 mph and faster. The topic of this Fifth Volta Conference was "High Velocities in

Aviation." The German engineer Adolf Busemann first revealed the swept wing as a means of high-speed wave-drag reduction. Within a year, the Luftwaffe had classified the swept-wing concept as a military secret. Little did the attendees know that work was then under way in both Great Britain and Germany on the prime mover that would make such high-speed flight a reality—the gas turbine jet engine.

DEVELOPMENT OF THE JET ENGINE

By the late 1920s, the combination of the reciprocating engine and the propeller was so totally accepted as the means of aircraft propulsion that other concepts were discounted. In particular, jet propulsion was viewed as technically infeasible. For example, NACA reported in 1923 that jet propulsion was "impractical," but at that time their studies were aimed at flight velocities of 250 mph or less. For such low speeds, jet propulsion is indeed impractical. Eleven years later, the British government was still holding a similar opinion.

Into this environment came Sir Frank Whittle, who as a young student in the RAF technical college at Cranwell in 1928 had written a senior thesis on the future of jet propulsion that aroused little interest. Although Whittle received a royal patent for his design of an aircraft gas turbine engine in 1931, it was not until 1935 that he was able to form a small company, Power Jets, Ltd., to develop the engine. In less than two years the engine was running successfully on a test stand, the first jet engine to operate successfully in a practical fashion.

It was not, however, the first to fly. Independently, Hans von Ohain in Germany developed a similar gas turbine engine. Working under the private support of the famous airplane designer Ernst Heinkel, von Ohain started his work in 1936. As with the governments of the United States and England, the German government at first showed little interest in jet propulsion. Using a von Ohain He.S-3b engine that produced 838 pounds of thrust, the experimental Heinkel He 178 completed the first successful flight of a jet-propelled airplane on August 27, 1939. On that day, just before the beginning of World War II in Europe, the He 178 flew to a maximum speed of 435 mph. On May 15, 1941, a Whittle engine delivering 860 pounds of thrust flew for the first time, powering the Gloster E.28/39 special-purpose test aircraft to 338 mph. The jet age had begun.

During World War II, the Germans made the most of jet propulsion. Beginning in 1939, Messerschmitt worked on the design of a twin-engine jet

The only jet aircraft deployed in any numbers by Germany during World War II was the Messerschmitt Me 262A, which had a top speed of 540 mph. The Me 262 first flew on July 18, 1942, but Hitler's attempt to convert the fighter to a vengeance bomber, problems with the turbojets, a deteriorating fuel situation, and Allied air attacks on the aircraft assembly factories combined to delay its appearance in combat until September 1944. Over 1,400 Me 262s were completed by May 1945, but less than 300 reached operational units, and even fewer saw aerial combat. The Me 262A-1a *Schwalbe* (Swallow) fighter version shown here is on display at the National Air and Space Museum. The fighter-bomber version, which accounted for about 30 percent of production, was the Me 262A-2 *Sturmvogel* (Stormbird).

The age of practical jet and rocket propulsion began in Gemany toward the end of World War II. This Messerschmitt Me 163 Komet, a rocket-powered interceptor with a top speed of 597 mph, was primarily intended to attack Allied bombers. Although it was used against B-17s on August 16, 1944, and had some successes, too few Me 163s reached combat units too late to have an effect on the outcome of the war. Persistent problems with the rocket motors delayed its development, as did personality conflicts between Alexander Lippisch, the designer, and Willy Messerschmitt, the builder. The Komet was a dangerous aircraft to fly, partly because of the explosiveness of the rocket fuel.

fighter later designated the Me 262. After a series of technical failures and politically induced delays by Hitler, the Me 262 went into production and entered service in the Luftwaffe in 1944. Powered by two Junkers Jumo 004 turbojet engines with a thrust of 1,984 pounds each, the Me 262 had a maximum speed of 540 mph and a service ceiling of 37,565 feet. In July 1944, a slightly modified Me 262 with a low-drag canopy flew at a record-breaking speed of 624 mph. In total, 1,433 Me 262s were produced before the end of the war. It was the first practical operational jet-propelled aircraft.

Another Messerschmitt design, the rocket-powered Me 163B Komet, complemented the Me 262. This airplane could fly for only 10 minutes before it ran out of fuel. In that time, it could climb to over 30,000 feet in just 2½ minutes and could reach a top speed of nearly 600 mph, all on the strength of the 3,748 pounds of thrust produced by its Walter HWK 509 rocket engine. Over 350 Me 163s were produced by the end of the war. Germany's jet- and rocket-propelled airplanes appeared too late to have a major impact on the outcome of the war. However, these airplanes later had a revolutionary impact on aviation, because all subsequent designs for fighter airplanes in the United States and Europe were to be jet-propelled.

JET FIGHTERS OF THE EARLY POSTWAR ERA

Late in the war, the United States began a frantic program to develop a production-line jet fighter. After a disappointing performance by the Bell P-59, the first American jet fighter, the government assigned a prototype development program to Lockheed in June 1943. Designed in Clarence "Kelly" Johnson's "Skunk Works," the XP-80 was ready for flight just 178 days later. This aircraft was subsequently put into mass production and became the first operational American jet fighter. Later designated the F-80 (the "P" for pursuit designation was changed to "F" for all American fighters in 1948) and named the Shooting Star, this aircraft became a major participant in the Korean war.

The Lockheed Shooting Star was a good example of the T − D relationship. It was so aerodynamically clean that its drag coefficient was 0.0134, lower than that of the best piston-engine fighters of World War II. Powered by an

THE SHOOTING STAR: THE FIRST SUCCESSFUL AMERICAN JET FIGHTER

Lockheed's chief research engineer, Clarence L. "Kelly" Johnson, and the "Skunk Works," his hand-picked team of designers and engineers, designed and built the prototype of America's first operational jet fighter, the Lockheed XP-80. This was done in just 178 days in the summer of 1943, at the urgent request of the U.S. Army Air Forces. Using a British turbojet engine with a 3,000-pound thrust, the XP-80 *Lulu Belle* first flew on January 8, 1944. Soon a better model, the XP-80A, with 4,000 pounds of thrust from a General Electric I-40 turbojet engine, (GE and Allison later produced the jet as the J33) flew on June 10, 1944.

Shooting Stars entered production in 1944 and began equipping the Army Air Forces' postwar jet fighter units in 1945. F-80s (the P for "pursuit" was changed to F for "fighter" by the U.S. Air Force newly created in 1947) served in the Air Force, Air Force Reserve, and Air National Guard until they were phased out in 1958. They saw action in Korea where they recorded the first Air Force aerial victories on June 27, 1950. Lt. Russell J. Brown scored the world's first victory in air-to-air combat between jets when he shot down a Soviet-built MiG-15 on November 7, 1950. The MiG-15, however, was vastly superior to the F-80 in aerial combat, and the Shooting Star was soon relegated to a ground-support role and replaced by the F-86 Sabre for air superiority missions. The Lockheed P-80A Shooting Star was powered by an Allison J33-A-17 turbojet which produced 4,000 pounds of thrust and had a top speed of 558 mph. The final F-80C version had a maximum speed of 594 mph. A total of 1,732 P-80s, F-80s, and experimental models were built from November 1943 and June 1950.

The fighter suffered a high accident rate in its early years as pilots used to propeller-driven aircraft moved to the faster and more powerful jets. This prompted Lockheed in 1947 to develop a jet-transition trainer—essentially a two-seat version of the Shooting Star initially designated the TP-80C and in 1949 called the T-33A. A total of 5,691 T-33s were produced through 1958, and all U.S. Air Force jet pilots were trained in them until the Cessna T-37A appeared in 1957 and the T-38A in 1961. T-33As were also provided to a number of air forces of nations friendly to the United States, and some of these aircraft are still in operation today. The last T-33As were ordered out of Air Force service by 1987—40 years after its initial development.

The U.S. Army Air Forces' P-80.

Developed from the F-80 Shooting Star in the late 1940s, the two-seat Lockheed T-33 was the primary jet trainer for the U.S. Air Force well into the 1960s.

Allison J33 jet engine with 4,000 pounds of thrust, the Shooting Star had a top speed of 558 mph.

Following on the heels of the F-80 was the North American F-86 Sabre, one of the most aesthetically pleasing of all aircraft. It was also one of the most technically pleasing because it was one of the first truly swept-wing fighters, sharing the honor with Mikoyan's MiG-15. As noted before, Adolf Busemann first advanced the concept of the swept wing for high-speed flight at the Volta Conference in 1935. During World War II, the Germans carried out extensive wind tunnel tests on swept-wing models and even designed several swept-wing prototype aircraft. The wings of the Me 262 were moderately swept not for aerodynamic reasons but to position the center of gravity properly to achieve stability. In the 1930s, the Douglas DC-3 exhibited mild wing-sweep on its leading edge for the same reason.

When the Allies occupied Germany in 1945, much swept-wing data and many German aeronautical engineers working in this area fell

The North American F-86 Sabre entered service in 1949 and was one of the best subsonic fighter aircraft of the early 1950s. The Sabre shown here on a 1948 test flight was one of three XP-86s built.

into American, British, and Soviet hands. The XP-86 was started in 1945 as a straight-wing design, essentially an outgrowth of the older piston engine P-51 Mustang. However, the XP-86 design was quickly changed when the German data and engineers became available after the war. The prototype XP-86 flew on October 1, 1947, several months after Mikoyan's early prototype MiG-15, and the first production P-86A flew with a 35-degree swept wing on May 18, 1948. The aerodynamic advantage of sweeping a wing is that the critical Mach number increases, delaying compressibility effects to higher Mach numbers. The zero-lift drag coefficient for the P-86, later designated the F-86, was a low 0.0132, and its top speed was 679 mph, almost 0.9 times the speed of sound at sea level. The F-86 was capable of exceeding the speed of sound in a shallow dive, which it first did on April 26, 1948.

Sabres entered squadron service in the U.S. Air Force in 1949 and remained through the 1960s. Hundreds of Sabres were provided to many Allied nations under the Mutual Defense Assistance Program (MDAP). The appearance of swept-wing Soviet-built MiG-15s in Korea in late 1950 quickly led to the transfer to the Far East of an F-86A wing, to be joined in 1951 by the advanced F-86Es and in 1952 by the F-86Fs, pictured here at a stateside base. Thus began the long months of MiG-Sabre dogfights in "MiG Alley" along the Yalu River over North Korea. The Sabre evolved through a number of modifications that enhanced its overall performance and ensured its reputation as an outstanding jet combat aircraft. It was also one of the most prolifically produced combat aircraft, with a total of 9,502 built by North American, besides being built under license in Japan, Canada, Australia, and Italy. Powered by a 5,970-pound-thrust General Electric J47 engine the F-86F was capable of 690 mph and had a ceiling of 50,000 feet.

THE BELL X-1 AND DOUGLAS SKYROCKET: SMASHING THE SOUND BARRIER

However, this was not the first supersonic flight. That honor went to then Captain Charles E. "Chuck" Yeager, who had flown Bell X-1 through the "sound barrier" on October 14, 1947. At the end of World War II, the Bell Aircraft Corporation was awarded a contract to develop an experimental airplane to fly faster than sound. At that time, flight at the speed of sound was an unknown quantity. No wind tunnels existed that could produce a good-quality flow near the speed of sound, and the Bell engineers thus had no data on which to base their design. Moreover, the aerodynamic theories in those days were not valid near Mach 1, and so the Bell engineers also had no basis for their design. In short, they were working in an information void.

In this situation, the fuselage of the X-1 was designed after a known shape that had flown supersonically in the past—a .50-caliber machine gun bullet. In combination with very thin straight wings, this mitigated the drag associated with shock waves on an airplane somewhat. However, a number of X-1 test flights experienced severe buffeting approaching Mach 1 and yielded critical information on the performance of the horizontal stabilizer and elevator that resulted in the adoption of a flying tail to give the pilot greater control at such speeds. This discovery was quickly transferred to the North American F-86 that was then being designed. The Sabre eventually incorporated a flying tail that gave the pilot better control at high subsonic and supersonic speeds. That degree of control was a primary reason why

Above and at right:
The Bell X-1 was the first airplane to fly faster than the speed of sound. On October 14, 1947, with Captain Chuck Yeager at the controls, the X-1 Glamorous Glennis achieved Mach 1.06 and forever dispensed with the myth of the sound barrier.

Breaking the Sound Barrier

BY GENERAL CHUCK YEAGER AND LEO JANOS

Test pilots like Chuck Yeager put their lives on the line every time they probed the limits of new aircraft. Yeager's mission on October 14, 1947 was to drive the rocket-powered Bell X-1 through the sound barrier into an unknown realm —supersonic flight.

Shivering, you bang your gloved hands together and strap on your oxygen mask inside the coldest airplane ever flown. You're being cold-soaked from the hundreds of gallons of liquid oxygen (LOX) fuel stored in the compartment directly behind you at minus 296 degrees. No heater, no defroster; you'll just have to grit your teeth for the next fifteen minutes until you land and feel that wonderful hot desert sun. But that cold saps your strength: it's like trying to work and concentrate inside a frozen food locker.

That cold will take you on the ride of your life. You watched the X-1 get its 7:00 A.M. feeding in a swirling cloud of vapor fog, saw the frost form under its orange belly. That was an eerie sight; you're carrying six hundred gallons of LOX and water alcohol on board that can blow up at the flick of an igniter switch and scatter your pieces over several counties. But if all goes well, the beast will chug-a-lug a ton of fuel a minute.

Anyone with brain cells would have to wonder what in hell he was doing in such a situation—strapped inside a live bomb that's about to be dropped out of a bomb bay. But risks are the spice of life, and this is the kind of moment that a test pilot lives for. The butterflies are fluttering, but you feed off fear as if it's a high-energy candy bar. It keeps you alert and focused....

Around eight, I climbed aboard the mother ship. The flight plan called for me to reach .97 Mach. The way I felt that day, .97 would be enough. On that first rocket ride I had a tiger by the tail; but by this ninth flight, I felt I was in the driver's seat. I knew that airplane inside and out. I didn't think it would turn against me. Hell, there wasn't much I could do to hurt it; it was built to withstand three times as much stress as I could survive. I didn't think the sound barrier would destroy her, either. But the only way to prove it was to do it...

I settled in to go over my checklist. Bob Cardenas, the B-29 driver, asked if I was ready.

"Hell, yes," I said. "Let's get it over with."

He dropped the X-1 at 20,000 feet, but his dive speed was once again too slow and the X-1 started to stall. I fought it with the control wheel for about five hundred feet, and finally got her nose down. The moment we picked up speed I fired all four rocket chambers in rapid sequence. We climbed at .88 Mach and began to buffet, so I flipped the stabilizer switch and changed the setting two degrees. We smoothed right out, and at 36,000 feet, I turned off two rocket chambers. At 40,000 feet, we were still climbing at a speed of .92 Mach. Leveling off at 42,000 feet, I had thirty percent of my fuel, so I turned on rocket chamber three and immediately reached .96 Mach. I noticed that the faster I got, the smoother the ride.

Suddenly the Mach needle began to fluctuate. It went up to .965 Mach —then tipped right off the scale. I thought I was seeing things! We were flying supersonic! And it was as smooth as a baby's bottom: Grandma could be sitting up there sipping lemonade. I kept the speed off the scale for about twenty seconds, then raised the nose to slow down.

I was thunderstruck. After all the anxiety, breaking the sound barrier turned out to be a perfectly paved speedway. I radioed Jack in the B-29. "Hey, Ridley, that Machmeter is acting screwy. It just went off the scale on me."

"Fluctuated off?"

"Yeah, at point nine-six-five."

"Son, you is imagining things."

"Must be. I'm still wearing my ears and nothing else fell off, neither."

The guys in the NACA tracking van interrupted to report that they heard what sounded like a distant rumble of thunder: my sonic boom! The first one by an airplane ever heard on earth. The X-1 was supposedly capable of reaching nearly twice the speed of sound, but the Machmeter aboard only registered to 1.0 Mach, which showed how much confidence they had; I estimated I had reached 1.05 Mach. (Later data showed it was 1.07 Mach—700 mph.)

And that was it. I sat up there feeling kind of numb, but elated. After all the anticipation to achieve this moment, it really was a let-down. It took a damned instrument meter to tell me what I'd done. There should've been a bump on the road, something to let you know you had just punched a nice clean hole through that sonic barrier. The Ughknown was a poke through Jello. Later on, I realized that this mission had to end in a let-down, because the real barrier wasn't in the sky, but in our knowledge and experience of supersonic flight.

I landed tired, but relieved to have hacked the program. There is always strain in research flying. It's the same as flying in combat, where you never can be sure of the outcome. You try not to think about possible disasters, but fear is churning around inside whether you think of it consciously or not. I thought now that I'd reached the top of the mountain, the remainder of these X-1 experimental flights would be downhill. But having sailed me safely through the sonic barrier, the X-1 had plenty of white-knuckle flights in store over the next year. The real hero in the flight test business is a pilot who manages to survive.

And so I was a hero this day.

U.S. Air Force F-86s in the Korean war achieved a 12:1 kill ratio over Soviet MiG-15s with a fixed horizontal stabilizer. The flying tail became a standard feature of all future transonic and supersonic fighters.

In terms of the T − D relationship, as explained earlier, D increases rapidly with increases in the Mach number once the critical Mach number is exceeded. Hence, the only way to maintain a reasonably large T − D is also

Only three of the U.S. Navy's rocket-powered Douglas D-558-2 Skyrocket supersonic research aircraft were built. In this picture, a modified B-29 mother ship releases a Skyrocket for a test flight early in 1951. The Skyrockets established a number of altitude and speed records while collecting important research data before they were retired in 1956.

Douglas test pilot Bill Bridgeman climbs into the Skyrocket.

to increase T greatly. The myth of the sound barrier was just that—a myth. An aircraft can fly faster than the speed of sound so long as there is enough thrust to push it through the barrier. The Bell engineers chose the Reaction Motors four-chamber, 6,000-pound-thrust rocket engine for this job.

On Tuesday, October 14, 1947, Yeager flew the X-1 in an attempt to surpass the speed of sound. Yeager was suffering from two broken ribs fractured during a horseback-riding accident the previous weekend, but he told virtually no one. At 10:26 A.M., at an altitude of 20,000 feet, the Bell X-1 was dropped from the belly of a B-29 carrier airplane. It then powered itself to Mach 1.06 at an altitude of 42,000 feet, the first manned supersonic flight in history. Less than a month later, Yeager reached Mach 1.35 in the same airplane. The sound barrier had been penetrated, and the myth was destroyed.

The next major barriers fell to the D-558-2 Skyrocket that Douglas built for the U.S. Navy and NACA as a supersonic research aircraft. Using captured German aerodynamic reports, the D-558 design team, headed by Ed Heinemann, produced a swept-wing rocket and turbojet version of the jet-powered Douglas D-558-1 Skystreak transonic research aircraft. In 1950 Douglas modified the second D-558-2 to take Reaction Motors' 6,000-pound thrust XLR-8-RM-6 rocket motor. On January 26, 1951, Douglas test pilot Bill Bridgeman was accidentally launched from the P2B-1S, a Navy-modified B-29 mother ship, over Edwards Air Force Base, California, and in a dive from 40,000 feet hit Mach 1.28. In six more flights during the summer of 1951, Bridgeman reached Mach 1.79 on June 11, Mach 1.85 on June 23, Mach 1.88 on August 7, and 74,494 feet on August 15. The Skyrocket had flown faster and higher than any manned aircraft ever—what the X-1 had broken, the Skyrocket smashed forever.

Under NACA control, the Skyrocket established a new world's altitude record on August 21, 1953, when Marion Carl reached 83,235 feet. Then, on November 20, 1953, A. Scott Crossfield became the first man to fly at twice the speed of sound when he dove his aircraft from 72,000 feet and reached Mach 2.005, or 1,291 mph. The last Skyrocket was retired in 1956 after accumulating much useful research data on supersonic flight. Appropriately, the record-setting D-558-2 is on display at the National Air and Space Museum with the Bell X-1.

THE CONTINUING QUEST FOR SPEED AND ALTITUDE

The quest for speed was insatiable. On May 25, 1953, the North American F-100 Super Sabre became the first fighter capable of sustained supersonic

The North American F-100 Super Sabre, the first of the U.S. Air Force's "Century series," was the first fighter designed for sustained supersonic flight. It first flew on May 25, 1953. Although it became operational before the end of 1953, a number of accidents and control problems led to modifications that slowed its introduction. Another problem was that pilots had to learn the nuances of supersonic flight. The F-100 had a maximum speed of 864 mph at 35,000 feet. An F-100C of the Air Defense Command is shown in flight near Holloman Air Force Base, New Mexico, in 1967.

The area rule was developed in the early 1950s as a means of reducing drag as an airplane flew through Mach 1. As originally designed, the F-102 Delta Dagger was based on Alexander Lippisch's research on delta wings in Germany and on Convair's experimental XP-92A of 1948. When the initial YF-102 flew at Edwards Air Force Base, California, in October 1953 and January 1954, it exhibited poor performance and was unable to go supersonic. However, Convair undertook a major investigation and soon redesigned the aircraft as the YF-102A, primarily by reducing the cross-sectional area of the fuselage in the wing region to produce the so-called Coke bottle shape, as prescribed by the area rule of NACA's Richard Whitcomb. The YF-102A achieved supersonic speeds on its second test flight, and Convair went on to build 975 Delta Dagger air defense interceptors for the U.S. Air Force from 1953 through 1957. This initial application of Whitcomb's area rule produced a successful supersonic airplane and saved Convair from a major design failure.

Facing page:
Four F-106 Delta Dart supersonic interceptors of the U.S. Air Defense Command.

speeds in level flight. It was powered by a Pratt & Whitney J57 turbojet with 16,000 pounds of thrust—four times greater than that of the Lockheed P-80 and three times that of the F-86. The T − D relationship was being stretched significantly simply by the addition of brute thrust.

At the same time, Convair was designing a delta-wing fighter, the F-102, that was having major difficulties breaking the speed of sound; the increase in drag near Mach 1 was simply too great. Fortunately, an aerodynamicist at NACA's Langley laboratory, Richard T. Whitcomb, had been conducting experiments on a unique concept for transonic drag reduction. By reducing the cross-sectional area of the fuselage in the vicinity of the wings, Whitcomb proved that the drag near Mach 1 could be reduced. This principle, called the *area rule*, was incorporated in a modified YF-102, and the airplane readily went supersonic with a maximum speed of 825 mph (Mach 1.25) and into service with the U.S. Air Force as the F-102 Delta Dagger. The follow-on F-102B—later designated the F-106 Delta Dart—was completely redesigned using the area rule to produce a much neater and more aerodynamically efficient aircraft. The F-106 also added a new Pratt & Whitney J75 turbojet engine with 50 percent more thrust that gave it a top speed of 1,525 mph (Mach 2.3) at 36,000 feet. In 1954, Whitcomb received the Collier Trophy for his pioneering work with the area rule, one of the most important advances in high-speed aerodynamics.

In February 1954, the first fighter capable of sustained flight at Mach 2, the Lockheed F-104 Starfighter, made its first appearance. In addition to those built for the U.S. Air Force, large numbers of F-104s were manufactured under license arrangements in Germany, Japan, Canada, Belgium, Italy, and the Netherlands, while the U.S. provided others to Denmark, Norway, Greece, and Turkey. In May 1958, an F-104 set a world's speed record of

This Lockheed U-2R of the Strategic Air Command's 99th Strategic Reconnaissance Squadron at Beale Air Force Base, California, was a complete redesign of the earlier versions that had emerged from Clarence "Kelly" Johnson's "Skunk Works" as high-altitude (70,000 feet and up) aerial photographic reconnaissance platforms during the mid-1950s. Used mainly by the CIA and the U.S. Air Force's Strategic Air Command to collect photographic intelligence over the Soviet Union, the U-2 was a supersecret aircraft that first came to world attention when a Soviet surface-to-air missile shot down Francis Gary Powers in his U-2B near Sverdlovsk on May 1, 1960. U-2 missions over Cuba in August 1962 confirmed the presence of Soviet intermediate-range ballistic missiles, leading to the Cuban missile crisis.

The SR-71A Blackbird is a further development of the U.S. Air Force's experimental YF-12A interceptor and the CIA's A-12 high-speed, high-altitude reconnaissance aircraft of the late 1950s.

1,404 mph as well as an altitude record of 91,243 feet. By the year 1960 supersonic flight was an everyday affair, not just the domain of research aircraft such as the X-1 and Douglas Skyrocket.

The quest for altitude was embodied in a special-purpose military airplane, the Lockheed U-2. Designed with an exceptionally large wing aspect ratio of 14.3, the U-2 was capable of flying at 90,000 feet. However, the quests for altitude and speed were combined in the U-2's successor, the Lockheed SR-71 Blackbird. This too was a special-purpose aircraft for high-altitude, high-speed reconnaissance, but unlike the subsonic U-2, the SR-71 was capable of sustained flight at Mach 3 at an altitude of about 100,000 feet. Designed at the Lockheed "Skunk Works" under Kelly Johnson, the same combination that produced the XP-80 and the U-2, the SR-71 broke new

Facing page:
The Lockheed F-104 Starfighter was the first American fighter designed for sustained use at Mach 2. This airplane contained the best supersonic aerodynamics: a sharp-nosed slender fuselage and an extremely thin, very-low-aspect-ratio wing to reduce wave drag. In May 1958, on separate flights, on F-104 set a speed record of 1,404 mph, and a record altitude of 91,243 feet. These photos show two F-104As over San Francisco Bay and an F-104 fitted with a refueling probe dropping away from a KC-135 tanker after refueling.

The SR-71A first flew in 1964, entered service with the Strategic Air Command in 1966, and has seen extensive global use ever since. With its sophisticated cameras and sensors, a Blackbird can photograph 100,000 square miles in a single hour while flying at Mach 3 above 80,000 feet.

ground in aerodynamics, propulsion, structures, and materials. It is still the fastest and highest-flying operational aircraft in the world, holding absolute world records for speed over 2,000 mph. The absolute altitude record for jet aircraft, however, belongs to Aleksandr Fedotov and the experimental Mikoyan Ye-266M (MiG-25 prototype), which set a record of 123,523.58 feet on August 31, 1977.

HYPERSONIC FLIGHT: FROM THE X-15 TO THE SPACE SHUTTLE AND THE FUTURE

Once the sound barrier had been broken, it was left far behind. The next goal became manned hypersonic flight at Mach 5 and beyond. This flight regime is characterized not only by high wave drag associated with the strong shock waves but also by high temperatures in the flow around the vehicle, thus introducing aerodynamic heating as a new technological challenge for the designer. With these problems in mind, in 1955 the American government awarded a contract to North American Aviation for the design and construction of three prototypes of a manned hypersonic research airplane, designated the X-15, that was capable of a nominal Mach 7 and a maximum altitude of 264,000 feet—about 50 miles. The X-15 has a basic internal structure made from titanium and stainless steel, but the skin is Inconel X, a nickel alloy capable of withstanding temperatures up to 1,200 degrees Fahrenheit.

The first X-15 rolled out of the North American factory at Los Angeles on October 15, 1958. Vice President Richard M. Nixon was the guest of honor at the rollout ceremonies. The mystique of high-speed airplanes as symbols of national pride (which started with the Schneider Cup races) was alive and well.

The X-15 flight program of 199 flights lasted until October 24, 1968, and was successful in all respects. On July 17, 1962, Major Robert White had zoomed to an altitude record of 314,750 feet, virtually at the edge of the atmosphere. The maximum Mach number achieved was 6.72 during a flight on October 3, 1967, with Air Force Major Pete Knight at the controls. Such flights formed the basis for claims that the X-15 was the Air Force's first manned "space vehicle."

The North American X-15 was the first hypersonic airplane. On October 3, 1967, it achieved Mach 6.72. On July 17, 1962, it had zoomed to an altitude of 314,750 feet. Like the Bell X-1 and Douglas Skyrocket research aircraft before it, the X-15 was carried into launch position by a modified B-52 mother ship.

Starting with the X-15, manned hypersonic airplane flight, although by no means commonplace, became a reality. The X-15 was the test bed from which the Space Shuttle was derived. On April 12, 1981, the NASA's *Columbia* became the first space shuttle to achieve an orbital flight, and on April 14 it returned to Earth, entering the atmosphere as a controlled glider at Mach 25.

The next steps in manned hypersonic flights are now being developed. There are ideas for transatmospheric vehicles—aircraft that will take off like ordinary airplanes from ordinary runways, accelerate through Mach 1, and then literally blast their way to Mach 25 and orbit strictly on the basis of air-breathing propulsion without rocket boosters. These transatmospheric vehicles will then carry out a mission in orbit, after which they will reenter the atmosphere at Mach 25 and, either as gliders or under power, return to a conventional airport. A project to develop such a transatmospheric vehicle in the United States, the National Aerospace Plane Project, was started in 1985 with the goal of producing a hypersonic test vehicle, the X-30. In addition, NASA is looking toward an eventual commercial hypersonic transport and is already conducting research toward this end. Even the idea of a "far" space shuttle is being considered, entailing a space shuttle that will go into very high geosynchronous orbit around Earth or a planetary mission to Mars or other planets and then return to Earth, entering the atmosphere at Mach 36.

The current realities of hypersonic flight are the milestones already attained, and the dreams of transatmospheric missions and vehicles only set out markers for the future. The quest for speed and altitude, which started on December 17, 1903, with a small, fledgling biplane struggling along at 30 mph barely 20 feet above the ground, has now progressed to flight far beyond the outer regions of the atmosphere at speeds of Mach 25 on the way to Mach 36. How proud Wilbur and Orville Wright would be of these achievements that have sprung from that first flight of December 1903, and how exciting the future prospects will be for the Orvilles and Wilburs of the twenty-first century. The many milestones so far laid down in the relentless quest for greater speed and higher altitude in manned, powered flying machines mark one of the crowning achievements of the human race. There is no reason why this quest will not continue indefinitely into the future.

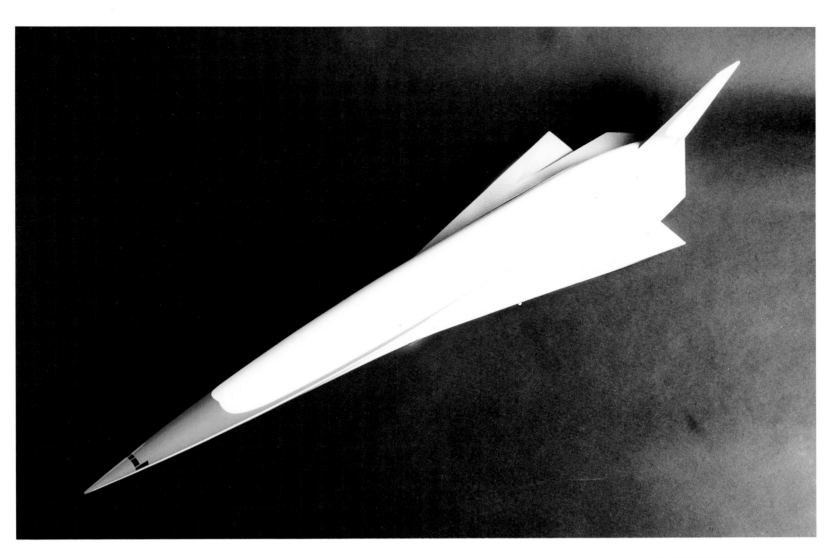

BIGGER

BIGGER
The Quest for Size

JAMES R. HANSEN

Pages 148–149:
A Lockheed C-5A Galaxy headed out past the Golden Gate Bridge at San Francisco, showing its four General Electric TF39 turbofan engines.

Facing page (top):
The six-engine Tarrant Tabor sits outside the balloon shed at the Royal Aircraft Establishment at Farnborough, where it was constructed in 1919. The triplane's most unusual feature, apart from its size (45,000 pounds) and engine arrangement (the four lower engines were mounted in tandem), was its use of braced wooden girders. Tarrant was a woodworking firm and building contractor in Surrey.

Some people just "think big": Alexander the Great, Julius Caesar, Napoleon, John D. Rockefeller, P. T. Barnum, Cecil B. deMille, and Wernher von Braun, to name a few. In different ways, each of these individuals thought big; nearly all of them paid a price for it.

The field of aircraft design has produced more than its fair share of big thinkers: Ferdinand von Zeppelin, Igor Sikorsky, Gianni Caproni, Walter Barling, Claudius Dornier, Howard Hughes, William Boeing, Oleg Antonov. All have earned a page in aviation history for designing *big* flying machines, and nearly all of them paid a price for it.

The rate of failure for big airplanes is nowhere near what it once was. Today, with systematic wind tunnel testing and computer-aided design, it is unthinkable that anyone would build an airplane that could not fly. A new airplane might be overweight or not make its specified cruise speed within one percent, but it is unthinkable for a company to build a plane that just won't fly.

In the early days of "cut-and-try" aircraft design, however, basic failures happened frequently, especially with big airplanes. Some of the earliest giants could not even get off the ground. This was fortunate, because if they had lifted off, aerodynamic forces would have prevented their pilots from exerting control over them. These big airplanes would have crashed to the ground, probably killing everybody aboard. On its maiden flight in May 1919, England's 44,600-pound Tarrant Tabor triplane bomber did exactly that; fortunately, all crew members but the two pilots had been kept off the airplane.

Four years later, the U.S. Army Air Service scrapped plans for another huge triplane bomber, Walter Barling's XNBL-1 "Barling Bomber," when the ungainly 42,569-pound prototype failed to demonstrate enough power, even with its six 420-horsepower Liberty engines, to make it over the Appalachian Mountains. That cancellation made Barling zero for two in designing large aircraft; he had also designed the Tarrant Tabor. Such failures of large military airplanes were a major factor inhibiting the development of strategic bombing for years to come; the state of aeronautical engineering and technology could not sustain the conceptual framework.

The largest aircraft ever built and flown, the Soviet An-225 transport plane can take off with a payload of 250 tons. It made its maiden flight from Kiev in December 1988.

Thinking Too Big

Ironically, some big thinkers about aircraft got around paying the price of failure by thinking *too* big. A case in point concerns an idea for a super airliner that the highly innovative American theatrical designer Norman Bel Geddes (1893–1958) conceived in 1929.

Earlier in the 1920s, Geddes had established an international reputation as the "Leonardo of the theater" by devising some of the most spectacular set decorations ever seen. The New York production of *The Miracle* in 1923 was the largest theatrical production staged up to that time and for a long time afterward. For it, Geddes magically transformed the gaudy interior of the Century Theater into a magnificent Gothic cathedral, complete with pungent incense, stained-glass windows, a richly carved altar, a profusion of lighted candles, and votive statues.

Six years later, on the eve of the Wall Street crash of October 1929, Geddes, now the head of a large industrial design firm, came up with an idea that was even more titanic than his spectacular medieval stage set. He conjured up the vision of a gigantic flying boat that could take several hundred "luxury lovers" quickly and regularly between New York and Paris.

Coming two years after Lindbergh's trans-Atlantic flight, Geddes's design was fantastic: a flying wing spanning nearly 600 feet (the length of two football fields), weighing 700 tons (1.4 million pounds), and powered by 20 large engines situated above the main plane on an attached separate wing that would carry 451 passengers and a crew of 155 across the Atlantic. Just as the audience in the Century Theater had experienced the mysteries of medieval Christianity while sitting in a Manhattan auditorium in their dinner clothes, passengers on his airliner would enjoy all the comforts and

Facing page (top):
The XNBL-1, better known as the Barling Bomber, was an ungainly 42,459-pound triplane intended for use in the U.S. Army Air Service as a long-range strategic bomber in the early 1920s. Walter Barling, a British engineer, designed the aircraft while working for the Air Service's engineering division at McCook Field near Dayton, Ohio. Barling had earlier served as chief designer for the ill-fated Tarrant Tabor. Although it did not crash before flying like its British brother, the XNBL-1 was also a failure.

Facing page (bottom):
The Barling bomber did well enough over the flat terrain of central Ohio, but it was too underpowered even with its six 420-horsepower Liberty engines to fly over the Appalachian mountains. The only way for the manufacturer, Witteman-Lewis Aircraft Corporation of Newark, New Jersey, to get the airplane to McCook Field was to ship it by rail in sections.

Perhaps Norman Bel Geddes's airliner was not so far-fetched. Some aeronautical experts today believe that the flying wing is the best aerodynamic configuration for large aircraft. Of course, such airplanes will not be outfitted with a gymnasium or a 200-seat formal dining room and will not be flying boats, but the aircraft of the twenty-first century may look something like Bel Geddes's idea of 1929.

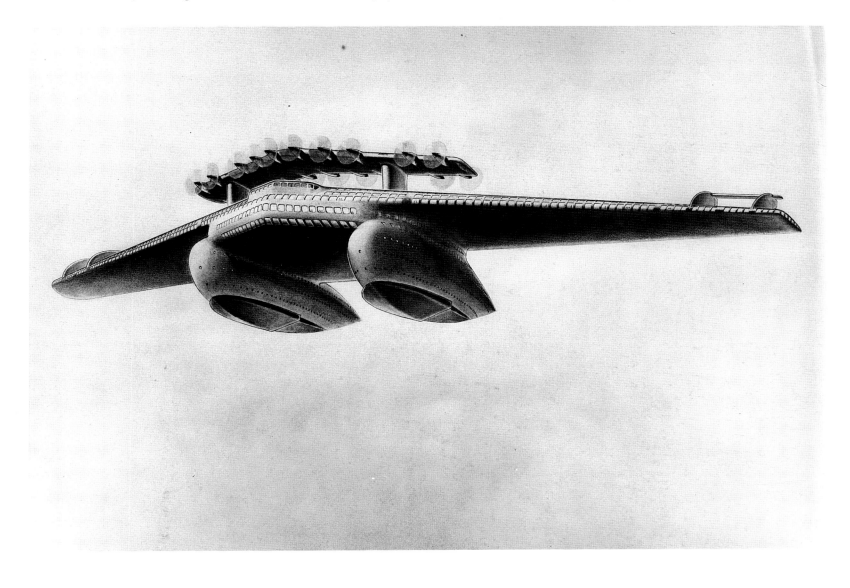

The Ocean Liner of the Sky

BY NORMAN BEL GEDDES

Imagination is an absolute necessity for any creative designer. Norman Bel Geddes's concept for his Air Liner Number 4, the great flying-wing seaplane of 1929, certainly was a futuristic fantasy of the greatest imagination. Today, the Boeing 747-400 is pushing toward the size of Geddes' dream machine, and Antonov's An-225 has actually achieved its gross takeoff weight of 1.3 million pounds.

For a number of years I have been working on plans for a big plane. It is not "big" for the sake of being big but for other factors which will be apparent as I describe it. It is my firm belief that this is in no sense a mad or foolish idea but sound in every particular. It represents my idea of what the intercontinental air liner of 1940 will be like.

As a premise, one must accept the fact that the air liner I am going to describe will fly, and fly just as readily as any other plane. In fact, I have every reason to believe that it will fly much more smoothly than any plane that has yet been built, if for no other reason than because of its enormous size....

Air Liner Number 4 is a tailless "V"-winged monoplane, carrying (sleeping accommodations) a total of 606 persons—451 passengers and a crew of 155. She has a total wing spread of 528 feet. On the water she is supported by two pontoons 104 feet apart, 235 feet long and 60 feet high. Better to visualize the size of this plane, imagine that if it were possible to stand her upon one wing tip against the Washington Monument, she would lack only 23 feet of reaching the top. Or imagine that the Public Library was removed from its site in Bryant Park at Forty-second Street and Fifth Avenue, New York. The plane could then settle comfortably in the park with a clearance of about 35 feet all around....

In the design of this plane, two major elements have had foremost consideration: first, safety; second, comfort of passengers. Both of these factors have been solved mainly by her immense size. As regards the safety factor, it has been possible to make elaborate provision. While twenty 1900 horsepower motors are required to raise her from the water, twelve are sufficient to fly her at cruising speed. Thus, counting the six reserve motors, she is equipped with more than twice as many motors as will be necessary after once rising from the water—a safety factor of over 100 percent....

No airplane or airship has yet offered to passengers comfort equal to that provided by steamship or even railway travel. Tomorrow's air liner will offer facilities and comforts that are in every respect identical with those offered by the most advanced ocean liner. Passengers aboard this air liner are able to move about as freely as on an ocean liner, enjoying recreations and diversions similar to those to which seagoing passengers are now accustomed....

On either side of the dining room and connecting the main lounge are two large foyers. From these foyers a wide corridor leads to the sport and recreation decks, with an area of four thousand square feet, providing space for four deck tennis courts, six shuffle-board courts, six quoits, and other games. These decks are entirely enclosed in glass. The gymnasium, which is also on this level, is twenty by twenty-five feet, and is provided with showers and private dressing rooms. Adjacent to the gymnasium is a solarium for men and another for women, each equipped with sixteen couches and with the necessary conveniences, including masseur and masseuse. On this deck are also the children's playroom, the doctor's waiting and consulting room and nurses' quarters, as well as the barber's and the hairdresser's shops....

The main promenade deck (Deck 7) is four hundred and fifty feet long and seventeen feet wide. Running nearly the full length of the main wing on the forward side, with large windows of shatterproof glass along its entire length, passengers are provided with the same view and conditions as on the finest ocean liner. Besides providing ample space for passengers to stroll, it accommodates at the same time one hundred and fifty deck chairs. On this deck there is a veranda café with tables for ninety persons....

This plane has been designed upon the basis of the latest developments in aviation known today. Every detail and every principle involved has been tested in one form or another. It is merely the combination that is new.

As to whether, exactly, this type of air liner is the next step in solving the problem of intercontinental aviation is beyond calculation. What can be reasonably anticipated is that a liner its equal in size, facilities, and comfort will be a common means of intercontinental transit in the not very remote future. Whether the development of such liners will follow the identical trend I have indicated is problematical. I am inclined to believe that the principles I have followed will be utilized for a few years and that engineers will then have at their command new principles which will make possible further advances and simplifications.

Air liners of a size that is not easily visualized today will eventually supplant ocean liners in intercontinental transportation of express traffic passengers and mail, but not freight. No such radical departure from a long-established mode of transportation can occur without bringing enormous consequences in its train. In many respects, getting the world on wheels has changed the face of the earth. With the prospect of air liners spanning the oceans on scheduled flights, one need not peer very far beyond the horizon to detect other changes that are stimulating to contemplate. Intercontinental aviation will change the whole structure of present-day world metropolises. This is not at all an exaggerated view. Chicago, for instance, under influences that will arise concomitantly with intercontinental aviation, may easily become as much of a world metropolis as New York.

Reprinted from *Horizons* by Norman Bel Geddes (Dover, 1977).

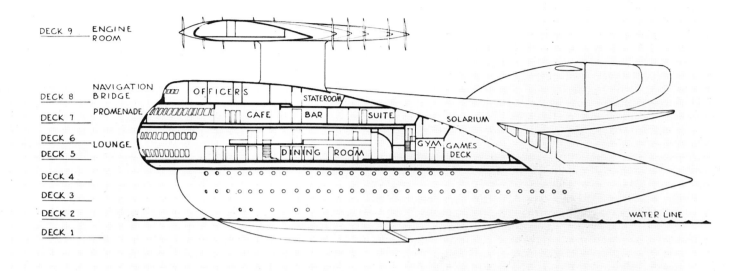

DECK 9 — ENGINE ROOM

DECK 8 — NAVIGATION BRIDGE — OFFICERS — STATEROOM

DECK 7 — PROMENADE — CAFE — BAR — SUITE — SOLARIUM

DECK 6 — LOUNGE

DECK 5 — DINING ROOM — GYM — GAMES DECK

DECK 4

DECK 3

DECK 2

DECK 1

WATER LINE

idle pleasures of the most lavish ocean liners while cruising through the air. Within the nine floors of this behemoth there was to be a dance floor, a gymnasium, a solarium, a 200-seat formal dining room, a café, a lounge, and a stateroom. There were even enclosed promenades and games decks. Three times a week, according to Geddes's plan, the airliner would make a trans-Atlantic trip, twice as often as the fastest steamship.

All this was to happen at a cruising speed of 90 miles per hour (mph). Clearly, Geddes had no idea that the primary reason for flying was to cross the Atlantic as quickly as possible. Ninety mph hardly qualified as a speedy trip. At that rate, it would take his fantasy airplane over a full day to reach London from New York. Lindbergh's cruising speed between New York and Paris in May 1927 had averaged 100 mph, and the *Spirit of St. Louis* had taken 33 hours.

In size, lavishness, and flying range, the only contemporary aircraft comparable to Geddes's hypothetical trans-Atlantic airliner was Germany's passenger-carrying *Graf Zeppelin* airship, which completed the first around-the-world airship flight in August 1929. The most amazing and the largest *airplane* to fly by the end of the decade—with sleeping berths, a bar, a restaurant, and a lounge—was the Dornier Do X flying boat. Although it resembled Geddes's airplane in some key aspects, Dornier's flying boat was much smaller. The maximum takeoff weight of the Do X was only 105,820 pounds, some 630 tons less than that of the machine proposed by Geddes. The Do X, a monoplane, possessed a wingspan that was almost four times shorter—only a little over 157 feet. It was powered by 12 engines instead of 20, and it accommodated a quarter of the passengers—only up to 150. More important, Dornier's flying boat could not lift any kind of payload over trans-Atlantic distances, the minimum such distance being roughly 2,000 miles. The maximum range of the Do X was 1,056 miles. Its first flight across the Atlantic from Germany to New York took 10 months—from November 1930 to August 1931—and encountered numerous hazards and mishaps.

In comparison with Geddes's plan, Claude Dornier's idea was a midget. But it flew, and in doing so it created an illusion of "tomorrow's" airliner today, although its operational performance provided little encouragement for the future. In terms of the aircraft technology and airline economics of the later 1920s and early 1930s, Dornier's flying boat was too big. The Do X did not have enough speed (134 mph) or range to operate successfully as a trans-Atlantic or transoceanic airliner. It would have been a commercial

The dining room of the Graf Zeppelin.

If the Do X's 12 engines, mounted in tandem in six nacelles, had been switched on during the launching ceremony at Altenrhein, Switzerland, no one in the crowd could have talked to his or her neighbor. The noise of the engines was compared to the sound of a squadron of pursuit planes passing by. Inside the luxurious cabin, however, the noise level was lower than in most airplanes of the era, and conversation was easy because the great wing separated the engines and propellers from the passengers.

failure, but only three were built, and none were ever placed in airline service. The Do X was more of a research and development exercise intended to explore the limits of large aircraft, and in accordance with good engineering mathematics practice, the X stood for "unknown quantity."

Not until 1935 did flying boats such as Pan American's Martin M-130 begin to cross the oceans satisfactorily on a regular airline basis. Even then, the Clippers carried no more than a few passengers, and they had to use intermediate stops for refueling.

As Geddes and many others would discover, it was one thing to design or even build a very large aircraft; it was another thing to see it fly, make it safe, have it perform a mission, and make its operations economically viable. No sane designer sets out to build a giant airplane unless it takes an airplane of such dimensions to accomplish the desired mission.

By and large, what has determined the size of an airplane in the minds of aircraft designers has been the range and the payload requirements. How far will the proposed aircraft need to fly before landing and refueling? What is the mission radius? What is the cargo, and how much does it weigh? How much fuel is necessary? What is the total payload weight? The answers to these and similar questions that relate size to function mostly determine the dimensions of the modern airplane.

Size Is Relative

In common parlance, "size" is a rather vague word that can refer to linear dimension, area, volume, mass, or even bulk. In relation to aircraft, it can and does mean all those things and more. Aeronautical engineers may even use power—i.e., horsepower and thrust—as a measure of an airplane's size. Typically, though, engineers think about size in terms of wingspan, wing area, overall length, and overall height.

Curiously, an analysis of the historical trends involving these linear dimensions does not reflect the really impressive changes in size that have been achieved in aircraft design since the Wright *Flyer*. In 1970, F.A. Cleveland, a distinguished aerodynamicist and executive with Lockheed, made such an analysis. He found that "growth measured by linear dimension has been fairly steady . . . with a flattening of the curves . . . after 1930." In other words, airplanes had definitely grown longer, higher, and wider over the years: The Dornier Do X of 1929 was more than six times longer than the Wright *Flyer* (131.4 versus 21.1 feet), with a wingspan roughly four times greater (157.5 versus 40.0 feet) and nine times more wing area (4,736 versus 510 square feet). When linear dimensions were used as a major criterion, however, the most dramatic historical progression in the size of aircraft was not apparent. This is especially true of the trend after 1930. As Cleveland pointed out, the wingspan of the Do X was not that much smaller than the 222.8-foot wingspan of his company's C-5A Galaxy, for many years the world's largest aircraft until its Soviet look-alike, the Antonov An-124, with a 240.6-foot wingspan, appeared in the mid-1980s.

When the analysis turns to weight— the most credible criterion of aircraft size—the perspective changes. The phenomenal increases in the weight of aircraft from the Wright *Flyer* to the C-5A, An-124, and the new 1.3-million-pound An-225 most clearly show the rapid progress brought about by major advances across a broad front of technologies.

At first glance, weight as a measure of size seems to simplify the matter only a little, because aircraft weight can be viewed in different respects. There is the empty, or "tare" weight, the fuel load, the payload, and the

useful load (which includes the payload, the fuel, and the crew), all of which are measurable in pounds or kilograms.

However, for simplicity's sake, one measure of weight can be used: the *gross weight* or *maximum takeoff weight* (MTOW). This figure refers to the total loaded weight of an aircraft, including fuel and oil, cargo, passengers, and crew. As the name implies, anything heavier than the MTOW will not be able to leave the ground. When dozens of passengers bring two or three pieces of heavy carry-on luggage each into the full commercial airliner on which you are flying, MTOW is the figure that should weigh on your mind.

The explosive growth in aircraft size since 1903 can be readily demonstrated by plotting the phenomenal increases in gross weight against the steady but relatively minor increases in the previously mentioned linear dimensions. These data show that while the wingspan of Lockheed's giant military transport is six times that of the little canard biplane of Wilbur and Orville Wright and its wing area is 12 times as large, in terms of gross weight, the C-5A is bigger by a factor of 1,000. Its gross weight is 764,500 pounds compared with the 765 pounds that flew over the sand dunes of Kitty Hawk. In terms of pitch inertia—that is, how the weight is distributed along the fuselage (in the Wright *Flyer*, most of the weight rested right in the middle, where the pilot and engine were located)—Lockheed's modern giant is bigger by a factor of 100,000.

In terms of weight, the C-5A is not ever the biggest thing around. In its new model 747-400 wide-body airliner, Boeing is now approaching a gross takeoff weight of over 900,000 pounds, and Antonov's An-124 tops the scale at 892,872 pounds MTOW. On November 30, 1988, the Soviets introduced an

A U.S. Air Force Lockheed C-5A flying off the coast of South Carolina in 1972, two years after it entered service with the Military Airlift Command.

airplane that significantly outsizes the C-5, the 747-400, and the An-124. The six-engine Antonov An-225—*Mriya*, Ukrainian for "dream"— with its huge interior space and capacity for carrying additional freight (the Soviet space shuttle *Buran* and *Energiya* rocket boosters) attached to points atop the fuselage, can carry up to 551,000 pounds of cargo. Its takeoff weight is an awesome 1.3 million pounds. This means we are now almost 90 percent of the way to the size of Norman Bel Geddes's super airliner of 1929!

EVADING THE SQUARE-CUBE LAW

How big can aircraft grow? Do terrestrial mechanics or the physics of atmospheric flight set an absolute limit? These are issues that aeronautical experts have debated for decades, only to have the assumptions on which they have based their answers shattered.

The most fundamental and persistent assumption that aeronautical experts have used to keep a hypothetical lid on the growth of aircraft size has been the *square-cube law*. This "law" is ancient, dating back to antiquity, when Hellenistic engineers used it as the basis for determining the right size of chariots and catapults. The basic premise of the modern law, as expressed by Sir George Cayley in the early 1800s and formalized by aeronautical engineers between the world wars, is that the structural weight of an airplane is the cube of its linear dimensions. In its more complete technical formulation, the law states that "the stress in similar structures increases with linear dimensions if the imposed load is proportional to the structural weight, since the latter grows as the cube of the linear dimensions and the material cross-section carrying the load grows only as the square."

Underlying this statement is a concern with *scale effects* and the problem of scaling up an object of a given geometry and structural density

On November 30, 1988, Oleg Antonov's An-225 *Mriya* first appeared. With a gross weight of 1.3 million pounds and a payload capacity of 551,000 pounds, the *Mriya* (Ukranian for "dream") is the biggest aircraft ever built. Designed in Antonov's bureau in Kiev, this newest Soviet transport for cargoes to Siberia and the Far East is powered by six jet engines. The An-225 will also carry on its back the Soviet space shuttle *Buran* and large parts of the *Energiya* booster rocket to the Baikonur space center. SOVFOTO

Facing page:
Six 29,000-pound, 60-passenger buses that would fit inside a Lockheed C-5A Galaxy's cargo compartment can easily park under one of its wings. When it entered service with the U.S. Air Force in 1970, the C-5A was, at over 750,000 pounds, the world's largest airplane. Though somewhat exaggerated by the camera, the C-5A's T-tail towers 65 feet above the ground.

Although Igor Sikorsky's giant biplane of 1914, the *Il'ya Muromets*, was quickly turned into a bomber and reconnaissance aircraft at the outbreak of World War I, it originally had a passenger cabin roomy enough for a small number of passengers to enjoy wicker armchairs, a sofa, a table, and a washroom.

Igor Sikorsky's pioneering four-engine *Il'ya Muromets*.

to a larger replica. The square-cube law suggests that certain objects, such as airplanes, can get only so big or they must become something else. An airplane has to be able to lift its own weight to fly; this is one of the things that makes it unique as a mode of transportation. If the weight of the airplane becomes excessive, there will not always be a way to make up for it with more lift. That is the message of the square-cube law.

Historically, the most interesting thing about this law has been the way aeronautical engineers have thought about, talked about, applied, and evaded it. To the extent that it has in fact kept the size of aircraft in check, the law has been largely a self-fulfilling prophecy of aeronautical engineers.

The first maverick to challenge and defeat the square-cube law was the Russian designer and eventually naturalized American Igor Sikorsky. Although more often associated with the invention of the helicopter, Sikorsky sparked the imagination of airplane designers all over the world just before World War I by building in tsarist Russia a number of exceptionally large airplanes. The first of these was the *Le Grand* (also known as the *Russkiy Vitaz*, or Russian Knight), a biplane that was the first airplane with four engines as well as the first with enclosed accommodations for pilots and crew. Powered by four German 100-horsepower Argus engines mounted on the lower wing, this giant flew for the first time in May 1913. It made 52 other successful flights, one lasting nearly two hours, before it was wrecked later in the year during army maneuvers. Ironically, the wreck occurred on the ground, when an airplane accidentally dropped an engine on it.

From the remains, Sikorsky built an even larger four-engine biplane called the *Il'ya Muromets*. About three times larger than the original Wright *Flyer* in terms of linear dimensions (67.2 feet long, with a wingspan of 113 feet and a wing area of 1,615 square feet), Sikorsky's airplane weighed 10,850 pounds gross weight, or roughly 14 times more than the Wright airplane. Its

During his early career in pre-revolutionary Russia, Igor Sikorsky designed the first successful large, multi-engine aircraft in the world. After fleeing the Bolsheviks, he established a thriving aircraft and helicopter company in the United States. Here he holds a model of his large CH-54 Skycrane that was used extensively by the U.S. Army for heavy cargo transport duties.

four engines produced a total of 400 horsepower in comparison to the 12 of the Wrights' one engine.

In a way, the *Il'ya Muromets* deserves the title of the world's first airliner. It had a flight deck, a roomy passenger cabin with sofas and tables, windows on both sides of the passenger cabin, and a toilet. For illumination of the interior compartments at night, there were electric lights driven by a wind-powered generator. Although it did not operate as an airliner, Sikorsky's airplane did fly as many as 16 passengers over the 400-mile distance between St. Petersburg (now Leningrad) and Moscow in early 1914. When World War I broke out in August, however, the Russian Army turned it into a reconnaissance aircraft and bomber. In a slightly altered form and with more powerful engines, 70 of these aircraft operated during the Great War.

World War I Giants

World War I saw the birth of strategic air power. Along with the dreaded German bombing Zeppelins that did little real damage except to British home-front morale, virtually all the combatants built a number of heavy bombers. Characteristic of these were two twin-engine biplanes, the German Gotha G.IV and the British Handley Page 0/400, and a three-engine triplane, the Italian Caproni CA 42. Like other contemporaries of the same type, including the *Il'ya Muromets*, they ranged in gross weight from 8,000 to 16,000 pounds. However, a few special-purpose bombers, such as Germany's R-planes and England's Handley Page V/1500, both of which were designed to attack each other's capital cities, tipped the scales at over 30,000 pounds.

The basic mission of these bombers was to drop a sufficient number of bombs on vital military and economic targets to inflict costly damage on the enemy's war effort, thereby weakening the morale and effectiveness of soldiers and civilians alike. This entailed a heavy payload. To make it hundreds of miles to enemy targets and back home again, these airplanes also had to carry hundreds of gallons of gasoline. With each gallon weighing more than six pounds, this meant carrying a heavy fuel load. The requirements of a bomber also came to entail carrying enough heavy defensive armament to protect itself against fighter attacks.

The 13,300-pound Handley Page 0/400 was intended to be the main heavy bomber of the Allied air forces in 1918, but the war ended before they could be used for strategic bombing.

The first man to fly Handley Page's colossal V/1500, Britain's biggest bomber of World War I, was Clifford Prodger, an American living in England who has been called the first free-lance test pilot. In one of Prodger's flights in 1918, the V/1500 carried a record 41 passengers. Adventurous passengers sat in the positions of the nose, dorsal, and the tail gunners.

Although 1,000-kilogram (2,200-pound) bombs like this were sometimes dropped from the largest of the German R-planes in World War I, their loads more typically consisted of 12 to 18 100-kilogram (220-pound) bombs.

Given the then adolescent state of aircraft technology, the only way to achieve all these things together and provide the structural weight needed to carry such a heavy payload was to increase wing area. The only acceptable way to give an airplane sufficient wing area yet make it small enough dimensionally so that it could be accommodated on the landing fields that were then available, was to give it two or more wings. Thus, nearly all the big aircraft built early in the century were either biplanes or triplanes.

The most extraordinary World War I airplanes in terms of size were the heavy bombers known as R-planes—"R" standing for Reisenflugzeuge, or "giant airplanes." As manufactured in Germany from 1915 to 1918 by Zeppelin-Staaken (successor of Versuchsbau Gotha-Ost, or V.G.O.), the Allgemeine Elektrizitäts Gesellschaft (A.E.G.), Linke-Hoffmann, and Siemens-Schukert, the majority of R-planes were multi-bay, strut and wire-braced biplanes. They possessed a conventional wooden framework and fabric covering. By the end of the war, however, designers with R-plane experience—notably Claude Dornier—were designing giant monoplane bombers incorporating thick cantilever wings. The plan was to build them of Düraluminium, a high-strength aluminum alloy called duralumin in American usage. After the war, Adolf Rohrbach, who had worked with Dornier, designed for Zeppelin-Staaken such a metal monoplane, the 19,000-pound E.4/20 Giant, which

Adolf Rohrbach's Zeppelin-Staaken E.4/20 required extremely heavy bulkheads in the fuselage to support its huge semicantilever monoplane wing of 138½ feet. Built into the very thick (ribbed and covered with duralumin) wing structure were four 245-horsepower Maybach engines. Inside each nacelle was a seat for a mechanic, who could reach the engine by crawling through a tunnel leading from the fuselage. The E.4/20 was a major advance in aircraft design using *Düraluminium* metal. Fearing its possible use as a bomber and the advance it represented, the Allied Control Commission in Germany ordered the E.4/20 destroyed in November 1922.

The Zeppelin-Staaken R-planes were powered by four Maybach engines mounted in streamlined nacelles between the wings. The nacelles were easily accessible from the fuselage so that crew-members could work on the engines and take care of other mechanical problems.

The German SSW R.VIII was the largest aircraft built during World War I. The large fuselage housed the engines, which drove two two-bladed tractor propellers and two four-bladed pushers. Note the absence of engines between the wings.

could carry 12 to 18 passengers up to 740 miles at a cruising speed of 124 mph.

What made the R-planes exceptional was not just their size but also the requirement to maintain and repair the engines *in flight*. For some of the German giants, such as the twin-engine A.E.G. R.I and the Linke-Hoffmann R.I and R.II, the designer had situated the engines fore and aft in the fuselage and then had used shafts, pulleys, gears, and clutches to drive propellers located outboard on struts between the wings. Others, including most of the planes built by Zeppelin-Staaken, possessed conventional engine-propeller arrangements set between the wings, but they also had ladders so that the crew members could climb out, stand on the ladder, and change spark plugs while flying.

The idea of working on engines in flight seems astonishing and even strange today, but engine technology was too unreliable in those days for airplanes to complete long-distance missions without in-flight maintenance and repair. Besides changing spark plugs, the wing-walking and ladder-climbing daredevils could also accomplish the greasing of rocker arm bearings and other simple tasks.

The R-planes were not unique in this. Many of the planes that set early endurance records had catwalks so that crew members could go outside

With room to spare, 34 men stand in front of the 128-foot wingspan of the Handley-Page V/1500. Immediately above and behind the pilot, in a tank built to conform with the contour of the upper fuselage, rested the 1,000 Imperial gallons of fuel for a round trip bombing mission against Berlin. Beneath the fuel tank, on racks in the lower half of the fuselage, hung a bomb load weighing as much as 7,500 pounds. Although the Royal Air Force ordered 225 of the huge airplanes, only three V/1500s had reported for action by the Armistice in November 1918.

Facing page (top):
The Boeing 247 that first entered service with United Air Lines early in 1933 was a sleek, twin-engined, low-wing monoplane of stressed-skin construction that was truly the first of today's commercial airliners. The fully enclosed cabin had room for 10 passengers, two pilots, and a steward. Its appearance prompted TWA to ask Douglas to develop what became the DC-2 and then DC-3. The 247 was restored in the early 1980s and is displayed in the Boeing Museum of Flight in Seattle.

Facing page (bottom):
The quality of the ride between London and Paris improved significantly in 1931 with the introduction of the Handley Page H.P.42 Hannibal. Slow but reliable, the safe and comfortable biplane served throughout the 1930s on British Imperial Airways routes to Europe, Egypt, India, and central Africa. When World War II started, it served briefly as a troop transport.

and examine the engines. Most of the large, multiengine aircraft, such as the Do X, had this feature. Even in the Boeing 314 flying boat of the late 1930s, the giant Convair B-36, and the Lockheed Constitution, a mechanic could crawl out into the engine nacelles and perform minor repairs on the accessory end of the engine while in flight.

Because these large airplanes required the combined power of more than one engine both to lift off and to stay in the air, everything possible had to be done to prevent loss of power. If they lost even one engine, many of these planes could not continue to fly safely and had to land. The 30,000-pound-gross-weight Handley Page V/1500, built by the British in 1918 for the purpose of bombing Berlin but never used in combat, possessed four Rolls-Royce Eagle VIII engines of 360 horsepower each, two tractor and two pusher. The huge biplane simply would not fly if it lost an engine.

Fighting for Control

Having the power of all the engines was one requirement; controlling that power was another. What caused the fatal crash of England's Tarrant Tabor triplane bomber on its maiden flight at Farnborough in May 1919 was the lack of such control caused by the poor arrangement of its six 500-horsepower Napier Lion engines. Four of the engines were in tandem on each side of the fuselage; each tandem drove a tractor and a pusher propeller. The other two were above, between the top two wings, driving tractor propellers. After taxiing out on the four lower engines, Sgt. Pilot "Dusty" Dunn opened up the two upper units for takeoff. The coupling moment caused the big triplane to nose over and catch fire, and both Dunn and his copilot died.

Pilots and aeronautical engineers learned a lot from such tragedies. Unfortunately, some of them learned how to do a better job of coaxing such aircraft into the air rather than ceasing to make them. In truth, only rarely have designers and engineers determined the "size" of their airplanes; usually, that has been done by prospective customers with more money than good sense. In the early 1930s, just a few years before the state-of-the-art Boeing 247 and Douglas DC-2 airliner were designed in the United States, Handley Page completed work on two large biplane passenger airliners: the 38-seat H.P.42 Hannibal and the H.P.45 Heracles. In comparison to the sleek new Boeing or Douglas airplanes, they were technological dinosaurs.

THE JUNKERS G38

One of the most remarkable big airplanes of the interwar period was the Junkers G38 of 1929. Although it weighed 52,911 pounds and had a wingspan over 144 feet, it was not really the size of the German transport that was extraordinary; it was the way that Junkers integrated the aircraft's size into a novel structure. Built primarily of metal, the G38 possessed wings so thick that small passenger cabins could be built into them. More importantly, the monoplane wings were thick enough to house the aircraft's four powerful engines. Besides the aerodynamic advantages of burying the engine nacelles in the leading edge of the wings, this meant that crew members could get to and attend to these engines in

flight without risking their lives by going outside, as R-plane mechanics had done during World War I.

Unfortunately, so much engine power was needed to lift the G38 into the air that it could accommodate only 34 passengers: three in each of two cabins in the wing root, two in the nose of the fuselage, and 26 in the main fuselage cabin.

Junkers produced only two G38s, and Lufthansa, the German national airline, operated both. Neither plane lasted for long: one of them, the *Deutschland*, crashed in 1936, and the other, the *Generalfeldmarschall von Hindenburg*, was destroyed by an RAF bombing raid in 1940.

The Junkers G 38.

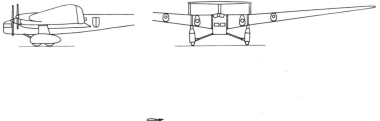

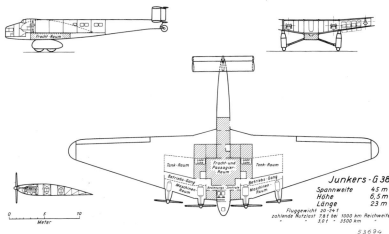

The Junkers G 38.

The Junkers G 38.

The Junkers G 38.

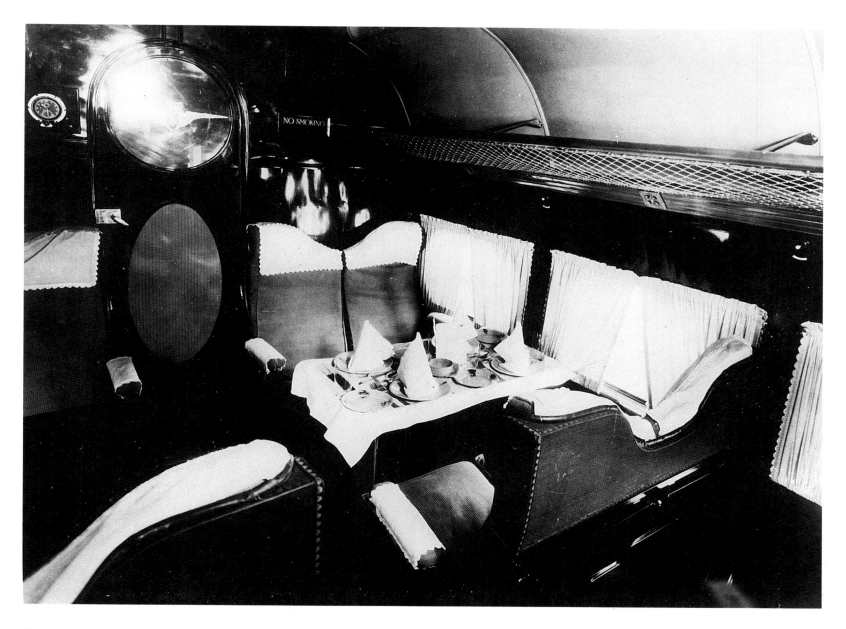

The H.P.42 was, however, one of the world's first four-engine airliners to enter scheduled service, along with the Fokker F.32 of 1929.

A gigantic biplane with a 130-foot wingspan, the H.P.42 cruised at a leisurely top speed of 100 mph on the power of four Bristol Jupiter engines, assuming there was no head wind. Two of the engines were on the upper wing, similar to the catastrophic arrangement on the Tarrant Tabor. Fortunately, when an H.P.42 pilot started a takeoff run, he was smart enough not to open up the top engines until the airplane had developed enough speed so that its tail could hold it down. This stopped the airplane from nosing over as the Tabor had done. The pilot could then open up the upper engines.

Given this dangerous condition, the airplane's lack of speed, and its overall obsolescent design in comparison to the modern airliners that were just appearing in the United States, it is astonishing how much success the H.P.42 enjoyed. A fleet of eight aircraft was used by British Imperial Airways from 1931 to 1939, and not a single passenger died or was seriously hurt in one. Moreover, passengers liked flying in them. Igor Sikorsky once remarked that British airliners were slow; even the flights between London and Paris took two and a half hours, so that the passengers would have time to enjoy a meal. Inside the H.P.42 there was enough room, and almost always enough time, to be served substantial and elegant meals. For many people, however, that leisurely pace beat spending all day on the train and crossing the unpredictable Channel by boat.

The operation of multiengine aircraft continued to be a problem for years to come, even when the airplanes were not very large. During the

The H.P.42's cruising speed was only 100 mph. When the much faster Armstrong Whitworth Ensign (170 mph) and the de Havilland D.H.91 Albatross began replacing the Hannibals in the late 1930s, many passengers on Imperial Airways complained that the flight from London to Paris no longer gave them their money's worth.

takeoff and climb of the Ford Tri-Motor, a moderate-size (13,500 pounds) high-wing monoplane produced for airline service between 1926 and 1933, the pilot and copilot had to keep both feet on the rudder pedals because they had no trim tab. If the Tri-Motor lost an engine, it took both men to hold the airplane straight.

Another serious problem has been the nervous exhaustion suffered by pilots. With the incredible size of some of the structures, the terribly high inertia and control forces, and the slow rates of response, the pilots' fear was totally justifiable. Many of these big airplanes were dangerously sluggish. For example, according to Cecil Lewis, the Royal Air Force's Handley Page 0/400 twin-engine bomber (gross weight 13,300 pounds) of 1918 behaved "like a lorry in the air. When you decided to turn left, you pushed over the controls, went and had a cup of tea and came back to find the turn just starting."

Slow-to-respond controls in combination with other extreme stresses facing pilot and machine led to many catastrophic failures. After several successful bombing raids to the eastern front, Zeppelin's first R-plane, the 21,000-pound V.G.O. I, crashed late in 1915, killing the crew. A little later, even before it could be delivered to the German Army, so too did the V.G.O. II. In early 1917, one of the Linke-Hoffmann giants broke up in the air when the wings collapsed. A year later, the A.E.G. R.I. also broke up in midair, when a propeller failed, killing the crew. In all, Germany produced over 50 R-series heavy bombers during the war. Only a handful were brought down in combat. A greater number were destroyed in some type of accident, like many of the other airplanes of World War I, which had similarly high accident rates. A few of these airplanes survived the war to give "joyrides" to naive paying passengers.

In the following decades, new technologies such as servo tabs, full-

A Ford Tri-motor rebuilt by American Airlines in the early 1960s hangs from the ceiling in the National Air and Space Museum's Air Transportation Gallery just in front of a Delta DC-3.

The 25,000-pound German Linke-Hofmann R.I. of 1917 was capable of some excellent maneuvers, but it was slow to respond to controls and very difficult to land because the pilot sat so high—near the top of a fuselage that was over 20 feet high.

power control systems, and aerodynamic balancing of control surfaces ultimately alleviated much of the difficulty of manually piloting these giants. But even with the development of electronic and automatic controls, it would still not be easy. On big commercial airliners today, the time it takes for the airplane to respond to controls still tends to be significantly longer than is the case for small airplanes.

EARTHBOUND LIMITATIONS

An important factor in the high accident rate of big airliners in the early days was the small size and poor condition of landing fields and their runways. Most airports amounted to no more than an open grass field with a few flimsy hangars in one corner. The usual shape of the field was square or rectangular so that a pilot could head the machine into the wind regardless of its direction. In metropolitan areas, it was also common for airports to be surrounded by buildings and power lines. Small wonder that the pilots of these colossal machines had serious qualms about takeoffs and landings.

Runways were made of sod or cinder or were nonexistent, even at military airfields. As late as the mid-1930s, the U.S. Army Air Corps base at Langley Field, Virginia, was only a big grass field with no runways. The only artificially hard surface was a wide concrete taxi ramp about a half mile long running in front of a row of hangars. Occasionally, test pilots from the NACA (National Advisory Committee for Aeronautics) Langley Aeronautical Laboratory, which shared the use of Langley Field with the Army, would use this ramp as a takeoff runway for small experimental aircraft. Concrete runways did not begin to appear even at the most vital military airfields until the late 1930s and early 1940s. Hard runways at major commercial airports had come only a few years earlier.

Although less directly related to flight safety, even the size and shape of hangars could work against large airplanes. During World War I, the Royal Air Force told its aircraft manufacturers that their airplanes had to fit inside the standard RAF hangar. This gave designers a fit. Handley Page, for example, had to find a way of folding up the big wings of the 0/400 bomber until they

The Handley Page 0/400 wings were foldable so that it could fit in the standard RAF hangar of the time.

The Short Stirling was an early mainstay of the RAF Bomber Command's night bomber offensive against Germany. An otherwise excellent aircraft with a payload capacity of 14,000 pounds of bombs at 590 miles, the Stirling was hampered by the shortening of its wings, which limited its service ceiling. This Stirling Mark III in its matte black night bombing paint scheme entered service in 1942, but by mid-1943 the Stirling was largely outmoded and had been replaced by Lancasters and Halifaxes.

The only DC-4E ever built arrives at New York's Floyd Bennett Field on June 1, 1939, after completing its test flight from Santa Monica, California. The redesigned triple tail is clearly visible.

almost rested flush to the fuselage. As one critic of this questionable dictate has observed, the RAF apparently felt that it was "more cost effective to complicate and perhaps compromise the aircraft than to build new hangars."

This particular shortsightedness continued to hamper British aircraft designers throughout the interwar period. When the Air Ministry issued its Specification B.12/36 for new heavy bombers in July 1936, it required that the aircraft's wingspan fit within the 100-foot opening of the standard large hangars. Because of this, Short Brothers limited their four-engine Stirling to a 99-foot wingspan. To obtain the necessary wing area to keep a reasonable wing loading for a bomber with a gross weight of 70,000 pounds, the chord was increased. In turn, this produced a very low aspect ratio wing that limited the big bomber's ceiling to 17,000 feet and severely affected its operational usefulness when war broke out in 1939.

The same thing held true in many other cases. Engineers had to reduce the overall height of both the Douglas DC-4E and the Lockheed L.049 Constellation, making it easier to push the aircraft under the lintel of hangar doorways, by employing a low triple-tail arrangement instead of one tall tail. Furthermore, the sizing of a number of military aircraft, including the McDonnell F-4 Phantom, has been done to accommodate these airplanes to the dimensions of the elevator that brings them to the flight deck on an aircraft carrier and to the limited storage space available on an aircraft carrier's hangar deck.

MORE WINGS, MORE WHEELS

Given these earthbound limitations on the physical dimensions of aircraft, designers did their best to come up with aerodynamic configurations that offered the greatest possible lift for a given length, height, and wingspan. During World War I, this was one of the factors that led to the triplane phenomenon.

The largest triplanes of the war were built by Gianni Caproni and used by the Italian Army (along with a number of Caproni biplanes) to bomb targets inside the Austro-Hungarian Empire. To make such raids, these airplanes not only had to make round-trip flights of over 500 miles but also had to cross the Alps.

The largest of the Caproni triplanes was the CA 42. One of the special design features required by its phenomenal size was the main landing gear, which consisted of eight wheels in two groupings of four. The idea behind such an arrangement was to help prevent the aircraft from becoming stuck in muddy fields by distributing its 17,700 pounds (MTOW) evenly across the 96.4-foot wingspan.

Just as large people often have trouble with their feet, large airplanes often have trouble with their landing gear. Here again, the criterion for what is large is weight. To modern aeronautical engineers, the problem of designing an efficient landing gear for a large airplane can be as vexing as it was 70 years ago to Caproni. The only experimental 162,000-pound Douglas XB-19 heavy bomber of the late 1930s had two huge wheels and exerted such ground pressure that it broke through concrete taxiways and aprons. The Convair XB-36, one of the largest piston-engine aircraft ever built, carried its full weight of 330,000 pounds on two 110-inch wheels. The ground pressure exerted by the prototype's wheels was so great that it badly cracked or broke through concrete runways, taxiways, and aprons. Convair engineers quickly changed to dual four-wheel bogie main undercarriages with the YB-36 and the production models. Even with the weight well distributed, the runway foundations at airfields built for B-36 operations,

It took 12 years for an aircraft to surpass the gross weight of the Dornier Do X of 1929. That aircraft was the Douglas XB-19, a 162,000-pound all-metal low-wing monoplane experimental strategic bomber that flew for the first time in 1941. Although this was the only XB-19 ever built, it served as a flying test bed, providing important data that were incorporated into the designs of the Boeing B-29 and Consolidated B-36. It was the largest American aircraft until the appearance of the B-36 in August 1946.

A mechanic works on one of the 110-inch wheels of the main landing gear on an XB-36.

One of the XB-19's two huge wheels breaks through the taxiway.

such as those at Limestone Air Force Base, Maine, had to be six feet thick to withstand the weight and constant pounding.

Lockheed rediscovered this problem in the 1960s, when its engineers were working out plans for the undercarriage of the 764,500-pound C-5 military transport. Supporting that kind of weight was going to take exceptionally sturdy feet—a total of 28 wheels.

But what really complicated the design of the C-5, as it had with the B-36 and B-52, was the airplane's *footprint pressure*, that is, the unit loading of the wheels on the runway. Air Force requirements called for the airplane to operate off a hard-surfaced runway and then land on an undeveloped

The C-5A Galaxy's complex of wheels gave it the capability to operate anywhere in the world.

A technological development essential to the construction of huge aircraft has been the creation of large forges, presses, jigs, milling machines, and other machine tools. Here a Lockheed machinist stands next to a 3,200-pound, 24-foot aluminum alloy rib fabricated by a 50,000-ton press for the C-5A. Eighteen of these forgings are milled down to 338 pounds and then used to complete the airplane's main frame structure. At Lockheed-Georgia's plant, finished and treated members can be seen in place forming the skeleton of a new C-5A that awaits the main wing center section.

Facing page:
Today the wide variety of machine tools, including presses 10 times heavier than this 5,000-ton Lake Erie press of 1941, produce large structural members of aircraft.

gravel or sod field in the third world. To meet this challenge, Lockheed came up with a very unusual and ingenious system in which each one of the airplane's 28 tires could be inflated or deflated in flight. That way, when the giant Galaxy transport was about to land on a soft field, the crew could reduce the pressure in the tires automatically.

Fortunately, the designers of the R-planes earlier in the century had not faced this requirement; otherwise, some poor acrobatic mechanic would have been ordered to slide off the lower wing and let air out of the tires manually.

"WHERE THERE'S A WILL, THERE'S A WAY"

Nothing in the history of technology illustrates the truth of this adage better than the story of large aircraft design. No matter what the barriers blocking the development of successful airplanes of enormous size, the desire for size always seemed to win out.

As for the square-cube law, what invalidated it time and time again were changes in design philosophy brought on by the development of new technologies. As F.A. Cleveland pointed out in his analysis of size effects in aircraft design, "technological advances have enabled consistently more progress in the size of aircraft than the square-cube law implies."

A major contributing factor to the defeat of the law has been the very significant increase in the stresses that can be maintained in an aircraft structure. This has been due partly to new and much improved materials and partly to the development of huge presses and machine tools to forge and mill parts of the airframe and skin. Specifically, the changeover from wood and fabric to aluminum and aluminum alloys, stainless steel and reinforced plastics, and recently to chemical composites has greatly affected the strength and weight of aircraft. Moreover, the huge presses, milling machines, routers, and electrochemical milling (ECM) processes now in common practice in airframe manufacturing did not exist to produce airframe structures of sufficient strength and size for assembly. Today, huge forging presses of up to 50,000 tons and extrusion presses can turn out complete fuselage frames, spar booms, root ribs, landing gear shock struts, and larger parts up to 50 by 30 feet as single pieces.

Based on his wartime experience with larger bombers, Gianni Caproni built the CA 60 *Trans-aereo* in 1920 and 1921. An enormous flying boat with nine huge wings in three triplane arrangements, powered by eight Liberty engines, this 55,115-pound airplane actually made one short flight over Lake Maggiore on March 4, 1921, before crashing into the water and suffering considerable damage to its hull. Caproni's idea was to determine whether a larger wing area would solve the problem of designing large airplanes. The CA 60 scored an early postwar "triple": the largest airplane of its time, the first triple triplane, and the first airplane designed to carry 100 passengers on trans-Atlantic routes.

Another factor in the defeat of the square-cube law has been the development of effective high-lift systems. Beginning in the late 1920s, the integration of features such as wing flaps and slots made possible by wind tunnel testing has enabled designers to increase their *wing loadings* (the weight per unit of wing area) by a considerable amount. When the wing loadings went up, it generally meant that the size of the wings could be kept down. This is why the wing of the C-5A is not that much bigger than that of the Dornier Do X. Higher wing loadings by themselves would have increased takeoff runs and landing speeds. What effective high-lift systems made possible were higher wing loadings without the need for monstrously large wings or runways 5 to 10 miles long. With such lifting systems, the designer no longer needed to add on a great amount of wing area, as the World War I designers did, by building biplanes and triplanes.

The square-cube rule aside, there was still the problem of the landing field's finite area to overcome. One possible way around it was to employ the broad unobstructed surface of water. As in the case of Caproni's eight-engine triple triplane CA 60 *Transaereo* of 1921, the Dornier Do X, the Latécoère 631, the Boeing 314, the Saunders-Roe SARO Princess, the Hughes-Kaiser H-4, and Norman Bel Geddes's hypothetical 700-ton super airliner, some of the world's largest aircraft over the years have turned out to be flying boats.

Boats in the Sky

The flying boat was a different type of machine, or so it seemed to many people. Two of its most important advantages were that it could take off and alight on the boundless sea rather than within the confines of an airfield and that it could be moored in only slightly protected harbors without the need for huge hangar accommodations. Another advantage was that it did not have the aerodynamic and structural nuisances of an undercarriage, relying instead for landing on a widely distributed water plane area. In the minds of some designers, this makes the flying boat a more "natural" creature, because there is nothing in nature with wheels.

In the minds of others, the flying boat's biggest advantage was its suitability for crossing the oceans. In reality, any plane could do that; the seaplane's advantage would be seen when it *failed* to cross an ocean. Then, unlike other airplanes, it could alight at sea, rest "safely," and even take off again.

The goal of the first really large flying boat, the Curtiss H *America* of 1913, was to be the first to fly across the Atlantic and thus grab the London *Daily Mail's* £10,000 prize. Although preparations for this ambitious flight were canceled when the war came, for the British in particular the war meant that there was an urgent military requirement for long-range naval patrol aircraft to use against German submarines. The Royal Navy Air Service (RNAS) took over the *America*, built some additional H-4s as Small Americas, and then ordered a number of H-8/H-12 Large Americas and H-16 Curtiss flying boats. From them, the RNAS evolved a series of "F" flying boats built at the Admiralty's air station at Felixstowe. The all-up weight of one of the later "F" boats, a triplane nicknamed the Felixstowe Fury, was 23,400 pounds. In 1919, this plane, overloaded with fuel, crashed on takeoff from Plymouth on its way to a nonstop flight to Lisbon.

In one of the most historic flights ever made, also in 1919, one of the U.S. Navy's Curtiss NC flying boats, the 27,386-pound NC-4, made it all the way across the Atlantic Ocean to Plymouth, England, albeit in a series of hops via

A U.S. Navy Curtiss H-16 flying boat on patrol.

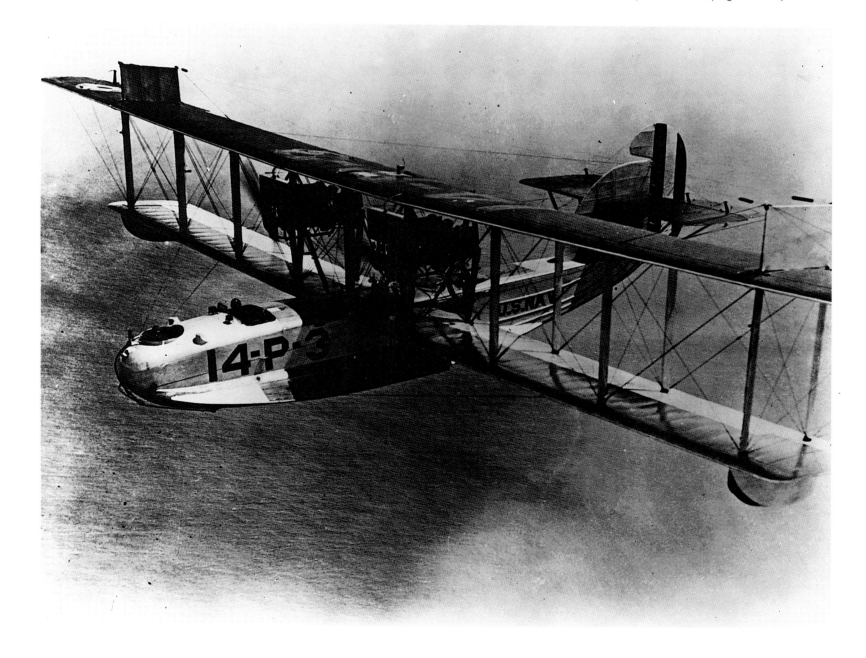

181

The Curtiss NC-4 flying boat that Commander A. C. Read flew across the Atlantic in May 1919 was one of only four NC class flying boats to serve in the U.S. Navy during and after World War I.

Sikorsky's 38,000-pound S-42 flying boats allowed Pan American Airways to develop its Caribbean routes and explore routes across the Pacific and Atlantic for commercial aviation.

THE COMPOSITE: ONE WAY TO BEAT THE DISTANCE PROBLEM

The Short-Mayo composite aircraft of 1938 is an example of early attempts to overcome the need for refueling stops. The large, launching aircraft was a short S.21 Empire-class flying boat named *Maia*. The small floatplane, a Short S.20 *Mercury*, would separate once safely airborne and fly to its destination; the mothership would return home. The designers intended to develop a viable trans-Atlantic mail run. Between

July 20 and 21, 1938, the Mercury, piloted by Captain D.C.T. Bennett, later an Air Vice Marshal with Bomber Command, completed the first commercial crossing of the North Atlantic by a heavier-than-air craft when it flew nonstop from Foynes, Northern Ireland, to Montreal, Canada, and then on to Port Washington, New York. That was its only flight to New York; the following year Pan Am's Clippers went into regular service.

At left and above:

The Short-Mayo composite aircraft.

Newfoundland, the Azores, and Lisbon. As any visitor knows who has seen the restored NC-4 at the U.S. Naval Air Museum in Pensacola, Florida, the most striking physical dimension of the aircraft is not its weightiness (it is hard to see weight) but its massive wing area. At 2,380 square feet, it is not much smaller (only about 18 percent) than the Boeing 707 jet transport. But even its weight is impressive; at 27,386 pounds, its gross weight exceeded that of the Douglas DC-3 of 15 years later by over 2,000 pounds.

Although the United States, Germany, and Japan were also very active, the country that had the most compelling reason to specialize in the construction and operation of flying boats between the wars was Great Britain. The British had a greater need for them because its far-flung empire included remote and forbidding terrain, far from the home island, where it was difficult to build airfields but where rivers, lakes, and harbors were abundant.

In the 1930s, as land planes became larger and heavier, but with few airfields capable of handling them, the flying boat enjoyed great success. With a fleet of Short C-Class flying boats, Imperial Airways moved passengers in comfort and style from London to South Africa, Egypt, and India and on to

Construction of a Boeing 314 flying boat on the huge assembly jig at Boeing's plant in Seattle, Washington. To speed production and cut costs for what was in 1938 the largest aircraft in the world, Boeing developed several new processes and methods of fabrication.

Singapore, Hong Kong, and Australia. Pan American Airways used Sikorsky's S-40 in its Caribbean service and then made trans-Atlantic and even trans-Pacific flights in its progressively larger four-engine Sikorsky S-42, Martin M-130, and Boeing 314 Clippers. Greater Japan Air Lines used the impressive Kawanishi H6K flying boats to fly the home islands as well as to connect them with vital port cities on the Asian mainland.

During World War II, flying boats of all sizes played an important role in maritime antisubmarine patrols and long-range reconnaissance. While the Short Sunderlands and twin-engine Consolidated PBY Catalinas of the RAF's Coastal Command hunted German U-boats in the Bay of Biscay and on the north Atlantic approaches to the British Isles, U.S. Navy Catalinas served in all theaters, especially the Pacific. The same vast operating distances in the Pacific that had spawned the Martin M-130 and Boeing 314 in the 1930s produced two of the largest naval flying boats of the war years—the Kawanishi H8K (gross weight 68,000 pounds, range 4,475 miles) and the Martin JRM-1 Mars (gross weight 145,000 pounds, range 4,700 miles). The five Mars JRM-1 and one JRM-2 flying boats that were built saw limited wartime duty as cargo carriers, but after the war they were used extensively as "water bombers" against forest fires. The 167 Kawanishis produced during the war saw heavy duty in transport and antisubmarine work.

Besides a comfortable dining salon, the Boeing 314 offered passengers the luxury of a private drawing room and separate dressing rooms and toilets. When the *Yankee Clipper* opened Pan Am's service along the north Atlantic route from Port Washington, New York, to Southampton, England, in July 1939 with 17 passengers, the fare was $375 one-way and $675 round-trip.

Facing page (bottom):
In service with Pan American Airways, the Boeing Clippers usually carried no more than two dozen passengers and had to make intermediate stops for refueling. With a full load of 74 passengers, the aircraft's maximum range was only about 1,900 miles. With 24 passengers and a much lighter overall load, the Clippers had a maximum range of over 2,400 miles. Boeing built six 314s and six 314As.

Some Great Flying Boats

Aircraft/Year	Wingspan (feet)	Length (feet)	Gross Weight (pounds)	Cruising Speed (mph)	Range (miles)
Dornier Do X (1929)	157.5	131.3	105,820	134	1,056
Sikorsky S-42 (1934)	114.2	64.2	38,000	170	750
Martin M-130 (1934)	130.0	90.9	52,252	163	2,400
Boeing 314 (1938)	152.0	106.0	84,000	184	2,400
Short S. 23 C (1936)	114	88	40,500	164	760
Short Sunderland V (1943)	112.8	85.3	60,000	134	2,980
Kawanishi H6K2 (1938)	131.2	84.1	35,274	150	2,567
Martin JRM-1 Mars (1944)	200.0	123.2	145,000	153	4,700
Saunders-Roe Princess (1952)	219.5	148	330,000	360	5,270

Only six Martin Mars flying boats were built. Designed in 1938 as a patrol bomber (XPB2M-1) for the U.S. Navy, the modified version (JRM-1) served primarily as a cargo aircraft in the Pacific. The Navy sometimes called the Martin Mars the "flying Liberty ship."

According to a Martin Company publicity release, the 200-foot wingspan of the Mars was so long that a Piper Cub could land on it.

The 45-foot-tall, 145,000-pound Martin Mars dwarfs its fellow amphibian, the Grumman Widgeon. Today, two of the Mars flying boats are used in Canada as water bombers to fight forest fires. The aircraft can refill by flying across a lake and scooping up the water.

EXIT FLYING BOATS, ENTER FOUR-ENGINE LAND PLANES

Excluding Howard Hughes's H-4 Hercules, the so-called *Spruce Goose* venture, the largest flying boat ever built actually flew, and flew very well. The 330,000-pound Saunders-Roe SR.45 SARO Princess was intended by the British Overseas Airways Corporation (BOAC) for luxury service on trans-Atlantic routes between England and New York and first flew in August 1952. Severe technical problems with the gearboxes and contrarotating propellers for its ten 3,780-horsepower Bristol Proteus engines, escalating development and production costs—an all too familiar story for such large aircraft—a cost-conscious British government, and BOAC's move away from large flying

At 330,000 pounds, the Saunders-Roe SRO45 SARO Princess of 1952 outweighed by 20 tons the Bristol Brabazon, which was then Britain's biggest land plane. Although construction of three of these large flying boats with the "double-bubble" hull was started, only one was completed and flown. BOAC backed out of its commitment to use the Princess in 1951, and by the time it flew in 1953, it had no future.

HOWARD HUGHES'S *SPRUCE GOOSE*

Howard Hughes's famous eight-engine H-4 Hercules flying boat of 1947, dubbed the *Spruce Goose*, was the largest aircraft built to its time. The original proposal for the big, 400,000-pound wooden flying boat, with its spectacular 320-foot wingspan, came from within the U.S. government. The idea, which surfaced not long after Pearl Harbor, was to build a cargo and troop carrier that did not require critical wartime materials; in other words, that substituted wood for metal. The steelmaker and shipbuilder Henry J. Kaiser picked up on the idea, and brought Hughes in as an aviation expert. Kaiser's shipyards were building Liberty ships at the rate of one a day, so he thought he might as well produce a large cargo-carrying airplane.

As Hughes kept meddling in the design, making things more complicated and causing lost time, Kaiser backed out. An urgent government project in 1942, the Hughes flying boat had lost all priority by 1944. When Hughes flew the H-4 for the one, and only, time on November 2, 1947, it lifted only 33 feet off the surface of Los Angeles harbor and flew about a mile before settling on the water. It was returned to its massive hangar and never flew again.

Hughes's motives for making things so complicated are not clear. They seem to have revolved around his idea for an "aerial freighter beyond anything Jules Verne could have imagined." It is possible he flew it that once just to prove that something that big could fly.

On November 2, 1947, the Hercules made its only flight—and that may have been an accident. When his chief designer asked Hughes, who was at the controls, whether he meant to lift it off the water, Hughes replied, "You'll never know." Today, the *Spruce Goose* is on public exhibition in Long Beach, California.

Powering the *Spruce Goose* were eight Pratt & Whitney R-4360 Wasp Major radial air-cooled engines. Each engine had 28 cylinders and generated 3,000 horsepower, every bit of which was necessary to lift the 400,000-pound aircraft off the water.

It has been said that not a single scratch was put on any of the big sections of the H-4 Hercules as they were moved very slowly from the factory in Culver City to the assembly site in Long Beach, California, in mid-1946.

Although he thought big, Howard Hughes paid careful attention to the smallest details. The eccentric Hughes would sit for hours in the cockpit of his great wooden flying boat deliberating the design of the control and the instrument panel. Unfortunately, as a perfectionist, he could not make up his mind, and his many delays finally caused a Senate committee to look into the project.

THE BRISTOL BRABAZON 1: ONE OF A KIND

J.T.C. Moore-Brabazon, Lord Brabazon of Tara, who in 1908 had been the first Briton to fly, chaired a special wartime committee that was to advise the government on postwar aircraft development policy. The committee recommended pushing ahead with land planes and flying boats with large passenger and cargo capacity that could fly the Atlantic nonstop. The aircraft endorsed for this mission were the Saunders-Roe SR.45 Princess flying boat and the Bristol Aeroplane Company's Type 167, later named the Brabazon in honor of Lord Brabazon.

The Brabazon that emerged from Bristol's design shops had a 230-foot wingspan, was 177 feet long, had a tail whose top was 50 feet off the ground, and weighed 290,000 pounds. Eight 2,500-horsepower Centaurus radial piston engines in pairs, with each linked to a contrarotating propeller, gave the giant a cruising speed of 250 mph and a range of 5,500 miles. The Brabazon 1 first flew in September 1949 and was intended only as a prototype; this was the only one ever built. The technical innovations designed into the aircraft, not the least of which was the complicated propeller gearing system, were a constant source of trouble and drove the development costs ever upward.

In the end, as it would also do with the SARO Princess, the British government terminated funding in the early 1950s, effectively killing the Brabazon. With the all-jet de Havilland Comet 1 already flying, the continued development and production of these expensive, technologically complicated, large piston-engine aircraft appeared to be unwarranted.

The Brabazon committee was not a complete flop, for it also recommended the development of two very successful Vickers aircraft. Almost 600 of the twin-engine Viking were sold. Powered by four Rolls-Royce Dart engines, the four-engine Vickers Viscount was the first turboprop airliner in the world when it appeared in regular service in 1953. It became the most successful British aircraft production program of the postwar era, with 444 built when production ended in 1964.

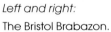

Left and right:
The Bristol Brabazon.

boats in November 1950 doomed the Princess. For many of the same reasons, a similar fate befell the 290,000-pound Bristol Brabazon.

The British government had envisioned the Brabazon as the land plane that, together with the Princess, would capture a sizeable part of the expected postwar international air travel business; this would help reestablish a strong position for the British aircraft industry in the European and world markets for commercial airplanes. The outbreak of World War II had effectively terminated the development and production of most large four-engine European commercial aircraft, including the promising British de Havilland D.H.91 Albatross and the Armstrong Whitworth A.W.27 Ensign, the largest of the prewar British airliners. The Luftwaffe pressed the Junkers Ju 90B and Ju 290 and the Focke-Wulf Fw 200A Condor into active military roles before their commercial potential was realized; the German defeat ended their commercial future. The fall of France in 1940 ended hopes for the Bloch 161, which emerged only after the war as the Sud-Est SE.161 Languedoc. In such circumstances, the continued development and production of commercial

Above:
In many respects a prototype of the modern airliner, the Armstrong Whitworth Ensign 14 could carry up to 40 passengers and cruise at 170 mph. Imperial Airways began using the Armstrong Whitworth Ensign in 1938, but persistent problems with the four 850-horsepower Siddeley Tiger engines limited its usefulness until it was re-engined during the war with Wright Cyclones.

Facing page (top):
The Douglas DC-4 was a scaled-down version of the DC-4E that proved to be a very successful civilian transport and passenger airplane as well as a military transport (C-54 Skymaster).

Facing page (bottom):
The Lockheed L.049 Constellation "Connie" entered commercial airline service in March 1946 with Trans World Airlines on its transcontinental route from New York to Los Angeles.

aircraft during the war gave American manufacturers and airlines a great advantage entering the renewed competition of the postwar years. The failure of both the Brabazon and Princess and the subsequent withdrawal of the de Havilland Comet in 1954 left the large commercial aircraft and air travel market almost entirely to U.S. manufacturers by the mid-1950s.

The golden age of the flying boat did not last long. By 1946, it was largely over except for the brief flight of the SARO Princess in the early 1950s. What brought about the demise of the flying boat as a major category of aircraft (flying boats are still used, of course) was the major event of the intervening period: World War II. Not only did the war witness the decline of the British Empire and the destruction of Japanese power and the German Reich; the vast requirements of fighting a war around the world also stimulated the construction, mostly by the United States, of a worldwide network of airfields with long, hard-surfaced runways as well as connecting and supporting airways, navigation aids, and communications facilities. In addition, wartime demands accelerated the development and production of a number of large, long-range four-engine American commercial aircraft outfitted with better engines and new airborne communications, navigation, and radar systems. As a result, the need for the flying boat disappeared.

Out of the war came a number of large four-engine land planes, such as the Boeing B-29 and C-97 Stratofreighter, Douglas DC-4 (C-54), and Lockheed L.049 Constellation (C-69) and later the newer, improved Douglas DC-6, Boeing 377 Stratocruiser, and Lockheed L.1049 Super Constellation. They could deliver heavy loads of passengers and freight to more locations

A SOVIET GIANT: UNCLE JOE IN THE SKY

One reason why major powers build phenomenally large aircraft is their political or propaganda value. In this context, airplane size even more than speed represents national power, prestige, a potential threat to others, and domestic as well as international legitimization and acceptance of the regime. While the Nazis sent their great passenger airships, the *Graf Zeppelin* and the *Hindenburg*, on international tours for exactly these reasons, Josef Stalin and the Communist Party used the obvious technological and aeronautical achievement of building very large aircraft to distract the Soviet people from internal turmoil and to confirm the legitimacy of his regime.

The most remarkable aircraft ever built expressly for propaganda purposes was the Tupolev ANT-20 *Maxim Gorki* of 1934. On board this gargantuan monoplane were a radio station, a printing press, and a photographic darkroom. Inside the cabin, there was a projector and screen for showing motion pictures. Under the huge all-metal wing (wingspan 206.8 feet, wing area 5,223 square feet) was illumination equipment for flashing Communist Party slogans on and off while airborne, a primitive version of the electronic message system for advertisements on the underbelly of the Goodyear blimps. In addition, there was an aerial loudspeaker system that could get political messages to people on the ground—but only when the airplane was parked with its eight 900-horsepower motors turned off. Even with 40 men and women orchestrating the propaganda, there was enough room in the 92,595-pound airplane for 70 passengers.

The *Maxim Gorki* collided with an I-5 fighter in the air near Tushino outside of Moscow on May 18, 1935; both aircraft were destroyed, killing 46. From the ANT-20 design, the Soviets built an even larger 64-passenger civilian airliner of 99,206 pounds, the ANT-20bis (PS-124), which went into service with *Aeroflot* in 1940.

The Tupolev ANT-20.

With a gross weight of 385,800 pounds, the Soviet Union's Tupolev Tu-114 Rossiya still ranks as the largest and fastest passenger-carrying turboprop aircraft ever built. Introduced in 1957 for the fortieth anniversary of the Bolshevik Revolution, the Tu-114 carried 220 passengers at a cruising speed of 480 mph and cut hours from the flying time from Moscow to Siberia and the Soviet Far East.

and across greater distances more quickly, reliably, and economically than could the flying boats. With bigger and more advanced versions of these land-based planes and new generations not yet designed, the two postwar superpowers, the United States and the Soviet Union, would contest for the postwar leadership in military and (less so) in civil aviation development, dominate significant shares of the aviation markets, and threaten each other with annihilation.

Big countries, it seems, tend to build big airplanes. The United States and Soviet airlines faced the awesome challenge of bridging vast continental distances interrupted by rugged intervening mountain chains, while the

The Boeing Model 377 Stratocruiser adopted the "double-bubble" configuration and had a long-range capability. The military version, the C-97 Stratofreighter, became the basis for the KC-97 Stratotankers of the U.S. Air Force.

SOME LARGE SOVIET AIRCRAFT: A DIFFERENT APPROACH

For a number of reasons, large Soviet aircraft have both followed western design leads and diverged along entirely different routes. The Soviet Union emerged from World War II with no large multiengine aircraft capable of striking targets outside Europe. By copying B-29s that were interned in the Soviet Far East, Tupolev created the Tu-4, the first postwar Soviet heavy bomber. But large, long-range aircraft came out slowly in the 1950s as Soviet designers absorbed German technology, both jet and turboprop.

Because early Soviet jet engines were unreliable and lacked power, Tupolev turned to Kuznetsov's powerful and efficient NK-12M turboprops (12,000 shaft horsepower, 15,000 in the Tu-114) with counterrotating propellers to drive the swept-wing Tu-20 long-range bomber and reconnaissance aircraft that appeared in 1955. With a gross weight of 385,000 pounds, the midwing military Tu-20 and its slightly different low-wing civilian counterpart, the Tu-114, had a maximum speed of over 541 mph at 26,000 feet and an operational range of 5,500 miles. A later version, the Tu-95, extended the range to 7,800 miles and is still used by the Soviet Air Force and Naval Air Force for maritime patrol and reconnaissance missions. These Tupolev planes are the fastest propeller-driven aircraft in the world.

Oleg Antonov also chose to use the powerful Kuznetsov turboprops for his heavy-lift high-wing transport, the An-22 Anteus, which, with a gross weight of 551,000 pounds, temporarily held the title of the world's largest aircraft before the appearance of the Lockheed C-5A. The An-22 and the IL-76 (350,000 pounds) and An-124 (892,000 pounds) heavy-lift jet transports serve in the Soviet Air Force's Military Transport Aviation and in the civil airline, Aeroflot. Along with long-range civilian airliners that double as troop transports, these airplanes provide the Soviet political and military leadership with a significant, rapid military airlift capability for projecting military power worldwide in support of its strategic objectives. Both the An-22 and the IL-76 played important roles in the quick Soviet move into Afghanistan in December 1979, then in sustaining the Soviet presence, and finally in facilitating the withdrawal in February 1989.

U.S. Navy F-4J Phantoms escort a TU-20/95 "Bear."

The Boeing B-29 Superfortress was the heaviest combat aircraft of World War II, with a gross weight of 120,000 pounds.

British had to span vast intercontinental distances to reach all the members of the Commonwealth. The only way to link such faraway places as New York and San Francisco (2,572 miles), Seattle and Miami (2,650 miles), Moscow and Tashkent (1,770 miles), Moscow and Khabarovsk (4,335 miles), London and Cape Town (5,989 miles), London and Melbourne (10,500 miles), Hong Kong and Montreal (7,736 miles), or Leningrad and Vladivostok (6,000 miles) was to design and build first-rate flying machines capable of carrying heavy payloads over long distances. Consequently, the aircraft industries of these countries often led the way, both before and after World War II, in the development of very large transport aircraft and bombers.

The American Heavy Bomber

A basic stimulus for the development of very large airplanes has been military aviators' desire for long-range heavy bombing capabilities. During World War I, the Germans, British, Russians, and Italians built the most impressive fleets of what would later be called heavy bombers. Between the wars, the Soviet Union's heavy bomber force of Tupolev TB-1s and TB-3s stood second to none. During World War II, the United States produced and deployed the greatest force of heavy bombing airplanes the world had ever known. To sustain these strategic bombers and their operations as well as those of the large new transport planes that brought weapons, supplies, and reinforcements to far-flung combat zones, the United States and its allies built a worldwide network of airfields and supporting airways.

One important American bomber of World War II was so heavy that the Army Air Forces designated it a "very heavy bomber"—this was the 120,000-pound Boeing B-29 Superfortress. A later version, the B-29B, weighed 137,000 pounds. Some of the other dimensions of the B-29 were also remarkable; its wingspan was 141.3 feet, 33 feet greater than that of a Boeing 727.

The most important dimension of the B-29's size, however, was its capacity to carry a payload—either a 20,000-pound load of bombs for 2,800 miles or a 2,000-pound load for 5,300 miles. These payload numbers—which, for bombers or commercial aircraft, are the ones that really count—far exceeded the capabilities of the "heavy" Boeing B-17 and

Consolidated B-24 bombers. Along with the Avro Lancasters and Handley Page Halifaxes of the RAF Bomber Command, these American bombers carried out the Allies' strategic bombing offensive against Nazi Germany with devastating effectiveness in 1944 and 1945. The B-29's payload numbers meant that the "Superforts," operating at first from airfields in China and then from hastily constructed runways on the bloodstained Pacific islands of Saipan, Tinian, Guam, and Okinawa, could reach critical targets in the Japanese homeland. With ever greater effectiveness from early 1945 on, B-29s dropped huge amounts of high explosives and incendiaries that caused great firestorms that incinerated Japan's fire-prone major cities and sapped Japanese morale and war-making capacity.

In the context of modern war, the large airplane was synonymous with large-scale destruction and death. The large airplane in combination with an atomic bomb (later a thermonuclear or hydrogen bomb) also meant the possibility of quick victory or sudden death. On August 6, 1945, the specially modified B-29 *Enola Gay* dropped the first atomic bomb on Hiroshima. Three days later, another B-29, *Bock's Car*, dropped a second atomic bomb on Nagasaki. The Japanese soon surrendered unconditionally, and World War II was over. The large B-29 had done more than its share to end the conflict. At the same time, it earned the dubious distinction of being the only airplane to drop atomic bombs in war.

Top of page:
The Boeing B-17 Flying Fortress was the workhorse heavy bomber of the U.S. Army Air Forces against Germany from 1942 to 1945. In its final versions, such as the B-17G shown here, the Flying Fortress reached a gross weight of over 65,000 pounds.

Midpage:
The *Enola Gay*, one of the few B-29s specially modified to carry atomic bombs and assigned to the 509th Composite Bomb Group (Very Heavy), dropped the first atomic bomb on Hiroshima, Japan, on August 6, 1945. It is currently undergoing restoration at the National Air and Space Museum's Silver Hill, Maryland, facility.

The B-29 looks small parked next to the Convair B-36 with its 162-foot wingspan. Both aircraft were propeller-driven strategic bombers capable of intercontinental missions, and both played important roles in the immediate postwar development of the U.S. Air Force's Strategic Air Command.

When the Consolidated-Vultee XB-36 first flew in August 1946, it was the largest aircraft that had ever flown. An idea of the size can be gained from the 65,000-pound Consolidated B-24 Liberator shown in the background. While it had great range, endurance, and bomb load capacity, the B-36 was already on the verge of obsolescence in the emerging world of jet aircraft.

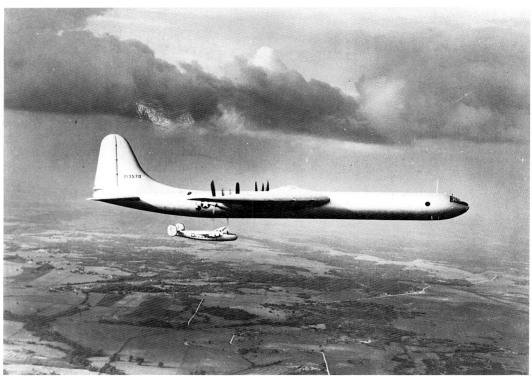

Facing page (top):
The performance of the original B-36As and B-36Bs with six piston engines (381 mph) left room for improvement, and so four General Electric J47 engines were mounted in the outer wing pods of 64 older model B-36Bs to make them B-36Ds. All subsequent aircraft had the jet pods added. The B-36D had a top speed of 439 mph after the modification.

Subsequent to the B-29, the superpowers designed a number of bigger, faster, and now "stealthier" airplanes whose purpose was to carry nuclear bombs across the continents to one another's homelands. Unlike the B-29, with its four 2,200-horsepower Wright R-3350 piston engines and huge four-blade controllable-pitch propellers, most of the American successors were jets, but some very notable Soviet long-range aircraft, especially the Tu-20/95, Tu-114, and An-22, have been powered by turboprops.

The Consolidated B-36 was a transitional aircraft. Designed during World War II for intercontinental missions of 10,000 miles with a 10,000-pound bomb load, the huge B-36 was powered by six 3,500-horsepower Pratt & Whitney R-4360 piston engines. When the 300,000-pound XB-36 first flew on August 8, 1946, it was the biggest aircraft that had ever flown. Its most advanced model, the jet-assisted B-36J, weighed 410,000 pounds, had a combat

range of 6,800 miles with a 10,000-pound bomb load (two early model A-bombs), a conventional bomb load capacity of 72,000 pounds, a wingspan of 230 feet, a crew of 15, and a cruising speed of 391 mph at 40,000 feet. Although it was big and had great range, the lumbering B-36 was almost obsolete when it entered service with the Strategic Air Command (SAC) in 1948. Eventually, over 300 B/RB-36s served in SAC until 1958, when the steadily increasing numbers of B-52s allowed the last B-36 to be retired. It had, however, bridged the gap between piston-engine and jet-powered strategic bombers.

Jet Aircraft

The postwar skies belonged by and large to the jet, at least outside the Soviet bloc. However, propeller-driven aircraft did not go the way of the dinosaur, nor did their technical refinement stop in its tracks. To this day, propeller-driven aircraft have remained vital parts of air transportation all over the world, and new technologies such as improved superchargers for reciprocating engines and the successive refinement of turboprops have continued to bring progress to the operation of propeller airplanes. But airplanes equipped with jet engines were capable of flying much higher, faster, and more economically over long distances than could those with propellers. For tourists, businesspeople eager to speed up their transactions, military forces,

The size of the B-36 can be extrapolated from the size of this Curtiss Electric propeller that was fitted to one of its six R-4360 Pratt & Whitney engines. For comparative purposes, a P-47 is shown next to the propeller.

and people intoxicated by the idea of speed, the advantages of the jet were in the end too great. By the 1960s, the jet came to predominate so much that many air travelers, including some very experienced ones, had never ridden a propeller-driven airplane.

Because it packages tremendous energy into single units weighing much less than piston engines, the turbojet engine has been the single most important new technology introduced since World War II. This is especially true when it comes to overcoming the adverse effects of larger aircraft size and thus getting around the square-cube law.

To demonstrate the favorable effects of the jet engine on aircraft size, F. A. Cleveland in his Wright brothers lecture compared the power plants used for the Wright *Flyer* and the Lockheed C-5A Galaxy. The *Flyer*'s crude little motor, a home-built four-cylinder gasoline engine with a four-inch bore and four-inch stroke, could develop no more than 12 horsepower for cruising flight. Yet the engine weighed 151 pounds, a hefty 20 percent of the aircraft's takeoff weight. In contrast, each of the C-5A's four General Electric TF39 turbofan engines—weighing 7,250 pounds apiece and together totaling only four percent of the Galaxy's takeoff weight (29,000 versus 764,500 pounds)—developed 41,000 pounds of thrust. Relative to the Wright *Flyer*, the ratio of engine power to aircraft weight had been increased by a factor of more than 5. Scaling up the *Flyer*'s engine to produce the useful power of G.E.'s turbofan brings its specific weight to more than twice what it was. Scaling back the power of the C-5A engine to the engine power/aircraft weight fraction of the Wright *Flyer* brings its total engine weight to almost 1.7 million pounds. As Cleveland emphasized, this amounts to 57 times the current C-5A engine weight. It is also 300,000 pounds more than the entire weight of Geddes's flying wing of 1929.

It took years for jet engine technology to mature to the point where it

A Lockheed C-5A Galaxy headed out past the Golden Gate Bridge at San Francisco, showing its four General Electric TF39 turbofan engines.

The Boeing 707 has seen extensive service around the world since its appearance in the late 1950s.

COMMERCIAL JETLINERS

A basic reason why a bomber has to be so big, in comparison to an airliner, is that a bomber has to fly round-trip nonstop. This means that, pound for pound, the bomber has to carry more fuel. Another basic reason is economics. While military requirements had often stimulated the development of very large airplanes, the stringent economics and required efficiencies of commercial aviation have always affected the size of passenger transports. Clearly, it made no sense to be flying big airplanes that were half filled, while smaller, more efficient aircraft could be operated more often and more profitably along the same routes.

Size did not become the focus of progress in transport aircraft design until the phenomenal increase in the total number of revenue passenger miles (RPMs in airliner terminology), airline economics, growing congestion of the airways, and improved technology prompted that change in the late 1960s. In 1949, the total number of RPMs flown by American carriers on all domestic and international flights together stood at 8.8 billion. By 1959, it had risen markedly to 32.5 billion. In the following 10 years, however, that number shot meteorically to 136.1 billion. By 1986, it had more than doubled again, to about 350 billion RPMs, as new markets were exploited.

Underlying these statistics was the revolution in air transportation that came with the refinement and widespread adoption of the jet airliner, more powerful and efficient high bypass turbofan engines with significantly lower specific fuel consumption, and the growing desire of tourists to spend more time at their vacation spots and less time getting to them. The only problem the airlines and the aircraft manufacturers had to solve was the pleasant one of how to serve the snowballing needs of the flying public more profitably.

Their answer in the late 1960s, specifically for nonstop cross-country, coast-to-coast, and transoceanic operations, was that "bigger is better." They created a new category of airplane, the jumbo jet, that represented a new generation of jet transports with wide-body fuselages up to 255.5 inches in diameter, sophisticated wings with high-lift devices, large passenger-carrying capacities, and much more powerful and efficient high-bypass-ratio turbofan engines. Among the preceding jetliners were a number of highly successful and profitable medium- and long-range, high-passenger-capacity aircraft on whose engineering and operational experience much of the jumbo jet's design would be built.

As de Havilland introduced, and then withdrew, its Comet 1 in the early 1950s, Boeing was building its Model 367-80 (Dash 80) prototype of what became the 707, its first commercial jetliner. In the Dash 80, Boeing adopted the successful design pattern of a swept-back wing and pylon-mounted underwing engines that it had established with the B-47 and B-52 bombers and with the Model 717 jet tanker prototype (KC-135). When the Boeing 707 entered airline service with Pan Am in 1958, it set the pattern for early jet transports. Primarily a long-haul aircraft that was most efficient on transcontinental (707-120 series) and international (707-320 series) routes, the 707 had less powerful and fuel efficient turbojet engines, which made it profitable on long flights but restricted its use to airports with runways over 10,000 feet long.

Boeing has built 917 aircraft in the 707 line, excluding military versions, which it is still producing (seven are planned for 1989), making it the most successful airplane of the early jetliners, and one of the most successful transports ever produced. In 1989, 219 Boeing 707s were still in use around the world, although none are now flown by scheduled airlines in the United States. At 257,000 pounds, the 707-120–series aircraft weighed more than twice as much as the pioneering de Havilland Comet, and was far more

In the late 1950s and early 1960s, the Douglas DC-8 seriously challenged the Boeing 707 for primacy in the commercial jet airliner market. Although an excellent aircraft, the DC-8 entered airline service in 1959, a year after the Boeing 707, which hampered its sales. United Air Lines put its first DC-8-11s into service between San Francisco and New York in September 1959.

The Douglas DC-8 Super 62.

productive, despite its operational limitations. Configured for high-density seating, the early 707-series aircraft was capable of carrying up to 179 passengers (147 seats standard) at speeds up to 600 mph over a nonstop distance of 3,000 miles.

Another successful early commercial jet transport, and competitor of the 707s, was the Douglas DC-8 series (556 built through 1972). At 273,000 pounds, it weighed slightly more than the 707 and could carry 179 passengers a nonstop distance of over 5,000 miles. In respect to aircraft size, however, the DC-8's life history is more interesting for what it shows about the possibilities of making an airplane bigger by stretching it.

The purpose of *stretching* is to create an airplane with greater passenger capacity without going to the time and expense of designing an entirely new structure. When stretching an airplane, all the manufacturer usually has to do is put a couple of "barrel sections" or "plugs" into the existing fuselage. Sometimes it has to do little more, except for some collateral redesigning of the tail surfaces and landing gear and perhaps adding some wing area and new engines for more power, none of which requires any major retooling of production facilities. The airplane is already designed. The cockpit, the wing (or at least a wing that can be modified), and the engines already exist. The financial and engineering advantages of this "cut and stitch" approach to making a larger airplane should be apparent.

In the mid-1960s, McDonnell Douglas stretched the fuselage of its DC-8 in order to add seats that would make the aircraft more attractive to the airlines and more competitive with Boeing's larger 707-320B/C models. Twenty-foot barrel sections were added ahead of and behind the airplane's wing, thereby creating a new family of higher passenger capacity aircraft known as the DC-8-60 series, or simply the "Dash 60" or "Super 60" series (262 built). One version, the DC-8 Super 63 (gross weight 355,000 pounds), entered airline service in 1968 and could carry nonstop a maximum of 259 passengers a distance of more than 2,000 miles at a cruising speed of 596 mph. It could carry a reduced payload nonstop a maximum of 5,400 miles.

At about the same time, Boeing tried to stretch its 707, but found that the design of the landing gear was such that with a stretched fuselage the airplane could not take off without banging its tail on the runway. From 1959 to 1969, however, the company built 154 of a smaller, and redesigned, third basic model of the 707, designated the Boeing 720 (230,000 pounds, 167 passengers, 5,200 miles), with full-span leading edge flaps to increase take-off performance and with the more efficient engines that made such large jetliners profitable for medium-haul service. The 720 intermediate-range jetliner entered domestic service with United Air Lines in July 1960, while American Airlines placed the first 720Bs (B indicates a model with turbofan engines) in service in March 1961.

The largest 707 variant, the 320C international model, which weighed 336,000 pounds and could carry 189 passengers a distance of 4,600 miles, began operations with Pan Am in June 1963 and quickly became the most popular model, with 337 built. Indeed, the three versions of the 707-320 series were by far the most numerous produced, totalling 570 of the Boeing 707s built. However, the stretched McDonnell Douglas Super 60s were so competitive with the 707-320 series, which had no growth potential, that in the mid-1960s Boeing moved ahead with the development of an entirely new series, the 747.

The new jetliners of the late 1950s and early 1960s were more attractive than piston-engine aircraft to the traveling public because they cut air travel time, and to the airlines because they were bigger, faster, more efficient, and cheaper to operate.

Boeing 707 versus Piston-Engine Airliners

	L.1049G	DC-7B	DC-7C	707-120
Range (miles)	4,140	3,280	4,605	3,000
Cruising Speed (mph)	305	360	355	571
Seats (max.)	102	99	110	179
Ceiling	22,300	27,900	21,700	38,000
MTOW	137,500	126,000	143,000	257,000

For the businessman, time saved was money earned; for the tourist, time saved was time and money enjoyed. Air travelers soon demanded jets on all major routes. For the airlines, the new jetliners meant greater passenger

Air Travel Times: New York–Los Angeles Flights

Year	Aircraft	Speed (mph)	Stops	Time Westbound	Eastbound
1940	Boeing 307	200	3/3	15:30	13:45
1950	Douglas DC-6	280	1/0	10:50	9:45
1955	Douglas DC-7	335	0	8:00	7:40
1960	Boeing 707 Douglas DC-8	570	0	5:20	4:40

capacities, lower operating costs, better reliability, less maintenance down-time, more frequent flights for higher operating rates, and greater profits. The turbojet engines of the late 1950s cost 20 to 25 percent less than piston engines to operate—they used kerosene fuel (Jet-A) at 9.25 cents a gallon, rather than aviation gasoline at 16 cents, and went 8,000 hours at 570 mph

(4,560,000 miles) between overhauls, rather than 2,000 to 2,500 hours at 300 mph (600,000 to 750,000 miles).

The jet engine was obviously the difference. The earliest jet engines used in commercial aircraft were modified military engines built for maximum thrust per pound of engine weight. Much less consideration was given to the low specific fuel consumption, economy of operation, low noise level, reliability, and maintainability the airlines needed. The early Boeing 707s had Pratt & Whitney JT3C-6 engines of 13,000 pounds thrust, which were derived from the J57 military engine of the B-52. Their lack of power meant a long takeoff run of over 10,000 feet, which limited the airports and routes the 707s could use; at the same time, their higher fuel consumption affected their range and payload.

The advent of the more efficient, powerful, and quieter JT3D-1 low-bypass-ratio turbofan engines of 17,000 pounds thrust, and a revised wing with high-lift leading edge flaps, significantly improved the overall performance and range of the 120B, which appeared in June 1960. In addition, the 120B cut its predecessor's takeoff distance by more than 3,000 feet, and thus it had much better route flexibility and could serve more markets. When fitted with the JT3D-3 engine of 18,000 pounds thrust, the new 320B, which first flew in January 1962, became an efficient intercontinental airliner with a range of well over 4,000 miles. The starkly different operating requirements of military and civilian jet engines took them along increasingly divergent paths after the early 1960s, although in at least one instance an engine originally built for a military purpose led directly to the creation of a commercial aircraft —the Boeing 747.

BOEING 727: KING OF THE AIRLINERS

The development of more fuel-efficient, reliable, and powerful low-bypass-ratio turbofan engines, which lowered seat-mile costs, paralleled the growing traffic demands for jet service on short- and medium-haul routes. Aircraft manufacturers quickly responded to the airlines' requirements with a series of new jetliners in the mid-1960s, among these the Douglas DC-9, British Aircraft Corporation BAC-111, and Boeing 727. The outstanding aircraft of this group has been the tri-jet Boeing 727 (with engines mounted in the rear of the fuselage rather than underwing), which is similar to the pioneering and popular French Sud Caravelle that first flew in 1955 and that entered airline service with Air France in 1959 and with United Air Lines in July 1961. Rear-mounting the engines made the aircraft quieter for passengers. It also provided a clean wing, to which Boeing fitted full-span leading-edge flaps and slots as well as new triple-slotted trailing-edge flaps that markedly improved takeoff performance and hence increased the number of airports and routes that the 727 could serve.

Because of its flexibility, the initial 152,000-pound 727-100 series became a best-seller with its introduction in February 1964. The airlines soon demanded greater capacity in this efficient tri-jet (94 seats standard, 131 maximum), and so Boeing stretched the basic 727 into the larger 727-200 series of shorter-haul, higher-capacity aircraft (145 seats standard, 189 maximum) that appeared in December 1967.

The airlines used the 727 profitably on almost any route (except long over-water flights, illegal anywhere in the United States), including all but the longest "stage length," or distance between air terminals. Eventually Boeing sold 1,245 passenger and 15 freighter versions (to Federal Express) of the 200 series, compared to 571 of the smaller Series 100. When it ceased production in 1984, the Boeing 727 was the industry's biggest seller, with a total

A Boeing 747 parked next to one of Pan Am's 727-100s shows that one of the distinctions of the 747, apart from its wide body and giant size, is the forward reach of the passenger cabin on the lower deck; it extends to the end of the fuselage because the cockpit is on the upper deck and is reached by a spiral staircase from the lower deck.

Facing page (top):
The 747-400, or "Dash 400," the newest version of the Boeing 747, which weighs 900,000 pounds and can carry over 600 passengers, entered service with Northwest Air Lines in February 1989. It is the world's largest commercial passenger aircraft.

Facing page (bottom):
The 747-400 prototype takes off for a test flight from the Boeing plant.

of 1,831—covering all variations built—although it is now second to the short-range, twin-jet Boeing 737 (1,672 of all models delivered, with orders for another 595 from 1967 through February 1989).

For years Boeing studied ways to stretch its best-selling 727 beyond the already stretched 727-200 and to add new, more efficient engines. What emerged in the early 1980s as the 727's replacement was the 220,000-pound 757, with two underwing high-bypass-ratio turbofans replacing the three rear-mounted engines, and with a capacity of 178 to 239 passengers. While the 757 retained the 727's basic fuselage cross-section, the new aircraft had more in common with the new wide-body 767 than with its narrow-body predecessor. Indeed, the airlines' operating experience with the 757 has indicated that it is far more efficient on longer routes than was originally estimated, so it is increasingly being used on such routes. Through early 1989, Boeing had delivered 210 of its 757 and had orders for 193 more.

The 727 has been the airlines' most flexible airplane, and Boeing certainly hopes the 757 will continue to fill that role. Airlines have been able to make money with the 727 flying nonstop from Philadelphia to Washington and from there on to Norfolk, Virginia, and Atlanta. They have also made money with the same airplane flying from Atlanta to Los Angeles. The jumbo jet, such as the Boeing 747 or DC-10, on the other hand, is more profitable for airlines on long-haul trips across the oceans or on transcontinental flights.

The size of an airplane is one thing, the right size for making money is

another, and is the most important consideration when it comes to success in the airline business. In nonsocialist economies, money is the reason airlines exist; they are a business like any other; they want to keep the flying public happy only insofar as that affects profits. Aircraft manufacturers understand this completely and operate accordingly. To them, a good airplane is one that sells. To sell, it has to be the right size to fill the holes in the airline market.

THE BOEING 747 AND THE JUMBO JET

In the mid-1960s, Boeing lost a hotly contested design competition for what became the U.S. Air Force's C-5A heavy-lift transport to Lockheed and then turned to developing the world's first jumbo jet, the 747. The driving forces behind this dramatic turn of events were Juan Trippe, the forward-looking president of Pan American World Airways, and Edward Wells, Boeing's brilliant vice-president of engineering and close advisor (some insiders have even said "guru") to Boeing's chief executive officer and board chairman, Thornton ("T.") Wilson. Trippe wanted to have an advantage over his competitors with a big new airplane having lower operating costs for flights on Pan Am's many long trans-oceanic stage lengths. Wells, Wilson, and Boeing president William Allen gambled that their engineers could design a huge new commercial jet transport that would satisfy not only Pan Am's wishes but those of most of the world's other major carriers.

In the opinion of many experts, the 747 was the greatest gamble in the history of the aircraft business. At risk were the lives of both companies, as well as the solvency of several private lending institutions. Financed with private money, if the 747 had failed, half the banks west of the Mississippi would have been badly shaken. Another important meaning of big aircraft is thus clear: big dollars go along with them.

When it first flew in February 1969, later to enter airline service on Pan Am's New York to London route in January 1970, the 747 dwarfed all earlier commercial aircraft. At 738,000 pounds, the certified takeoff weight of the initial 747-100 series exceeded that of all other aircraft ever built except the Air Force's behemoth Lockheed C-5A of 764,500 pounds. Advanced versions of the 747-200, which first flew in October 1970, added fuel and range, pushing the gross weight to 833,000 pounds and passenger capacity to 484 in standard, and 516 in maximum, seating. This made the 200 series considerably heavier than the original C-5A Galaxy and about the same size as the new C-5B that weighs in at 837,000 pounds. With an extended upper deck capable of seating 69, the 747-300 series introduced in 1982 pushed seating capacity to 526. The new 747-400 long-range version now in production at Boeing approaches a gross takeoff weight of 900,000 pounds and has a range of 8,400 miles with a full load of 402 passengers. Boeing delivered the first 747-400 to Northwest Airlines on January 26, 1989, and entered it into airline service in February 1989 on Northwest's New York to Tokyo route. At $125 million each, the 747-400 makes used 747s and DC-10s very attractive propositions to new and to smaller carriers.

Early in 1989, Pan Am's *Clipper Pride of the Sea*, the first 747 to be delivered to an airline (January 1970), completed its 17,000th landing. In less than 20 years of service, Boeing 747s have flown over 20 million hours and 10 billion miles while carrying over 700 million passengers—a great record for a milestone airliner.

What distinguished jumbo jets such as the 747 and C-5A from other transports were their incredible weights, wide fuselage cross-sections, and powerful high-bypass-ratio turbofan engines, which made them possible in the first place. With a width of 255.5 inches, compared to 148 in the earlier 707/727/737 series, 747 series aircraft are very aptly described as *wide body*,

The Boeing 767-300 has two extra fuselage plugs to increase its passenger payload.

a term that clearly indicates its material advantages over narrow-body transports. Indeed, the 747 was originally intended as a cargo freighter capable of holding two 8 x 8-foot containers side-by-side on its main flight deck, thus many of its most popular variations are convertible between cargo and passenger configurations (called a Combi for "combination").

As with the design and operation of other modern aircraft, engines made the critical difference in jumbo jets. The C-5A design competition in the mid-1960s produced the world's first high-bypass-ratio turbofan engine of over 40,000 pounds of thrust, the GE1/6 (later the TF39). To assure itself a source for engines, Boeing married the losing engine, Pratt & Whitney's 41,000-pound thrust JT9D, to its new wide-body design to produce the 747. In later 747 models, Boeing has offered a variety of engines to suit the buyer's requirements, including General Electric CF6s, Rolls-Royce RB.211s, and improved JT9Ds with up to 53,000 pounds of thrust. The huge new Boeing 747-400 gives the purchaser three engine options, with the Rolls-Royce RB.211-524C providing as much as 58,000 pounds of thrust. For comparison, the Soviets' giant Antonov An-225 uses six Lotarev D-18T turbofan engines, each of 51,590 pounds thrust, to haul its 1.3 million pounds around the sky. While the first Boeing 707s weighed 257,000 pounds and had a total of 52,000 pounds of thrust, the 747-400s weigh up to 900,000 pounds and have engines that produce 232,000 pounds of thrust.

It has been much easier technically to stretch an airplane than to shorten one. Airline economics (market considerations) have normally not justified the time and expense of shortening larger aircraft to suit a market in which a sufficient supply of aircraft already exists to satisfy seat requirements. One problem for the manufacturer in shortening the length of an airplane presents itself in modifying the tail properly; normally, making it bigger. Boeing found this out when it designed the 747SP (Special Performance), a smaller version of its 747 jumbo jet (47 feet shorter, 702,000 pounds versus 833,000) which, while it carries fewer passengers (321 maximum versus 452), is capable of longer full-payload distances (6,736 miles versus 5,800). To assure control on the ground in the event an engine were lost on takeoff, Boeing ultimately had to give its 747SP a new tail that was 10 feet wider and five feet longer. Boeing demonstrated the 747SP's range when it delivered a new aircraft to South African Airways by flying it nonstop 10,290 miles from Seattle, Washington, to Cape Town with 50 passengers and spare parts on board, finishing with over two hours of fuel on board.

The Boeing 747SP (Special Performance) was designed specifically for long-range flights.

The new McDonnell Douglas MD-11, slated for initial flight testing in 1989.

When Boeing designed and built its new 767 wide body (249 delivered, 103 on order as of February 1989), which appeared in the early 1980s to compete with the Airbus A300 series for use on medium-range, high-density routes, they broke away from the fuselage cross-section uniformity of the 707/727/737/757 series' narrow bodies by adding four feet to cross-section width, which allowed eight-across seating and a standard passenger load of 220 (maximum 250 or 290). They had also learned the lessons of stretching from the 707 and 727. A 10-foot plug was added in front of, and an 11-foot plug aft of, the wing to make the original 300,000-pound twin-engine 767-200 into the 345,000-pound Model 767-300, which could carry 269 passengers in its standard seating configuration (290–330 maximum). The new 767-300 entered service with Japan Air Lines in 1986. Two extended-range versions of the 767-300 with additional tankage, designated 300ERs, brought the maximum weights up to 380,000 and 400,000 pounds.

To borrow from computer terminology, the wide body was "user friendly," whether for passengers or handling air cargo shipments. How many of us have tried to get seated in a stretched DC-8 with its one long aisle? It takes a long time to get back to row 40, and we have to fight through a lot of people and their luggage to do it. When the airplane lands, it takes even longer to disembark. One good thing about the wide body, in comparison to the narrow body, is that there are two aisles and a larger door that let people in and out side by side. The wide body is simply a lot handier for the passenger—not to mention what it does to alleviate the serving problems of overworked flight attendants.

The cabin width of the wide body does one more thing that is important for passengers: it creates the illusion that they are not in an airplane. For nervous air travelers, this is psychologically very reassuring, and the airlines know it.

From the point of view of the airlines, what made the jumbo jet such an attractive airplane was that it combined phenomenal payload capacity with the greatly improved operating efficiencies of its engines and airframe. In all of its models, the Boeing 747 has an exceptional passenger capacity, which makes it extremely attractive and profitable to the airlines on long-haul trips such as New York to London, Chicago to Honolulu, and Washington to Frankfurt. Airline executives must always worry about the percentage of airplane seats that are filled with paying passengers. The 747 allowed airlines to make money with only about 50 percent of its seats filled. To put that figure into perspective, in the 1930s, to make any money flying the revolutionary DC-3, airlines needed about 80 percent of seats sold.

Boeing and Pan Am won their gamble. Through early 1989, Boeing had delivered 712, and had orders for 198 more 747s of all variations; it remains the market leader in wide-body transports. Just as in the early 1930s when the 247 spurred the building of the Douglas DC-2 and DC-3, Boeing's competitors at the time of the 747's institution were already developing wide bodies of their own, such as the 510,000-pound Lockheed L-1011 Tristar (246 seats, 330 maximum) and the 575,000-pound McDonnell Douglas DC-10 (250-270 seats, 380 maximum), transports designed specifically for U.S. domestic carriers and markets. A total of 446 DC-10s had been produced through 1987, when production ended. McDonnell Douglas already has orders for 263 of its new, larger (602,500 pounds) MD-11 long-range large-capacity (321 seats, 405 maximum) transport (based on the DC-10) that entered full-scale development in December 1986, with its first flight scheduled for 1989. Lockheed terminated production of the L-1011 in 1984 after building 250.

Although the 747's large capacity and efficiency is most attractive to airlines for long distance use, other wide bodies have proven profitable on shorter, high-density routes because they better fit market demands. It is much easier to fill the 250 to 270 seats of aptly named "airbuses" such as the DC-10, Tristar, and A300 on many routes than it is to fill the 452 seats of the 747-100 or the 484 seats of the 200 and 300 series. in the complex world of airline economics, however, stage length, route, traffic density and demand, and aircraft capacities and range have blurred the once clear advantages of matching equipment to route demands. In an era of deregulation, airlines that can make the best matches, win; those that cannot, disappear.

While in the United States the 747 is normally used only on transcontinental or long-haul routes, the same is not true for other nations and airlines. Boeing introduced a lighter and strengthened (603,000 pounds; 516 seats) short-range version, the 747SR, which entered service with Japan Air Lines in October 1973 on its short, high-density routes of less than 500 miles. A later version of this aircraft, the 747-300SR, can carry 624 passengers—in Boeing's highest-density seating configuration of 10-abreast (3-4-3)—seats no first-

THE DC-10 FAMILY

250—380 Passengers

MEDIUM RANGE

LONG RANGE

STRETCHED FUSELAGE
360+ Passengers
Long Range

Major Options:
● General Electric or Pratt & Whitney Engines
  (only GE on Medium Range) — Thrust Levels
  of 40,000 to 54,000 Lb
● Customized Interiors and Lounges
● Upstairs or Downstairs Galley
● Inertial or Area Navigation

ALL FREIGHTER
182,000 Lb Payload
Long Range

CONVERTIBLE FREIGHTER

Medium or
Long Range

The DC-10 Family has the flexibility that aircraft manufacturers offer in today's wide-body jet transports to enhance their attractiveness to the airlines. The DC-10 family was designed for easy conversion to a variety of functions, from passenger to cargo transporting as well as for use on various routes and for different market demands.

class passengers, and has an extended upper deck. The Douglas DC-10 and Lockheed Tristar, while smaller in gross weight and passenger load (250–270) than the 747, were more versatile in combining long-range attributes with the ability to fulfill a wider variety of traffic and route demands.

In recent years, the smaller 313,000-pound A300 and A310 wide-body airliners built by the European consortium, Airbus Industrie, has provided strong competition for the DC-10, MD-11, L-1011, and Boeing 757/767, but not for the 747. This is particularly evident in quickly expanding markets demanding big airliners for use on high-density routes outside the United States. Some 300 A300s (267 seats, 375 maximum) and over 100 smaller A310s (170,000 pounds; 218 seats, 280 maximum) have been sold to customers worldwide. New A330s of 450,000 pounds, with a range of 5,700 miles (305–338 seats, 375 maximum), and international A340s of 540,000 pounds, with a range of 8,000 miles (282 seats, 375 maximum), are planned for delivery in the early 1990s. Despite its growth, Airbus has yet to supplant Boeing as the major supplier of the world's largest long-haul airliners. The 747 and its derivatives will probably be around well beyond the year 2000.

The Future of Bigness

There is a cloud hanging over the safety of very large airplanes, of course: the sad fact that the big, high-capacity passenger transports provide the most sensational targets for hijackers and terrorists. When passengers get on a jumbo jet for an international flight, this danger is something they must at least privately acknowledge. Big attracts attention—and those seeking attention—as the Pan Am Flight 103 disaster of December 1988 proves.

There is no telling how much bigger airplanes will get. Perhaps there is an absolute physical limit. During the development of the Boeing 747, the director of aeronautics at the National Aeronautics and Space Administration's Langley Research Center, Laurence K. Loftin, Jr., asked Boeing's Ed Wells whether the square-cube law was catching up to him with regard to big airplanes. Wells answered that he did not know but that it seemed to be getting harder and harder to meet the design structural weight on airplanes of that size.

But that has not stopped visionaries from studying the possibilities of aircraft much larger than even the 747. They have named their hypothetical aircraft, simply enough, very large vehicles (VLVs).

The most interesting VLV possibilities are span-loading aircraft with wings capable of holding more than half a million pounds of cargo, flying wings with multiple fuselages, air-cushioned vehicles (ACVs), and surface-effect ships (SESs) that skim along the ocean in ground effects. In fact, it is thought that VLV technology will be most useful in sea-based operations. This way the aircraft can use the dock-handling systems and other port facilities already devised for large container ships.

VLVs would be enormous. One flying-wing multibody concept being studied at Lockheed-Georgia has a gross weight of 1,350,000 pounds. This puts it in the same weight class as Norman Bel Geddes's imaginary 700-ton flying-wing airliner of 1929 and Oleg Antonov's existing An-225. Surface-effect ships would be significantly bigger, with projected gross weights up to 900 tons. If their excessive use of energy can be solved and they can be made to pay off for investors and operators, it is likely that VLVs as big as this will someday be built and flown.

Some people just think big. Norman Bel Geddes's dream of a superbig trans-Atlantic airliner with gymnasium and dance floor, though unreal for its time, is no longer so far-fetched.

One way to design bigger aircraft is to give them multiple fuselages. In the early 1980s, engineers at Lockheed-Georgia conceived this 1,348,410-pound multibody transport capable of carrying 441,000 pounds—the equivalent of eight Boeing B-17 heavy bombers of World War II. The projected wingspan of 346 feet was 26 feet longer than the wing of Howard Hughes's *Spruce Goose*.

221

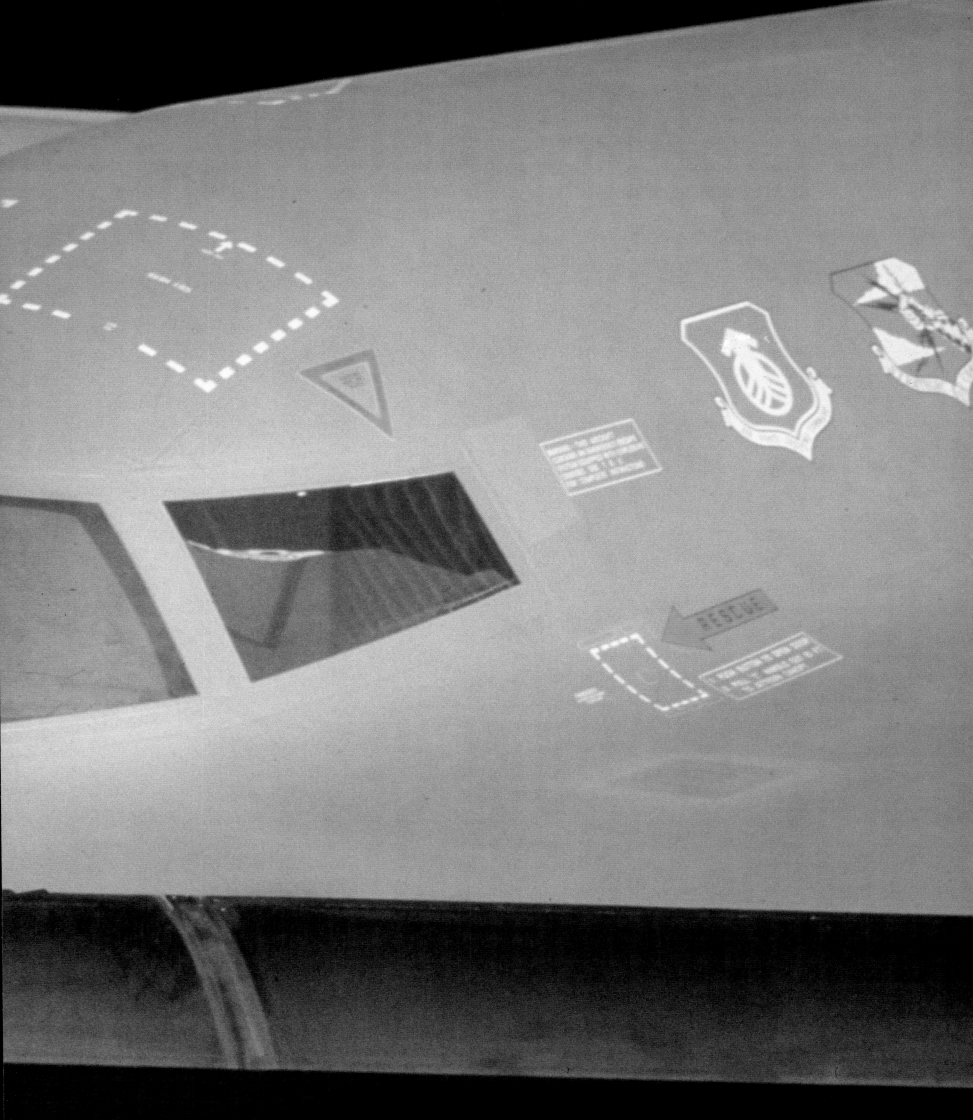

BETTER

BETTER
The Quest for Excellence

RICHARD K. SMITH

At Hunaudières racetrack in August 1908, Wilbur Wright publicly demonstrated the new two-seat Wright Model A.

Pages 222–223:
The exterior of the cockpit area of the Stealth bomber.

In the half century between 1903 and 1953, well within the life span of a single generation, human ingenuity transformed a fragile, clumsy, and unreliable vehicle of no practical utility into a magic carpet that routinely served global transportation. It is a tale of engineers, mechanics, and artisans, and their cumulative labors to master the mechanics of flight, extracting dramatic measures of energy from a minimum of material, and manipulating structures to maximize the machine's productivity. Science did not have much to do with it. Indeed, the airplane did more for science than science ever did for the airplane.

Although it is customary to date the beginning of mechanical flight at December 17, 1903, when the Wright brothers made their powered flight at Kitty Hawk, the curtain raiser, in fact, occurred on August 8, 1908. On that day, at Hunaudières racetrack near Le Mans, France, Wilbur Wright demonstrated to a startled world that the airplane could be controlled and flown. This was modern aviation's starting point.

The Weight Envelope: Weight, Power, and Payload

In the dawn of mechanical flight, the airplane was of necessity a fragile machine of sticks and wire. The small power then available in internal combustion engines, and their poor ratio of power to thrust, dictated this. Although the Wrights and many of the pioneers of flight often built their own, engines were ordinarily a "shelf" item provided by an outside supplier whose bread-and-butter in 1908 was typically engines for automobiles, in which engine weight was not critical to performance. The manufacture of aero engines quickly became a specialty unto itself, and was disciplined toward designing for maximum power from a minimum of material. After selecting an engine with the best power-to-weight ratio, the only area in which an airplane designer could save weight was in the airplane's structure.

In no other machine is weight as critical as it is in the airplane. Francis R. Shanley (1904–1969), a legendary professor of aerostructures at the University of California, Berkeley, liked to puzzle his classes with the question: "In an airplane structure, do we wish to aim in the direction of infinite strength, or in the direction of zero weight?"

Shanley gave his students a few minutes in which to mull this over.

At nearly 900,000 pounds, the Boeing 747-400 is now the largest commercial airliner in scheduled airline service in the world.

The Gossamer Dream

BY BRYAN ALLEN

Human-powered flight has been a dream since the imaginations of primitive people first took wing with the birds. On June 12, 1979, Bryan Allen flew his Mylar-covered *Gossamer Albatross*, powered solely by himself, across the English Channel.

A sea gull wheeling above cries plaintively, perhaps puzzled by the giant man-made bird resting on the concrete embankment before me. It is the Gossamer Albatross, a remarkable airplane composed of thin carbon-filament tubing covered in a transparent Mylar film only .0005 inch thick. Its huge wing extends 94 feet, yet it weighs only 75 pounds. My challenge is to fly it by my own muscle power across the Channel to Cap Gris Nez, France....

After months of intensive training, I accompanied the Albatross to England, where we waited for the weather service to predict a wind-free day.

Today, June 12, 1979, is it.

The gleaming Albatross is ready. Every ounce of weight has been carefully checked. Just enough drinking water to replenish my vital body fluids for the two-hour flight is stored in a plastic container with a drinking tube. Even the electric batteries powering the altimeter and air-speed instruments are sized to a two-hour capacity.

As I look out over the water, which laps quietly at the rocks below, I wonder, Will I make it? I remember what my coach, Joe Mastropaolo, said about the undreamed-of capabilities within us. An Olympic rowing coach, Joe said his experience had shown him that these reserves are available if we call on them.

"Having faith is knowing," he said. "Know that you'll suc-

ceed and you will."...

I thrust on the pedals with smooth, even strokes, and the propeller begins its steady, silent turning. Ten feet...15...20...30. Then up! The pavement and rocks fall away, and the Albatross and I are 25 feet above the gray water.

An exhilaration fills me. The launch crew below rush into motorboats to keep pace. Ahead, a cabin cruiser, plowing through the water toward Cap Gris Nez, will be my guide. I pedal with less power to descend and take advantage of the reduced air-drag near the water. Faint shouts of people in boats drift up. Inside, I hear nothing but my own breathing.

Pedal-pedal-pedal. Thirty minutes have passed. Our air speed is now 14 miles per hour. The Albatross begins to veer from course, and I gently twist a steering lever to correct it. Glancing down at the water, I note small wavelets. It's obvious we're facing a light wind. Not too bad, but if it builds, we're in trouble.

Still pedaling. It's getting harder to maintain height. A voice crackles in my radio receiver. "What's your speed and altitude?" I glance at the instruments. "Altitude six feet, speed fourteen!" I gasp. But no one replies that they have received me.

I call again. Still no response. My transmitter has failed, though I can still hear incoming voices.

"Altitude two feet...."

Is it my imagination or are the wavelets building? The Albatross yaws. I pedal harder just to stay level.

The chase boats now rise and fall on three-foot swells. I must pedal harder. But how long can I keep this up? I'm expending every ounce of energy just to stay above the waves that reach for the bottom of the Albatross. If one of

Instinctively, most of them were driven to find an answer in terms of strength. Then Shanley gave the answer to his question: "Although neither goal is obtainable, there is no question as to which would be the more desirable— zero weight!"

From the days of the Wright brothers to our own, airplane designers have striven to achieve maximum strength from an artfully manipulated minimum of material in quest of Shanley's ideal of zero weight. The purpose of this determined effort at weight control has been to maximize payload: In an airliner, passengers and their baggage; in a bomber, tonnage of explosives and ordnance necessary to defend the airplane; in a fighter, guns and missiles and the electronics necessary to make the airplane an effective weapon. The primary function of an airplane is to carry a payload to a destination with all practicable speed.

Without payload an airplane is a plaything created for the visual entertainment of others. A lovely example is a Pitts Special, a tiny aerobatic machine whose only payload is the weight of its pilot and his parachute.

The Wrights were the first to come to grips with the flying machine's problems of utility. Their proof-of-concept Kitty Hawk machine of 1903

them touches it, we are disqualified.

I stare fixedly ahead. Sweat stings my eyes, fogs my glasses. My churning legs feel leaden. Gasping, I sink lower.

"Two feet!...one foot!" screams the voice of Sam Duran, flight manager.

My vision begins to fade; I taste blood in the back of my throat—signs of complete exhaustion. The wind turbulence is too much. I cannot go on....

Gritting my teeth, I pump with my last surge of strength...and the Albatross begins to climb. "Altitude four feet...ten feet...fifteen feet."

An amazing thing happens. The turbulence has stopped! In that frantic effort, I have climbed from the turbulence into calm air.

I can go on....

Now I maintain progress with less effort. As I pedal on, slowly recovering strength, I am intrigued by what has just happened. Somewhere within I have found a surprising reservoir of new strength....

One hour and 45 minutes have gone by. I search the hazy horizon for France. The sun is higher, and again I sense fatigue building. I've already gone past my limit. How much longer can I hold out?

"Altitude two feet." I pump faster, watching my altimeter and air-speed indicator. But they're no longer working. The batteries have given out. I reach for more water, only to suck dry air.

Two hours. Of course. The flight was not designed for any longer time. Computations had proven that my body would never even make it this far with all that we've encountered.

Where is the shore? Why is it taking so long? Then I realize the obvious. We have been fighting a continual head wind, a gentle one, but enough to hold us back....

Two and one-half hours have passed since Folkestone. I have been flying 30 impossible minutes. Thirty little miracles.

Eighty times a minute my legs continue to turn. What's that ahead? A thin shoreline. France! Breathe deeply...now my left leg begins to cramp and I shift more to the right. Tall cliffs slowly rise up from a sand beach. But it is still over two miles away. My knees feel like lead; I can hardly keep them going around....

Now, I can see a crowd of people on the beach. But the Albatross trembles and rocks. Wind surging down the high beach cliffs pushes the Albatross to the right. She creaks and groans....

But something urges me on to the bright sand beach. I narrow my eyes and pedal harder...harder. Suddenly, there is angry roaring below me; I glance down to see white foaming breakers. Looking up I see people waving and cheering. One final wrench of my muscles and I coast.

The beautiful white sand rises to meet us and I level the plane out to a feather-soft landing. The crowd surges around the Albatross....

We have made it—in two hours and 49 minutes. We've won the richest prize in aviation history.

But I have gained something far more important that will help me in every good thing I attempt from now on. I see now what Coach Mastropaolo meant by the power of knowing. I have seen it work 49 little miracles.

carried no payload except for its pilot. The same was true of their training machine of 1904, but the Wright *Flyer* of 1905 had a seat for a passenger. However, no one sat in that payload seat until May 14, 1908, when Wilbur took their mechanic Charlie Furnas up for a few circuits of Kitty Hawk. This flight initiated the difference between flying and the business of aviation.

The most significant aspect of the Wright *Flyer* of 1905 is the ratio between its useful load and the dead weight of its structure. These are the primary constituents of an airplane's "weight envelope." The 1903 Kitty Hawk machine's ratio was 20:80. The 1904 machine improved to 27:73. In their 1905 *Flyer* the Wrights achieved 32:68, and in the 1909 airplane that they sold to the U.S. Army, this ratio was further improved to 34:66. This is to say that relative to its gross takeoff weight, the airplane's useful load—which included fuel, oil, crew, and miscellaneous items—was 34 percent of the whole.

Without an appreciation of relative weights, there can be no understanding of the airplane, especially the differences among good, bad, or mediocre airplanes. It makes no difference if it is a stick-and-wire apparatus of 1908 or a billion-dollar hypersonic dream machine of the twenty-first century. An airplane can be endowed with maximum thrust and the best

In the 1920s, aircraft manufacturing was still a painstaking process that involved numerous skilled people, many of them woodworkers. Here workers at the Dayton-Wright Airplane Company at Dayton, Ohio, are fabricating wing structures.

aerodynamics imaginable, but if the designers have not controlled its weight to achieve the specified payload it may be adjudged "good enough," but certainly less than the best.

In the significant ratio of 34:66 of 1909 is indicated that a useful load of 34 percent was obtained. This is to say that 66 percent of the airplane's takeoff weight was solid vehicle and that only 34 percent was involved in establishing its payoff. More significantly, a quarter of a century later, in 1934, a ratio of 34:66 was still typical among most airplanes. In this, as in so many other points of the airplane, the Wrights were first. Although by 1934 the achievements of some airline designs were dramatically better than 34:66, among fighter planes this ratio has remained practically a constant from that day to our own.

The Vegetable Airplane

From the Wright brothers' machine of 1903, and for more than a quarter of a century thereafter, the airplane was typically a wood structure braced by wire and covered with fabric treated with varnishes. The most favored structural material was Sitka spruce. Lumbered in Alaska and the Pacific Northwest where humidity is high and summers are short, this small, slow-growing tree produces a fine, straight-grained wood with a minimum of knots. Its elasticity is excellent—spruce is not given to splitting—and it weighs just 30 pounds per cubic foot as compared to 60 pounds for most oaks. White pine was a good second best, but it tends to have numerous knots and pitch pockets, making for a high percentage of waste in usable lumber. Ash was favored for landing-gear struts. Until the pusher engine configuration—in which the engine is behind most of the structure's weight rather than in front of it—was superseded during World War I, many of these airplanes had their rudder and elevator assemblies suspended on tail booms made of bamboo, which is tough and resilient. Whatever type of wood was used, it had to be seasoned to rid it of its internal moisture. This meant letting it cure naturally in timber sheds for at least six months, preferably longer.

The airplane's structure was covered with fabric. Although many books describe the airplanes of World War I as being covered with canvas, this is nonsense. Canvas is tent and awning material, and is too porous and much too heavy for aircraft. The preferred covering was finely woven linen. Cotton, which could not be woven as tightly, was a second best; long-strand Egyptian cotton or Sea Island cotton from Georgia was preferred as compared to short-strand fibers from more common sources. After being laced to the airplane's structure, the fabric was painted with an acetate or cellulose varnish known as "dope." Both were highly flammable, but they

Once the basic wing structure was finished, thin linen or silk cloth was stretched taut over the wing and sewn to the structure. Then it was painted with acetate to waterproof and stiffen the wing.

Like other airplane manufacturers during the early years of aviation, Dayton-Wright produced many of the components of its aircraft. The workers shown here are milling fixed-pitch, laminated wooden propellers.

229

In terms of design, the Deperdussin racer of 1912, which pushed the world speed record beyond 100 mph, could have been an airplane of 1922. In 1914, the monoplane seemed to be the airplane of the future, but the structural requirements of World War I put the monoplane in temporary eclipse.

sealed the fabric's pores and shrank its threads to create a drum-tight surface and a tough outer cover.

Until the end of World War I, propellers were invariably hewn from solid blocks of wood: ash, walnut, or oak. Later, propellers were typically laminations of fairly small pieces of diverse woods with their grains laid at angles to one another.

Aside from its engine, and fasteners such as screws, carriage bolts, doubler plates, angle braces, sockets, wires, and turnbuckles, the early airplane had very little metal in its structure. Prior to the 1930s the airplane was typically an assemblage of wood, flax, cotton, cellulose, and rubber; it was essentially a conglomeration of vegetable products. Indeed, until the early 1920s, many aero engines were lubricated with castor oil. An advantage of this high-quality lubricant from the castor bean was that it resisted dilution by gasoline. Animal tallow was often used as grease. It was not until the mid-1920s that innovations in the petroleum industry made mineral oil lubricants universal.

The Speed Envelope

No one yet knew what configuration an effective airplane should have; therefore, the airplane of the earliest years of flight had almost as many distinctive forms as there were designers. Whereas the unforgiving "numbers" of an airplane's weight envelope are invisible to the eye, the dictates of its speed envelope have always been subject to interpretation and speculation. Its speed envelope shapes an airplane's external form.

Whereas the airplane of today is about as interesting to behold as a chicken egg, the flying machine of 1908 had almost as many external flourishes as a Gothic cathedral, and the eye could study it for an hour with small risk of boredom. However, the magnificent clutter of the early airplane was practicable only so long as intrepid birdmen were content to stutter through the air at less than 50 mph. As men were driven to fly faster, the airplane's external form was gradually reduced from the obviously complex to the apparently simple.

In the 1920s the German architect Walter Gropius coined the expression "form follows function," which quickly degenerated into a cliché. However, the external form of an airplane is determined absolutely by the dimensions of its speed envelope—its function. The larger the speed envelope, the more that all airplanes that fly within it will appear to be similar, if not essentially the same.

In 1909 the American newspaper impresario James Gordon Bennett endowed the Coupe Internationale d'Aviation, commonly known as the Gordon Bennett Trophy. For more than 10 years its lavish prizes served to establish the measure of ultimate speed in the air.

The first Gordon Bennett speed contest was flown at Reims, France, August 28, 1909, which Glenn Curtiss won with a speed of 47.65 mph. Four years later, on September 29, 1913, Marcel Prévost pushed the world speed record beyond the 100-mph mark, winning the Gordon Bennett Trophy with a speed of 124.8 mph while seated inside a semienclosed cockpit of a Deperdussin racer's fuselage. This form of open cockpit prevailed among high performance airplanes until cruising speeds crossed the 200-mph mark in the mid-1930s.

The French Influence

Designed by Louis Béchereau of the Société pour Aviation Deperdussin (SPAD), the Deperdussin racer's fuselage was a departure from the norm. Instead of being a framework covered by fabric, it consisted of a sleek plywood shell built up from three layers of thin strips of tulip wood painstakingly formed and glued differentially around a mandrel. When the glue had dried and the mandrel was withdrawn, the result was a strong, seamless, tubular fuselage. The French called it a *monocoque* (single shell). Unlike a fuselage of built-up trusses whose fabric covering provided only a weather-tight flying surface, a monocoque's skin carried the entire structural load. It was lighter, stronger, and almost impervious to distortion, providing a superior enclosure and flying surface. However, the making of a plywood monocoque shell was tedious, time-consuming, and expensive. Although some German biplane fighters of World War I, notably certain of the Albatross and Pfalz series, used semi-monocoque designs, true shell structures experienced relatively little use until the 1930s, when they could be wrought in metal.

The Wright brothers' canard configuration of the airplane—with its elevator in front, the foreplane—was soon abandoned. The Wrights had designed an unstable airplane because they wanted absolute control at their fingertips—and they got it. Self-educated experts that Orville and Wilbur were, this was good enough for them, especially at the relatively slow speeds of 1908–1909. However, it was too much for novices to master easily. The foreplane was too sensitive and the airplane too easily flown out of control and into the ground. Fatal accidents became too possible and too frequent, especially as speeds moved toward the 100-mph mark.

After 1910 an airplane with elevator and rudder integrated "in trail" at the after-end of the fuselage became universal. The pusher engine, with the pilot sitting in front of the power unit, largely gave way to the "tractor" powered airplane with the engine in the nose and the pilot sitting behind the engine. Louis Blériot can be credited with originating the successful seating of the pilot within the fuselage, leading the way to the tractor engine with the elevator in trail, and popularizing the monoplane configuration.

It is no coincidence that Blériot was a Frenchman. After 1908 it was the French who took up the airplane with greatest enthusiasm. In 1904, A. Gustave Eiffel, the engineer who is remembered in the Parisian tower that

The first airplanes Glenn Curtiss built were classical pusher biplanes with the motors centrally mounted between the wings and the propellers fixed behind the wings to push the flying machine forward rather than pull it, as in the tractor airplane. Curtiss built his first biplane pusher, Curtiss Number 1, for the Aeronautical Society of New York early in 1909. This first airplane was called the *Gold Bug* because of the goldish tint that the varnish gave to its fabric covering; only later was it renamed the *Golden Flyer*.

Facing page (top):
This Deperdussin, entry F2 in the 1913 Gordon Bennett Trophy race, was one of the best examples of the pre—World War I monoplane. This was the sleekest version of Louis Béchereau's monoplane racing airplanes, complete with a windshield and headrest. Troubles with the Gnome engine slowed its speed to 119.5 mph, which was good enough for third place.

Facing page (bottom):
T.O.M. Sopwith and F. Sigrist built the Sopwith Tabloid in 1913 as a fast tractor biplane for military use. In flight tests, Harry Hawker reached 92 mph in the new Sopwith before he flew it to Hendon near London in late November 1913 for a public air meet. Sopwith then added two floats so that the Tabloid could qualify as a seaplane for the second Schneider race. Howard Pixton flew the Tabloid to victory at an average speed at 86.78 mph on April 20, 1914, at Monaco.

bears his name, established a laboratory dedicated to aerodynamics, one of the first of its kind. Eiffel's *Résistance de l'Air* (1910), widely translated into other languages, was for many years the textbook on the subject. For almost a decade French aviation had few rivals. The leader in technology inevitably leaves a lasting mark on its vocabulary, and this early French leadership has left us with such elementary aeronautical terms as *aileron, ballonet, empennage, fuselage, longeron, monocoque, nacelle*, and even *hangar*.

Monoplane or Biplane?

With Blériot and Béchereau leading the way for the French, there was an ongoing debate of monoplane versus biplane. There are no biplanes in nature; all birds are "monoplanes." This inevitably raised a question of why mankind required biplanes when for thousands of years nature had been doing a marvelous job with monoplanes.

The answer was in wing area, wing loading, and structural strength. Before the early 1930s, when engine horsepower crossed the one-thousand mark and its application was made ever more versatile by the controllable-pitch propeller, wing area—the elementary flight surfaces—was a partial but important substitute for power. For want of power, airplane designers laid on more wing area—or they took the risk of a higher wing loading—that is, the weight carried by each square foot of wing.

Unless one is familiar with the weights, wing loadings, and power loadings (weight per horsepower) of the flying machine, one will understand very little about any particular airplane. A history of the airplane could be written solely in terms of the relationships among these three elements: a tale of how the finite characteristics of available power at any point along the aerostructure timeline, combined with demands for improved performance and the availability of better aerodynamics, forced the aerostructure to carry ever-increasing measures of flight load.

233

The Wright brothers faced this problem of wing loading versus power loading, and their coming to grips with it as they did is another of their many firsts. Between their flying machine of 1903 and their airplane of 1909, they experienced a 60-percent increase in horsepower, permitting them to reduce wing area by 18 percent while concurrently accepting an 18-percent higher wing loading. However, the Wrights did this within the "envelope" of a biplane structure.

Within any given wingspan, a biplane yields almost twice as much wing area, or lift, as a monoplane. To obtain the same wing area, a monoplane requires an inordinately long and clumsy wingspan. Furthermore, the biplane's wing structure, joined by struts and braced by wires, was inherently strong. It was similar to the structure of a trussed bridge, whose design, by the twentieth century, was well understood. The biplane also created more aerodynamic drag, but for a quarter of a century after 1903 this was an acceptable price for structural integrity.

Although the monoplane's wing could be built inherently stiff, with internal bracing as a cantilever, the resultant structure was usually too heavy for a pre-1918 airplane. Aeroelastic divergence—the inevitable tendency of aerodynamic forces to make the wing rotate around and away from its attachment to the fuselage—often sorely afflicted the early monoplane, which had thin, wire-braced wings. Out of control, divergence results in catastrophic failure. The deadly problem of flutter, a phenomenon in which the flying surface extracts energy from the moving airstream and develops self-destructive vibrations, occurs simultaneously. However, one problem masks the other, and divergence was not fully understood until the mid-1920s. Flutter was also identified as a problem, but the many forms it took within wing and tailplane structures and their movable surfaces required more years to recognize. It is a problem that continues to be dealt with in any airplane design.

Tony Fokker's E.III *Eindecker* ("one wing" or monoplane) gave the German air units a fighter faster and more maneuverable than the British and French biplanes it faced over the western front in August 1915. With the E.IIIs came the "Fokker scourge," which continued into 1916, when the Allies introduced new fighters.

World War I

In the summer of 1914, on the eve of World War I, at least half the airplanes in the world were monoplanes; by the end of the war in 1918 practically all airplanes were biplanes. The urgent demands of war locked in the rugged reliability of the biplane. Indeed, for a moment during the war, the triplane, providing ever more wing area within the same or less wingspan, enjoyed a brief vogue. On this point, airplane design of 1914–1918 was emphatically regressive.

Wing loadings experienced the least improvement. The wing loading of the Fokker E.III Eindecker and Morane-Saulnier Type N monoplane fighters of 1914 was 8 pounds per square foot; that for the SPAD XIII and Fokker D.VII biplane fighters of 1918 were 8 and 9.6, respectively. Available power, however, had more than tripled. In 1914 the typical aero engine yielded 90 horsepower; by 1918 engines of 300 horsepower were not unusual—the Rolls-Royce Eagle producing 360, the American Liberty 400. Airplane gross weights were also increasing, and whereas the power loading of a 980-pound Morane-Saulnier monoplane fighter with 100 horsepower was 9.8 pounds per horsepower, the SPAD XIII.C1 had the best power loading of 1918 at 8.2 pounds per horsepower. The average power loading of World War I fighters was 10 pounds per horsepower.

Most disappointing was that although available power tripled, maximum speeds failed to double. The fighter plane of 1914 did well to flash across the sky at 80 mph; the fastest fighters of 1918 were the French SPAD XIII and Italian Ansaldo A-1 Balilla and S.V.A.5 that approached 140 mph. A generalized 250-percent increase in horsepower yielded only a 75-percent increase in speed. These may have been good fighters, but they were not aero-

The Royal Aircraft Factory S.E. 5a was one of the fastest fighters of World War I.

dynamically efficient. Something was wrong, and it was all the struts, wires, and other protuberances that the biplane dragged along with it.

The same may be said of the large, multiengine bombers built during the war. Although their gross weights were as high as 32,000 pounds, wing loadings were typically less than 10 pounds per square foot; power loadings varied from 16 to as much as 24 pounds per horsepower. Some of the bombers were huge. The four-engine Handley Page V/1500 had the external dimensions of a Boeing 727 jetliner, but with its wing loading of 10 and power loading of 20, it was practically a powered glider. Like most of its contemporaries, with its power off it was an extremely marginal glider. These bombers did well laboring through the air at a cruising speed of 85 mph—as often as not, within 20 mph of stalling speed. Their crews were brave to fly these machines into combat, and their courage was demonstrated by their consenting to fly them under any circumstances. Despite such problems, these aircraft were still remarkable creations. A mere 15 years after the Wrights first struggled to fly 852 feet in a 765-pound flying machine, the Handley Page V/1500 had a range of 1,300 miles, could fly for 17 hours, and carried a crew of five to seven men, defensive machine guns, and a bomb load of 7,500 pounds.

More concerned with production than contributing to improvements in airplane design, World War I contributed less to the airplane than it did to aviation. It took aviation out of the hands of inventors, tinkerers, and sportsmen and created the foundations of an industry. It trained thousands of young men in design, manufacture, operations, and maintenance, and enabled them to seek careers in these areas after the war. Finally, it firmly established aviation as a vital aspect of national security.

This rebuilt S.E.5a belongs to the Royal Air Force Museum at Hendon outside of London.

Postwar Aviation

After the Armistice of November 11, 1918, there were great expectations for a postwar aviation boom—an "air age"—but these naive hopes were wiped out by the vast stocks of war surplus aviation equipment dumped on the civil markets of the victorious Allies. Unlike the automobile, an airplane was not, and never would be, a consumer product with a mass market. In Europe, governments subsidized commercial aviation operations, which the short intra-European distances made practicable. In the United States, however, vast continental distances, powerful railroad interests, and difficult terrain had defeated the fragile pre-1919 airplane in any effort to demonstrate its commercial utility. Curiously, after 1919 these same factors created an environment that stimulated the creation of a more advanced airplane.

The United States combined the territory, the demanding terrain and meteorological environment, the wealth, natural resources, industrial potential, and the proper distribution of a middle-class population for the airplane to develop, demonstrate, and finally validate its capabilities on a daily basis. The rectangle delineated by Boston, Miami, Los Angeles, and Seattle established a demanding aeronautical laboratory of continental dimensions.

Except for the Alps, in Europe there are no mountains of consequence in the 4,000 miles between Velentia in westernmost Ireland and the Urals in easternmost European Russia. However, between New York and California there was no avoiding the Alleghenies, the Rockies, the Sierra Nevadas, and the Cascades, and in between were mile-high airports such as Cheyenne, Denver, Albuquerque, Salt Lake City, and Reno. Furthermore, North America is practically a continental island, separated from Europe and Asia by vast oceans and from South America by the island-studded Caribbean. The North American condition made formidable demands on the airplane; by 1935 those demands had transformed the airplane into a high-speed instrument of intercontinental capability.

Henry Ford's Contribution

One of the great aviation events of the 1920s was Henry Ford's entry into aviation. Ford's name is invariably remembered in terms of his all-metal tri-motored airliner, the legendary *Tin Goose*. However, Ford's most important contribution to airplane design was his building of the world's first concrete runways at the Ford Airport in Dearborn, Michigan. Ford knew that automobiles run better on a smooth surface—so should airplanes. In addition, the hard runway improved drainage and in wintertime made snow removal easier.

Henry Ford set a new standard for airports. By the end of the 1920s every progressive city in America felt the need for an airport, and most of these airports had hard runways. Even small cities met this expense. Joliet, Illinois, with a population of only 35,000, built an airport with a concrete runway in 1931. No airport in Europe had concrete runways until Bromma-Stockholm opened in 1936.

The hard runway revolutionized an airplane's ground handling. Before the hard surface, an airplane's only braking system consisted of tire friction and a tailskid that dragged through an airfield's turf. For want of brakes, taxiing had to be extremely cautious, often requiring people on each wingtip to guide the airplane. A concrete runway made both a tailwheel and brakes in the main wheels mandatory; with differential braking an airplane could be turned within its own length.

This is the only Ford 9-AT (Air Transport) built. It was essentially a Ford 4-AT with a modified windshield and three Pratt & Whitney Wasp Jr. engines. The basic 4-AT was a 10,130-pound airplane that seated 10 passengers. The three Wright J-6 engines provided 1,800 horsepower, which produced a remarkable power-to-weight ratio of 1:5.6. However, with the drag of its three uncowled engines, fixed landing gear, and other excrescences, it did well to cruise at 110 mph.

When Ford Airport in Dearborn, Michigan, opened in 1926, it was the first commercial airport with concrete runways. Hard runways dictated the use of wheel brakes in airplanes. Ford-Dearborn set the standard for American airports. By the late 1930s, there were hundreds of airports in the United States with hard runways, whereas in Europe grass airfields were commonplace until after 1945. In the upper left-hand corner is a mooring mast for airships, which was seldom used.

The requirements for a tailwheel and brakes marked the beginning of "systems" and an airplane that would become increasingly complicated with things that had little to do with aerodynamics. Demands for better braking led from mechanical systems to hydraulic systems and from drum brakes to disc brakes, and finally to retracting systems. The concrete runway also required better shock absorbers in landing gear than the rubber cords commonly used. The development of oleo-hydraulic landing-gear struts was transformed from desirable to necessary. Until the 1920s an airplane's engine was customarily started by turning the propeller over by hand, forcing it to life against its own compression. By 1927 the inertia starter was available; by the early 1930s electric starters were commonplace in large airplanes.

Night operations made powerful landing lights mandatory, requiring larger generating capacity in engines. By the 1930s night operations were extensive in the United States, at least partly because of the lighted airways system developed by the U.S. Post Office during the 1920s. By as late as 1934, landing lights were still rare in European airline equipment. For radio to be effective, engines required insulating harnesses around their ignition systems to prevent their radiations from blanketing the radio signal. Efforts to establish around-the-clock schedules regardless of weather made icing of the airplane a frequent hazard, forcing the development of de-icing equipment for wings, tail surfaces, and propellers.

These and other new systems and accessories put new weights into the airplane, complicating matters for the designer. The relative simplicity of the pre-1918 airplane gave a designer control over almost 50 percent of the machine's empty weight, namely, the basic structure. The only "shelf" items were engine, propeller, wheels, and tires; in military airplanes there was also

Before hand-cranked inertia and electric starters became available in the late 1920s, this Rube Goldberg–like device, invented by the British aviator B. C. Hucks during World War I, was the best means of getting a quick engine to start. Through a clutch, the airplane's propeller and engine were spun up quickly by the automobile's engine. Hucks starters were used widely by European air forces until the 1930s. The Soviet Air Force used them during World War II for cold-weather starts, and the Japanese used them as well. The starter shown here is mounted on a Ford Model T at NACA's Langley research facility.

armament. By the 1930s, as the airplane's structure accumulated systems that were necessary accessories to flight—all of which were shelf items provided by outside vendors—this area of control was reduced to 30 percent. Fortunately, the airplane was being cleaned up aerodynamically and more power and dramatic improvements in the thrust systems were becoming available.

NACA and Aircraft Development

In the years 1928–1938 no other institution in the world contributed more to the definition of the modern airplane than the Langley Laboratory of the U.S. National Advisory Committee for Aeronautics (NACA). Established in 1915 purely as an advisory committee, by the end of World War I it had a small professional staff and the beginnings of a research laboratory.

NACA's contribution started with its variable-density wind tunnel (VDT), which became operational in March 1923. Most wind tunnel testing is still done with small-scale models of the airplane or its parts, but the density of the air in which the models prior to 1923 were tested was "full scale." Inevitably, there were discrepancies between the promises yielded by these wind tunnel tests and the performance of full-scale airplanes. However, the VDT was enclosed in a pressure chamber that compressed the air to the scale of the model, producing data that corresponded more closely to reality. Until the early 1930s there was no other VDT in the world. As a result of data from the VDT, by the end of the 1920s American aerodynamicists and designers were getting more accurate information than their foreign counterparts.

In the early 1920s the world's airfoils were many, and none of their data was uniform. For example, there were the Eiffel, Göttingen, Royal Aircraft

During the 1920s, NACA used its variable-density wind tunnel to rationalize basic airfoils into "families," coincidentally reducing wing section data to shelf information for the convenience of airplane designers.

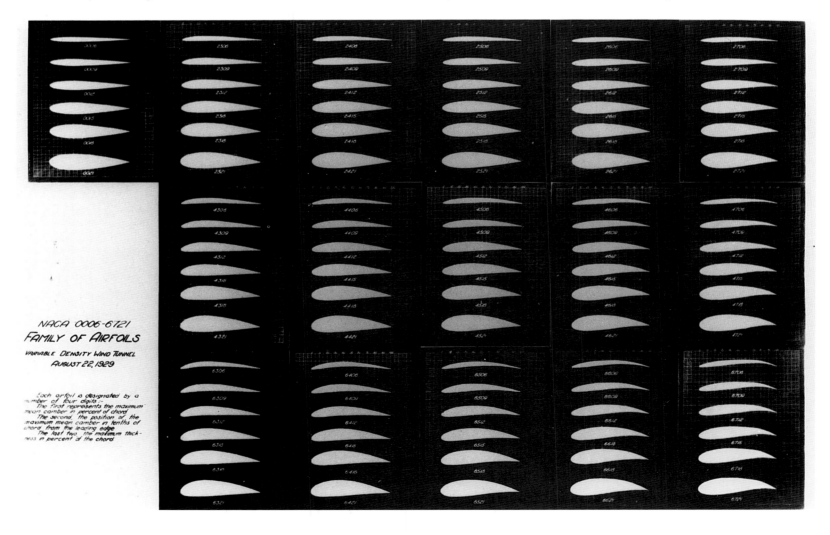

NACA 0006-6T2I
FAMILY OF AIRFOILS
VARIABLE DENSITY WIND TUNNEL
AUGUST 22, 1929

Each airfoil is designated by a
number of four digits :-
The first represents the maximum
mean camber in percent of chord
The second, the position of the
maximum mean camber in tenths of
chord from the leading edge
The last two the maximum thickness in percent of the chord

240

Factory, U.S.A., and Clark series of airfoils, among many others. They constituted a hodgepodge of data. NACA spent some 10 years analyzing these and other airfoils in the VDT, standardizing their information and rationalizing them in terms of "NACA numbers." In 1933 the first results of these data were published, creating a worldwide sensation among aerodynamicists. These and subsequent results created a continuous "mail-order catalogue" of airfoils. No longer did an airplane designer have to hunt and scrape through dozens of obscure publications for the airfoil properties he sought, reworking their data to determine what was desired. The growing catalogue of NACA information had it all, and the properties of available airfoils were reduced to a shelf item.

NACA also built a wind tunnel for testing propellers. Twenty feet in diameter, it was used primarily to study the relationship between propeller flow and the fuselage or wing, but the Propeller Research Tunnel (PRT) served many other purposes. Put into operation in July 1927, the most significant products of the PRT were: (1) quantifying the aerodynamic drag of protuberances such as struts, wires, engines, and fixed landing gear; (2) developing the NACA cowling for the air-cooled radial engine; and (3) determining the installation of a wing-mounted engine relative to propeller flow in the vicinity of the wing. These data constituted further shelf information, and they served to fix a generalized shape for the airplane.

Everyone knew that fixed landing gear created substantial aerodynamic drag, but no one knew exactly how much. In 1928 NACA engineers put a

In 1928, using the new propeller research wind tunnel at Langley Laboratory, Virginia, NACA engineers developed and validated the deep chord engine cowling to improve the streamlining of the airplane and the cooling of the radial air-cooled engine. It was among the most significant aviation developments of the interwar years.

241

The exposed cylinder heads of this air-cooled Pratt & Whitney Wasp radial engine used in a Boeing P-12 pursuit airplane of the U.S. Army Air Corps were great sources of aerodynamic drag in aircraft of the 1920s. Much of NACA's research effort was directed toward solving this problem.

cluttered Sperry Messenger biplane with its landing gear removed in the PRT, and then informed the world that landing gear meant a breathtaking 40 percent of an airplane's drag. The exposed cylinders of an air-cooled engine contributed another 17 percent.

Having quantified a landing gear's drag, NACA could leave its correction to the industry. The drag of the air-cooled engine was different: It was not enough to throw a streamlined shroud around it; provision also had to be made for adequate airflow to cool the engine. The NACA method consisted of two cowlings, an aesthetically pleasing wrapper that greets the eye and an unseen inner cowling that controls the airflow within the enclosure. Carefully designed baffles were placed between and behind the engine's cylinders to further control airflow. This was a crude beginning of what some 20 years later would be called internal aerodynamics. The cowling not only added to the airplane's streamlined form, it made for more uniform heat exchange, permitting the engine to run at somewhat higher and more efficient temperatures.

In most single-engine airplanes powered by radial engines, the NACA cowling contributed to at least a 10-mph increase in speed. However, its results on multiengine airplanes were generally disappointing. This inspired the study of propeller and nacelle effects relative to airflow across the wing. Dozens of engine locations relative to the wing were examined, the most practicable proving to be in the wing's leading edge with the propeller a substantial distance ahead of the wing. Boeing soon used this data to design the engine locations for its B-9 bomber and then the 247 airliner of the early 1930s. The Glenn Martin Company used a similar engine placement for its B-10, but added the NACA cowlings, an enclosed cockpit, and fully retractable landing gear to push the plane's speed to 200 mph and win an

Air Corps production contract over the B-9. Engine location research in the 1930s fixed the shape of most multiengine propeller-driven airplanes from that time to our own.

Jimmy Doolittle stands next to a Lockheed Vega 5A Executive, owned by Shell Oil Company from 1930 to 1934, that he used in a number of speed and distance races. The streamlined NACA cowling over the engine reduced its aerodynamic drag and increased its speed significantly.

The Aircraft Designer

Although the designing of airplanes occasionally draws on the stuff of theoretical science, it ordinarily depends on the techniques of engineering, which consist more of perspicacity, perspiration, and imagination than of inspiration. This work of NACA consisted of running the same tests again and again—each time under new circumstances—measuring the results, and working up comparative analyses of the data. This has come to be known as *parameter variation*, but engineers call it "cut-and-try." Airplane design is of necessity scientific, but it has less to do with pure "science" than it has with art—the art of the engineer.

Nevil Shute, best remembered for the novels he wrote for his personal entertainment, was an aeronautical engineer by profession. With pencil, paper, and slide rule, he designed airplanes and later managed their manufacture. Indeed, in 1931 he managed the production of the Airspeed Courier, the first British biplane with retractable landing gear. In his novel *No Highway* (1947) Shute summed up airplane design with the remark: "A beautiful aircraft is the expression of the genius of a great engineer who is also a great artist."

Instead of a palette of colors, the aeronautical engineer has his own artist's palette of options. How he mixes these engineering options on his technological palette and applies them to his canvas (design) determines the performance of his airplane. When the synthesis is best it yields synergism, a result that is dramatically greater than the sum of its parts. This is hailed as "innovation." Failing this, there will result a mediocre airplane that may be good enough, or perhaps an airplane of lovely external appearance, but otherwise an iron peacock that everyone wants to forget.

Better Engines, Better Propellers

At the end of World War I, the horsepower available in an aero engine was typically 300. In 1926 it crossed the 500 mark; the 1,000 point was reached in 1933; by 1939 1,500 horsepower was on the shelf and 2,000 was becoming available. Of itself this would mean little without the engine's power-to-weight ratio also improving. The 9-cylinder 160-horsepower Gnome R-970 engine that powered a Sopwith Camel fighter of 1918 had a power-to-weight ratio of 1:2.4; the 14-cylinder 2,000-horsepower Pratt & Whitney R-2800 Double Wasp of 1940 had a ratio of 1:1.2.

An engine is only half an airplane's thrust system; the other half is the unglamorous propeller. The engine generates power; the propeller transforms power to thrust. A propeller blade is simply an airfoil rotating around a fixed point, but instead of generating lift it generates thrust. The blades' angle of attack, or pitch, relative to the flight axis, determines the thrust's characteristics. During takeoff or climb, a low pitch delivers the most efficient thrust; in cruising, high pitch provides maximum thrust. This is similar to shifting gears in an automobile. Prior to 1932 the typical propeller was of fixed pitch, imposing distinct limitations on airplane performance.

In the mid-1920s a successful hydraulically actuated controllable-pitch propeller was developed in England, meeting nothing but apathy or resistance from most British designers. However, until the early 1930s, the biplane prevailed in British aviation and a biplane's thicket of aerodynamic drag could not adequately demonstrate the propeller's versatility. Many arguments were also made against the propeller's weight, complexity, and cost.

It was the demands of the North American environment that, after 1932, finally pushed the controllable-pitch propeller into common use. The less dense air of mile-high airports among the Rocky Mountains, combined with ever higher wing loadings among American airline equipment, forced the airlines to seek something that would improve takeoff and climb performance. The controllable-pitch propeller from Hamilton Standard was the answer.

Duralumin in Structural Development

In 1927 two events did great things for the airplane: durable aluminum alloy was confirmed as the best material for aircraft structures and the Lockheed Vega appeared. A year earlier NACA initiated an annual conference with designers from the aircraft industry. Given the isolation of NACA's Langley Laboratory on the edge of a swamp in Tidewater, Virginia, this facilitated an intense cross-pollination between researchers and users of NACA's research product that would not have occurred otherwise. These annual conferences were eminently useful and fruitful events; nothing similar to them occurred in Europe. On May 24, at the 1927 conference, E. H. Dix, Jr., a metallurgist of the Aluminum Corporation of America (ALCOA), announced the validation of Alclad, a new technique for the protection of aluminum aircraft alloys. In the history of the airplane, this was a great milestone.

PROPELLER PROGRESS

From the earliest days of metal propellers to the perfection of the quick-feathering type, Hamilton Standard Propellers have made possible continued improvement in the performance and safety of modern aircraft.

1925 METAL PROPELLERS. Hamilton Standard develops a practical adjustable-pitch metal propeller, first outstanding advance over old style fixed-pitch wooden propellers.

1933 CONTROLLABLE-PITCH PROPELLERS. Hamilton Standard achieves world leadership through the development of the first practical controllable-pitch propeller, awarded the Collier Trophy as the year's most important aeronautical achievement.

1936 CONSTANT SPEED PROPELLERS. Offering improved performance through automatic change of pitch, Hamilton Standard constant speed propellers become the most universally used item of aviation equipment in the world.

1939 QUICK-FEATHERING PROPELLERS. The immediate and general acceptance of the Hydromatic quick-feathering propeller for use on military airplanes and on the nation's airlines shows it to be worthy of a place in the distinguished record of Hamilton Standard achievements.

HAMILTON STANDARD PROPELLERS
ONE OF THE FOUR DIVISIONS OF
UNITED AIRCRAFT CORPORATION
EAST HARTFORD, CONNECTICUT

The controllable-pitch propeller is a vital constituent of the modern airplane. Without it, the redesign of the aerostructure, streamlining, and all the other significant aspects of the modern airplane would have been impossible. The propeller constitutes one-half of the airplane's thrust system; it transforms the engine's power to thrust. The ability to vary propeller pitch gave designers control over the thrust delivered. Controllable pitch shortened the takeoff run, reduced the landing run and rollout, and increased engine efficiency at cruising speeds. In the 1930s, the principles of the Hamilton Standard hydraulic controllable-pitch propeller were licensed to manufacturers in Great Britain, Germany, France, Italy, and Japan. By the end of the 1930's, other manufacturers had developed techniques for propeller control that evaded the Hamilton Standard patents. Most notable was the Curtiss electrically actuated propeller.

This aluminum aircraft alloy is duralumin. (Pronounced "d'*ral*-uh-mun," in the industry it is usually called dural, pronounced "d'ral.") It was discovered in September 1906 by Alfred Wilm, a German chemist employed by an agency of the Prussian War Ministry, who was in quest of a lightweight metal to supplant brass in cartridge casings. In one experiment, Wilm alloyed pure aluminum with 3.5 percent copper, 0.5 percent manganese, and 0.5 percent magnesium. Wilm's laboratory assistant started testing the material on a Saturday, but at noon he quit for the day, accidently permitting the alloy to "age" over the weekend. When testing resumed on Monday, it was discovered that the material's strength had multiplied by a factor of five. This seemed incredible, but the experiment proved to be repeatable. The material was not acceptable for cartridge casings, but Wilm knew he had something good and he patented it.

In 1908 Wilm quit the government agency and licensed his patent to the Dürenmetallwerke A.G. of Düren. The company marketed the alloy under the name Düraluminium. The alloy's primary application to aeronautics was in the structures of Zeppelin airships. Among the multiple redundancies of a

245

Zeppelin's lightly loaded structure, Düraluminium performed well, but it eventually became apparent that it was flawed. Exposed to the atmosphere, the alloy was susceptible to intercrystalline embrittlement, sometimes called exfoliation, and generally known as corrosion.

Employed in an airplane's determinate structure, which is inevitably exposed to the atmosphere, Düraluminium's vulnerability posed an eventual hazard. This did not prevent Dr. Hugo Junkers, Claudius Dornier, and Adolf Rohrbach, the world's leaders in all-metal aerostructures, from using the material. They acknowledged the alloy as an experimental metal; it was important to learn from its applications. It is noteworthy that during World War I both Dornier and Rohrbach were employees of the Zeppelin Company; it was Zeppelin's use of Düraluminium that introduced these two men to the material and that propagated its use.

Shortly after World War I, at the Zeppelin factory at Staaken-Berlin, Rohrbach designed and built the Zeppelin Staaken E.4/20, a 4-engine 18-passenger airliner of 18,700 pounds and all-metal construction that flew in 1920. By the standards of 12 years later, many aspects of its external form were crude: the poor location of its engines and propellers relative to the

HUGO JUNKERS

Dr. Hugo Junkers (1859–1935) was 49 years old when Wilbur Wright flew at Hunaudières in 1908. He was already well known for his work on internal combustion engines and had made a fortune manufacturing small gas-operated hot water heaters for domestic use. For almost 20 years his name was synonymous with the all-metal airplane. The trademarks of Junkers were a low-wing monoplane configuration and a corrugated skin. In 1915 Junkers built his J-1, an all-metal airplane fabricated from sheet steel. It flew, but was too heavy to be a practical airplane; in 1916 Junkers switched to duralumin. Junkers's designs consisted of a duralumin framework covered by unstressed, duralumin corrugated sheeting. Although

the corrugated skin inevitably made a contribution to stiffness, its primary function was simply to serve as an outer cover. In the 1920s and 1930s Junkers built a series of eminently successful airplanes—the F13, G23, G24, W33, Ju 52, Ju 86, and Ju 160—that became worldwide sales successes. Truly sensational was his four-engine G38 of 53,000 pounds, which some years after 1929 was the largest land plane in the world. After his finances became overextended, Junkers gradually lost control of his company, which became virtually nationalized under the Nazis. Hugo Junkers died near Munich on February 3, 1935, on his 76th birthday.

Hugo Junkers.

The Junkers G 31.

CLAUDIUS DORNIER

Claudius (often given as Claude) Dornier (1884–1969) designed and built bridges in Germany until 1910. He then became a structures engineer for Luftschiffbau Zeppelin, which was at that time the only firm in the world working with duralumin for aerostructures. During World War I Dornier was in charge of the Zeppelin works at Lindau, which developed large, all-metal flying boats. Because of the original limitations on German aviation in the Treaty of Versailles, after 1919 Dornier created companies in Italy and Switzerland in order to build his airplanes without restrictions. In the 1920s Dornier developed a family of commercial flying boats that culminated in the rugged and versatile twin-engine Wal. In 1929 he produced the Do X, a 12-engine flying boat that was the largest airplane in the world for almost a decade. The Do X was a white elephant, but a magnificent beast. During the early years of World War II, the Dornier company produced a series of twin-engine bomber and reconnaissance aircraft—Do 17s, Do 215s, and Do 217s—which were workhorses for the Luftwaffe. With the Allied victory in 1945, Dornier was put out of business, but his business gradually revived beginning in the mid-1950s. Dornier died in 1969 at the age of 85, but the company that bears his name continues to build airplanes.

Claudius (Claude) Dornier.

ADOLF ROHRBACH

Adolf Rohrbach (1889–1939) was born in Gotha, Germany. After graduating from engineering school, he took up naval architecture. When Luftschiffbau Zeppelin expanded into airplane design and manufacture during World War I, he became an engineer for the Zeppelin-Staaken works near Berlin. Here he developed an all-duralumin wing designed around a single box spar (the leading and trailing edges being cantilevered from it) and covered with duralumin sheeting carrying most of the structural loads. The four-engine E.4/20 airliner that Rohrbach built in 1920 is generally regarded as the prototype of the modern airliner. Under the terms of the Treaty of Versailles, it was seized and destroyed by the victorious Allies in 1922. When Allied controls on German aviation were relaxed after 1926, Rohrbach built a series of large, multiengine flying boats and airliners for Lufthansa. A scandal within the government relating to Germany's secret rearmament efforts of the late 1920s practically destroyed the company. In 1929 Rohrbach established an American company, but the effects of the Depression quickly consigned it to oblivion. Rohrbach failed to find a significant place for himself in Hitler's Germany in the 1930s; he died in Berlin in 1939.

Adolf Rohrbach.

The all-metal Rohrbach Roland II began service with Lufthansa in 1929.

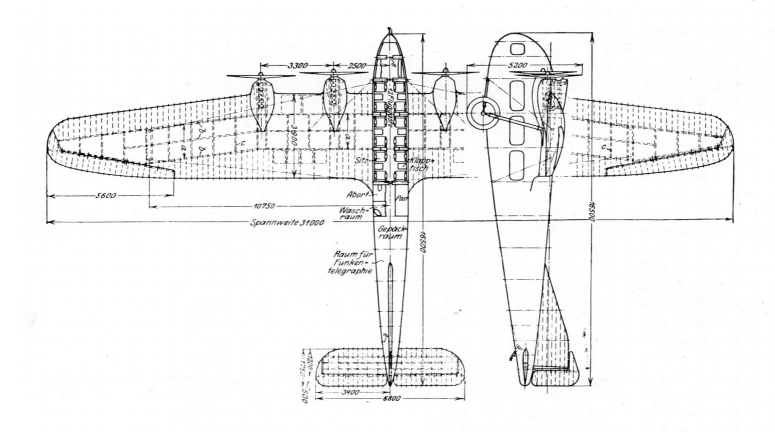

In terms of aerostructure, the Zeppelin-Staaken E.4/20 of 1919 was the great-grandfather of the modern airplane. Its gross weight of 18,740 pounds and wing area of 1,141 square feet produced a wing loading of 16.4 pounds per square foot, slightly higher than that of the Boeing 247 airliner produced 13 years later. Four 245-horsepower Maybach engines produced only 980 horsepower, less than that of the single Wright R-1820-G2 used in the early-model Douglas DC-3s. The E.4/20 cruised at 120 mph and carried 12 passengers.

wing surface, and a fixed landing gear that radiated extraordinary drag. By the standards of 1920, however, the E.4/20 looked like something from a science fiction story: a flying machine created by some extraterrestrial civilization.

Most unusual was the E.4/20's wing design. It consisted of a massive, full-span central box-section Düraluminium girder from which an all-metal leading edge and trailing edge were cantilevered; the whole was covered by stressed Düraluminium sheeting. The vertical and horizontal stabilizers employed similar cantilever construction. Wing loading was 16 pounds per square foot, unusually high for 1920. In terms of its elementary stressed-skin cantilever wing structure, the E.4/20 was the great grand-daddy of the "modern airplanes" of the 1930s.

Except for its use of metal, the E.4/20's fuselage was not unusual. It consisted of a conventional framework made of Düraluminium and covered by metal sheeting, the sheeting displacing the diagonal crosswires ordinarily used to give stiffness to a wooden structure. Clearly, in this "first cut" at such an extraordinary airplane, Rohrbach built as strongly as possible and the E.4/20 was a heavy machine. Its load-to-tare ratio of 28:72 was only a trifle better than the Wright brothers' airplane of 1904, and substantially less than the norm of 34:66. Nevertheless, the E.4/20 was an extraordinary airplane, and on this point deserves comparison with the Douglas DC-2 of 14 years later.

Unfortunately for Rohrbach, in 1920 Germany was a defeated nation. The victorious Allies were determined to keep Germany disarmed, and thus the Treaty of Versailles included crippling restrictions on the development of German military and civil aviation. In 1922 the Allies decreed that the E.4/20s had to be destroyed.

The British, French, and Americans experimented with Düraluminium, tinkering with its formula to improve its characteristics and to get around the Wilm patent. ALCOA sold it in the United States under the designation 17S. Its applications were made with great caution. Outside Germany it was

Cutting a door in the side of a Zeppelin-Staaken E.4/20 of 1919 would have created a large interruption in the hull structure, requiring reinforcements that would have increased the structural weight. Adolf Rohrbach got around this problem by having passengers enter at the front of the fuselage's "tube" through a door in the nose.

typically used in unstressed parts of the airplane—such as fuel tanks, fairings, seats, and instrument panels—but not in primary structures. Meanwhile, Düraluminium's spelling was simplified to the more pronounceable *duralumin*.

While high-strength duralumin is vulnerable to corrosion, pure aluminum develops an oxide that renders it impervious to corrosion. ALCOA developed a technique for cladding duralumin sheeting with microscopically thin coatings of pure aluminum that protected it from corrosion. In effect, the duralumin was sandwiched between pure aluminum coatings. The improved material was trademarked as Alclad, and this is what Dix announced at the NACA industrial conference of 1927. At the same time, in England, a technique was developed for anodizing duralumin. ALCOA's cladding was used on duralumin sheeting; anodizing was most effectively used on forgings and castings or pieces with irregular shapes. The protection given by cladding and anodizing served to establish a dramatically new baseline for aerostructures. After 1927 aluminum aircraft alloys became commonplace in aerostructures, and improved variants went from strength to greater strength.

The Lockheed Vega

Another critical event of 1927 was the appearance of the first of Lockheed's famous Star series, the Vega. A high-wing single-engine monoplane of 3,400 pounds designed for airline service, it seated six passengers. With an internally braced wing covered with stressed plywood and with a plywood stressed-skin fuselage, the Vega presented an extraordinarily well-streamlined form. The Vega's semi-monocoque fuselage was feasible only as a result of the Loughead brothers, Malcolm and Allan, and their chief engineer, John K. Northrop, developing a technique for manufacturing prefabricated fuselage shells that avoided the time-consuming handwork previously associated with that form of construction. The result was an airframe of light weight, great strength and stiffness, and unusual aerodynamic cleanliness.

The Vega prototype had a load-to-tare ratio of 45:55, and although this deteriorated to 40:60 in its final version, the Vega's useful load was increased

John K. Northrop, who later created Northrop Aviation, designed the Lockheed Vega. The plane's unusual performance resulted from its clean cantilever wing and unusual technique for manufacturing very light prefabricated wooden fuselage shells. Here Vega fuselage half shells are being readied in the fuselage room.

This early Lockheed Vega 5 (Lockheed serial number 23, NC 7953) was manufactured in December 1928 with a Pratt & Whitney Wasp engine but without a NACA cowling. Its maximum speed was 165 mph.

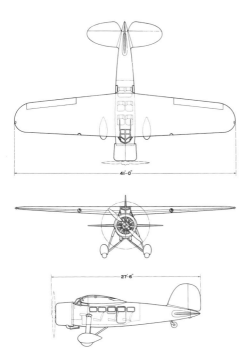

This three-view drawing clearly shows the clean lines that gave the Vega the lowest drag coefficient of any operational airplane in 1930. Lockheed's detailed multiview drawing provides a résumé of all the salient technical features of the various Vega models.

The Lockheed 5C Vega, a 4,750-pound airplane with seats for six passengers, was the fully refined version, with a NACA cowling and aerodynamic wheel pants fitted. It cruised at 160 mph with a top speed of 185 mph. From 1928 to 1931, it was the world's fastest airliner and pound for pound carried a greater payload than did any similar airplane. The Vega shown here belonged to the Standard Aircraft Company of Hackensack, New Jersey.

19 percent by doubling its horsepower and increasing its wing loading. The Vega's original wing loading was 12.6; the final variant's was 17, a 34 percent increase. In other words, Lockheed took the Vega through the same process that the Wright brothers had taken their airplanes during the years 1903–1909. This is a path that any airplane design experiences as its engineers develop it from good, to better, to its best.

The Vega was not only a good load carrier, it had speed. In a day when most airplanes cruised at 100 mph, the original Vega cruised at 115 mph and had a top speed of 135. Its final variant cruised at 160 mph and had a top speed of 185, with much of this increase due to the adoption of the NACA cowling.

From the Vega to Orion to DC-2

In 1927, the same year the Vega appeared, Charles Lindbergh startled the world by flying nonstop from New York to Paris, 3,600 miles, in 33.5 hours, averaging 107 mph. This was a magnificent achievement, but compared to the Lockheed Vega, Lindbergh's *Spirit of St. Louis* was a "yesterday's airplane."

When Lindbergh sought a new airplane in 1929, he went to Lockheed;

This Lockheed Orion (NC 12222, Lockheed serial number 180) "flies" today as a restored exhibit at the Swiss Transport Museum in Lucerne. It began as an experimental Altair DL-2A in September 1931 but was converted to an Orion 9C Special in June 1932. For the next six years, Jimmy Doolittle, Shell Aviation Corporation's aviation manager, piloted it around the country as the *Shellightning*. After it had gone through a number of other owners, the Swiss Transport Museum purchased it in 1976. It was restored and repainted with the markings of one of SwissAir's original Orions, CH-167 (Lockheed serial number 189).

the results were the Lockheed 8 Sirius, which was essentially a low-wing Vega, and, later, its twin the Lockheed 8 Altair, which was equipped with retractable landing gear. Out of the Sirius and Altair experience Lockheed developed the Orion; it was designed for high-speed airline service with seats for six passengers.

The Orion, which first flew in early 1931, was simply a low-wing Vega, but with a profound difference. The Orion had retractable landing gear. Whereas the Vega's maximum speed was 185 mph, the Orion cruised at 200, and its more numerous 9 and 9D models had a top speed of 226 mph. An Orion could run away from any fighter plane in the world—all of which were still biplanes replete with struts, wires, and fixed landing gear. Europeans assumed that the Orion's performance was grossly exaggerated until 1932 when Swissair put two into service between Zurich and Vienna. Relative to European airline equipment, their daily performances were mind-boggling and soon inspired the design of the British Airspeed AS.5 Courier and Ernst Heinkel's He 70 in Germany. The plywood Orion pioneered the shape of today's airplane, but not its materials.

After 1932 all the constituents suddenly came together in America. Boeing built the twin-engine B-9 bomber based on its two Monomails. In 1933 Martin produced the B-10 bomber for the Army Air Corps. The B-10 delivered a ton of bombs at 190 mph, after which it sped away at 225 mph; its speed made all existing fighter planes obsolete. Boeing delivered its 247 airliner to United Air Lines in 1933, and then Douglas built the DC-1 for Transcontinental and Western Airlines (TWA), which went into production as

The Heinkel He 70 Blitz, developed for Lufthansa in 1932 as a response to the Lockheed Orion, was a 7,630-pound airliner with seats for four passengers. Although it had a metal semi-monocoque fuselage, the He 70 had a wooden wing covered with stressed plywood. With a top speed of 220 mph and a cruising speed of 190 mph, the He 70 was the fastest airplane produced in Europe in 1932.

The Boeing 247, which first flew in February 1933 and soon entered service with United Air Lines, was the first modern airliner. A 13,000-pound airplane with seats for 10 passengers, it was the first airliner to reduce coast-to-coast travel time to 20 hours. A more advanced model, the 247D, had a top speed of 200 mph and cruised at 180. However, the 247 was soon eclipsed by the superior performance of the 18,500-pound Douglas DC-2. This Boeing 247, which Roscoe Turner and Clyde Pangborn flew to a third-place finish in the MacRobertson Air Race of 1934, is on permanent display in the National Air and Space Museum.

the DC-2 in 1934. In August 1934, TWA's DC-2 Sky Chief service from Newark to Los Angeles slashed American transcontinental transportation to 18 hours, including en route fuel stops only at Chicago, Kansas City, and Albuquerque.

The updated airplane coincidentally created a distinct division of labor between the design of military and civil aircraft. Before 1933 any airliner was readily converted to a bomber simply by adding bomb shackles and defensive armament. With aircraft such as the Heinkel He 111 and Junkers Ju 86 and Ju 90, European airline fleets were often regarded as convertible, *ad hoc* bombers. However, the streamlined airplane dictated internal bomb stowage, and because bombs necessitated substantially less space than a human payload, hereafter fuselage cross-section designs of bombers and airline equipment would move in opposite directions.

The Douglas DC-2, which first flew on May 11, 1934, and went into service with TWA shortly thereafter. It was a smashing commercial success, with more than 190 built.

The Junkers Ju 90B went into service with Lufthansa in 1938.

THE MARTIN B-10'S COMBAT AIRPLANE REVOLUTION

A B-10B of the 6th Bombardment Group from France Field, Canal Zone, Panama, cruises over the Caribbean in November 1937.

Three B-10s from the 7th Bombardment Group at Hamilton Field, California, fly formation on air mail route 18 (note the marking "A.M. 18" on the fuselage) in then–Lt. Col. Henry H. Arnold's Western Zone during early 1934, when the Army Air Corps was responsible for flying the mail.

The Boeing Model 299 four-engine bomber made its first appearance in July 1935. The aircraft crashed taking off from Wright Field, Ohio, while undergoing flight tests by the Army Air Corps. The Flying Fortress was the backbone of the American strategic bomber force against Germany from 1942 to 1945. By the time production finally ended, 12,731 Flying Fortresses had been built.

The Glenn L. Martin Company's Model 123, generally remembered as the U.S. Army Air Corps' B-10 bomber, first flew in February 1932, started rolling off production lines in late 1933, and by the end of 1936 had established a global revolution in bomber design.

Prior to the B-10, multiengine bombers were typically angular biplanes without retractable landing gear, and although they usually had a metal structure, it was covered with fabric. Their crews sat in open cockpits, and the bombload was carried externally. Their best speed might be as fast as 120 mph; cruising speed was 95 mph. Except for much-improved reliability, their performances were only marginally superior to the rickety and treacherous multiengine bombers of World War I.

The Martin B-10 was a sleek, stress-skinned all-metal monoplane of 16,400 pounds with a load-to-tare ratio of 40:60. It had retractable landing gear, its crew sat in enclosed cockpits, and the bombload was carried internally behind streamlined doors. At a B-10's takeoff weight, two 775-horsepower R-1820 engines provided a power-to-weight ratio of 1:10.5; with almost half its fuel consumed and its bombs gone, this ratio improved to 1:8.6. In 1935 the best fighters among all air forces of the world were biplanes, improved variants of World War I fighters, and a best power-to-weight ratio among these combat planes was 1:7; their best speed was 190 mph, but a B-10 could rush in at 185 mph to strike its target with a ton of bombs and speed away at 210 mph. As of 1935 there was not a fighter plane in the world that could catch a Martin B-10.

Once this fact was established, its portents came as a terrible shock to the military establishments of the world. The Martin B-10 inspired a global revolution in bomber design, immediately yielding the Heinkel He 111 and Dornier DO 17, Germany's workhorse bombers of World War II; the Japanese Mitsubishi G3M-1 and Ki-21; the Soviet Tupolev SB-2; the French Bloch 131; and the British Handley Page Hampden and Bristol Blenheim. It also inspired Boeing to double the number of a bomber's power units from two to four in its Model 299, the prototype of the legendary B-17 Flying Fortress that first flew in 1935.

All of these modern bombers were into production or flying in prototype before the end of 1936. All were first-line equipment when World War II started in September 1939, and most of them soldiered on to the end of the war in 1945.

Most significantly, B-10 performance provoked a revolution in fighter design, finally forcing it to part from the biplane. With the knowledge that it would require more firepower to destroy a faster bomber of all-metal construction and in minimal time, the threat of B-10 performance initiated a heavying-up of fighter armament from two to four, from four to six, and then from six to eight guns, as well as a movement toward guns of larger caliber. Most immediately, Martin B-10 performance inspired the designs of the Messerschmitt Bf 109, the Hawker Hurricane, and the Supermarine Spitfire, the principal antagonists of the fateful Battle of Britain in 1940.

KLM's *Uiver* at Waalhaven Airport, Rotterdam, after winning the MacRobertson London-to-Melbourne Air Race in 1934. It placed first in the transport division; in the overall competition it placed second to a custom-built race plane.

The cabin cross section and floor plan of the Douglas DC-2 were practically the same as those of the Ford and Fokker Tri-motors. However, the DC-2's cruising speed of 180 mph was 70 mph faster, and it required only two engines.

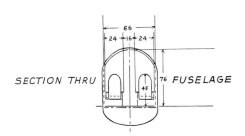

SECTION THRU FUSELAGE

14 PASSENGER INSTALLATION

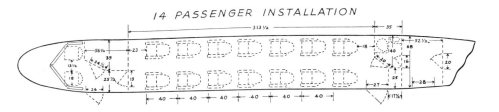

The Lockheed 188 Electra four-engine, turbo-prop airliner was designed in the mid-1950s to meet an American Airlines requirement. The first Electra flew in 1957, and Eastern Air Lines and American initiated airline service with it in January 1959. In 1959–60, however, three Electras crashed and public confidence in the aircraft seriously eroded. The development of medium- and short-range jet airliners in the early and mid-1960s spelled the end for the Electra as a civilian airliner after production of 232 aircraft. The U.S. Navy, however, developed the Electra into the extremely successful P-3 Orion land-based anti-submarine patrol aircraft. Through 1986, 611 Orions had been delivered to the U.S. Navy and a number of navies and air forces around the world.

The military airplane would take on many of the characteristics of a racehorse; a high-strung thoroughbred that was carefully stabled, exercised, and otherwise fussed over, to be ready for the bugle on race day. On the other hand, an airliner had to be a tough, reliable workhorse capable of earning its keep every day.

1934: The Year of Transition

In October 1934, the MacRobertson Race was flown, an intercontinental contest covering 11,300 miles between England and Australia. In England, the de Havilland Company developed its D.H.88 Comet racer expressly for this event. Three Comets were entered, and one won the race, but a Douglas DC-2 came in second and a Boeing 247 took third place. It was a terrible shock for British and European aircraft manufacturers to realize that these American airliners, designed to haul people through the sky efficiently, had matched the performance the of what was the world's finest long-distance racing plane.

The Sikorsky S-42, a four-engine flying boat of some 40,000 pounds, also took to the air in 1934, for Pan American Airways' South American service. Whereas a Boeing 247's wing loading was 15 pounds per square foot, and

One of Pan American Airways' 19-ton Sikorsky S-42 Clippers at the Pan American International Airport, Miami.

In November 1935, the Martin M-130 *China Clipper* inaugurated trans-Pacific air mail service from San Francisco to the Philippines via Hawaii and the islands of Midway, Wake, and Guam. Weighing 52,000-pounds, the M-130 was unusual in having a useful load of 23,500 pounds, 45 percent of its gross weight. The 2,410-mile San Francisco–Hawaii flight is the longest nonalternative over-water flight in the world, and an airplane that can fly it can continue to any other point in the world. The Martin M-130 was thus the first intercontinental airliner.

the DC-2's was 19.5, the S-42 was a startling 30. By making the structure carry more load, the S-42 achieved a load-to-tare ratio of 42:58. Ordinarily, such a high wing loading resulted in a high landing speed, but this was avoided in the S-42 by artful use of a large, trailing wing flap. The intense development and employment of wing flaps as auxiliary lift devices in the 1930s permitted airplane designers to exploit ever higher wing loadings.

Martin's M-130 also made its first flight in 1934. A flying boat of 52,000 pounds, the M-130 was intended to pioneer Pan American's trans-Atlantic service, but because of political problems the airline had to use it for trans-Pacific service. Among large airplanes the weight control achieved by the M-130's designers was extraordinary. As a bare airplane stripped of cabin furnishings, an M-130's load-to-tare ratio was 51:49, 44:56 with a fully equipped cabin.

In November 1935, Pan Am's M-130 *China Clipper* demonstrated its capabilities by inaugurating trans-Pacific air mail service. The 2,410 miles between California and Hawaii constitute the longest non-alternative over-water route between commercial destinations in the world. An airplane that can fly this distance can continue to any part of the world; it is an intercontinental vehicle. Although an M-130's payload over this distance was only some 2,600 pounds, no other airplane of these years could begin to equal it. The Martin M-130 was the world's first intercontinental airliner.

Having developed a streamlined shape that after 1934 became universal among new designs the world over, many small refinements became worthwhile: filleting junctions between wing and fuselage where minor air turbulence might occur; designing windows with frames that were flush with the exterior skin; insetting door handles and putting door hinges inside a door's opening; eliminating the thousands of tiny, drag-producing rivet heads by replacing them with countersunk, flush rivets; butting metal skin panels to eliminate the small discontinuities of airflow created by lapped skin junctions; and making tailwheels retractable.

Fred Weick, an NACA engineer working on his own, validated in 1934 the superiority of tricycle landing gear and a steerable nosewheel relative to the conventional tail-dragging configuration. Tricycle landing gear not only concluded the revolution in an airplane's ground handling initiated by the concrete runway and brakes, it also made vital improvements to takeoff and landing characteristics. Although a novelty in the 1930s, within a decade

The one and only Douglas DC-4E (E for Experimental) first flew on June 7, 1938. It was a 66,500-pound airplane with two-by-two seating for 42 passengers. The DC-4E was one of the first airplanes to have tricycle landing gear. Douglas would have preferred to have built the DC-4E with a single vertical stabilizer and rudder, but it would have been too tall to clear the lintel of hangar doors. The triple tail was dictated by the necessity of hangar door clearance. The American airlines finally decided that the DC-4E's performance was poor (cruising speed 200 mph), its systems were excessively complex and required too much maintenance, and its operating economics were unacceptable. Only one was built and used by United Air Lines for proving flights on its routes before being returned to Douglas, who sold it to Mitsui Trading Company in late 1939 for use by Greater Japan Air Lines. Although originally reported to have crashed in Tokyo Bay, the DC-4E was actually disassembled by the Nakajima Aircraft Company and became the basis for its four-engine long-range G5N Shinzan bombers used by the Japanese Navy. The Shinzan performed poorly, and only six were built. Douglas revised the DC-4E specification to a less complex aircraft that became the successful DC-4 (C-54) series.

A United Air Lines DC-3 over the northeast corner of New York's Central Park, demonstrating its ability to fly on one engine with the propeller of the other engine feathered. With a feathered propeller, the blades in the hub were rotated edgewise to the direction of flight. Without feathering, the dead propeller would continue to rotate in the wind, turning the dead engine and creating a great increase in aerodynamic drag.

American Airlines initiated the development of the Douglas Sleeper Transport (DST), a larger and faster version of the DC-2, in 1934. Two years later, the DST and the day transport versions of the DST fitted with Wright R-1820 engines, designated the DC-3, entered service with American Airlines and set the pattern for today's airliner service and reliability.

tricycle gear would be conventional, and the tail-dragger would be representative of the past. Until 1944 tricycle landing gear was also unique to American airplanes.

The year 1934 was the *annus mirabilis* of the airplane. The American aircraft industry gained a technological lead that the rest of the world did not catch up to until some 30 years later. The swift absorption and use of new foreign technologies, such as the turbojet engine, swept wing, and delta wing planform, only served to build on that lead in the years after World War II.

Increased Sophistication in Aircraft and Production

Until the 1930s the airplane was essentially a low-altitude machine. Although supercharging would support engines in the progressively thinner atmosphere above 10,000 feet, the problem was sustaining the human operator. Humans are comfortable enough up to altitudes of 10,000 feet (e.g., Mexico City is

THE C-46, THE C-47, AND THE LEGEND OF THE DC-3

The DC-3 legend is owed to this airplane being an extraordinarily well-designed flying machine, to its more than 13,000 productions, to the tens of thousands of aviators who flew it and loved it, and to the teething problems of the Curtiss CW-20.

However, it was the Douglas DC-1 that was a truly great airplane—a dramatic departure from the past. The DC-2, of which 193 were built, was the great demonstrator. The DC-3 is noteworthy for being the great economic vehicle. Although the 18,650-pound DC-2 had 75 percent more speed than the angular tri-motors it displaced, its cabin cross section measured only 66 inches. This was about the same as the old tri-motors, and it seated 14 passengers, seven on each side of the aisle. The 25,200-pound DC-3's cabin cross section measured 92 inches, permitting three-seat rows, 2 + 1 divided by the aisle, multiplying seating from 14 to 21.

For a 35-percent increase in gross weight, the DC-3 yielded a 50-percent increase in payload. The airlines were fond of saying that it was the first airliner with which they could make money by carrying passengers only. Assuming that they could fill a DC-3's 21 seats, an air mail subsidy was not necessary.

After the DC-3 first flew in 1935, the Curtiss-Wright Corporation initiated the design of a DC-3 replacement, its CW-20, which flew in March 1940. It weighed some 40,000 pounds, gigantic for a twin-engine airplane of this era. It had a pressure cabin that pioneered the "double-bubble" fuselage cross section. Its 118-inch cabin cross section accommodated 40 passengers in 2 + 2 seating and 50 passengers in 2 + 3 seating; the lower section of the double bubble had a generous capacity for cargo.

As a load carrier the CW-20 was not only superior to the DC-3, in 1940 it seemed clearly destined to replace it. However, Curtiss design staffs were notoriously conservative, and they sold short the CW-20's long-term future by designing it as a tail-dragger at the moment when tricycle landing had been validated. Needing a large-capacity troop carrier and cargo plane, the Army Air Forces rushed to order the CW-20 which it designated the C-46 Commando. Although the C-46's shell was designed to be pressurized, the Army never installed pressurization equipment.

The C-46 was a troubled airplane. It did not go into production until 1942. Rushed into service, the airplane had no body of test experience behind it and there were inevitably many resultant difficulties. Meanwhile, for want of a load carrier, the Army ordered DC-3s, designated C-47 in military service. Continued problems with the C-46 generated more stopgap orders for the C-47 and its variants. In lieu of the "best," the Army had to settle for "good enough"; the Navy adopted the DC-3, which became the R3D. By the end of the war, some 13,000 DC-3s and its military variants had been built; meanwhile only some 2,000 C-46s were produced.

Almost half a century after 1940 there are still a few hundred DC-3s in commercial operation, flying among the far pavillions of the world. Only a dozen or so CW-20s still exist, hauling freight around the Caribbean, but if it were not for the CW-20's teething problems, not nearly so many C-47s would have been produced and the legend of the DC-3 would not have achieved the magnificent dimensions it has.

The C-47.

The C-47.

The C-47.

The interior of the C-46.

The Curtiss Wright C-46 production line.

The C-46.

The Boeing 307 Stratoliner, a 42,000-pound airplane that seated 32 passengers, used the wing, engines, and tail group of the B-17 bomber. It was the first airliner with a pressure cabin, and its barrel-shaped fuselage permitted it to hurdle the Rocky Mountains at 20,000 feet. In coast-to-coast service from Los Angeles to New York, the 307 could fly the Los Angeles–Chicago leg nonstop.

7,600 feet above sea level), but above that altitude oxygen content falls off rapidly. Airliners such as the Douglas DC-3 did not fly over the Rockies; trying to stay below 10,000 feet, they flew between mountains, following valleys—and giving passengers a breathtaking view of mountains off each wingtip.

As early as 1930, Junkers in Germany and Farman in France demonstrated airplanes for high-altitude operations that had special pressurized chambers for their crews. In 1937 the U.S. Army Air Corps validated a pressure cabin in the Lockheed XC-35 that was inherently part of the airplane, its exterior skin serving as the pressure shell. Building on this technology, Boeing built its 307 Stratoliner as the world's first airliner with a pressure cabin. When Boeing went into transcontinental service with TWA in 1940, for the first time the North American continental divide could be routinely overflown at cruising altitudes in excess of 15,000 feet.

By the eve of World War II, all the basic constituents of the modern airplane were on the shelf for the use of airplane designers. In the course of the 1930s the airplane became an increasingly complex machine. Only nine months were required to design, build, and fly the Douglas DC-1 (September 20, 1932–July 1, 1933); in May 1934, just 22 months after the DC-1 contract award, production models of the 19,000-pound DC-2 were being delivered to TWA. However, three years were required to move the four-engine 73,000-pound Douglas DC-4 from preliminary design in 1939 to its first flight in February 1942. During this period, the entire industry expanded. In 1933 only some 7,800 persons were directly involved in the design and

manufacture of airplanes in the United States, whereas by 1939 the beginning of major prewar military expansion had pushed this number to more than 48,000.

By the end of the 1930s, manufacturers had organized the necessary divisions of labor among design teams into specialized groups: aerodynamics, structures, power plant, landing gear, various "systems," and armament, among others. Each had its piece of the airplane. Over them all, like a grim policeman, hovered the "weights group," which was always ready to invoke its First Commandment: Simplify and add a bit of lightness. Each area became a vital specialty, and after 1940 an engineer might devote a career of 30 years to designing landing gear, an absolutely unforgiving part of the airplane whose design was a demanding art unto itself.

Profiting from its experience with the DC-4E, Douglas Aircraft designed a completely new four-engine aircraft, the DC-4, that could accommodate 40 passengers. The outbreak of war with Japan prompted the U.S. government to take over DC-4 production. The Army Air Forces designated the new aircraft the C-54 Skymaster, which was heavily used in the Air Transport Command throughout the world. After the war, many wartime C-54s were converted to civilian use and additional DC-4s were built to serve the postwar needs of airlines worldwide.

World War II

Like the World War of 1914–1918, the Second World War was a period more noteworthy for production—expanding aviation's industrial base—and a determined exploitation of available technology than for unusual contributions to airplane design. Once again, war did more for aviation than it did for the airplane. In the United States alone, factory floor space increased from 9,455, 000 square feet in 1939 to 168,000,000 square feet in 1945; the labor force rose from 77,500 persons in 1940 to a peak of 1.3 million in late 1943.

Whereas in 1940, 12,871 airplanes were produced, 53 percent of them civilian aircraft, in 1945 some 97,000 were produced, all of them military. More descriptive, however, of the aircraft production leap was the common denominator of airframe weights, which multiplied from 24.6 million pounds produced in 1940 to 1.1 billion pounds in the peak year of 1944. Engine production paralleled this growth, jumping from 11,172 units in 1939 to more than 256,000 in 1944, while controllable-pitch propeller output grew from 23,000 in 1940 to almost 244,000 in 1944.

Aviation in World War II was essentially a story of the refinement of the shelf technology of 1939. Most of the airplane designs used in the war were either already flying or being tooled for production in 1939. One outstanding example was the Boeing B-17 bomber, whose 42,600-pound gross-weight Y1B-17 second prototype of 1936 grew into the 65,500-pound B-17G by 1945. This colossal weight growth was made possible only by concurrent growth in the Wright R-1820 engine's horsepower from 930 to 1,200. Another example was the B-17's German nemesis, the Messerschmitt Bf 109 fighter. In 1936 the Bf 109B prototype had a maximum loaded weight of 4,740 pounds and a 720-horsepower Junkers Jumo 210Da engine; it finished the war with one of its most advanced models, the Bf 109K-4, weighing 7,440 pounds with a 2,000-horsepower Daimler-Benz DB 605ASCM engine.

Exceptions to this weight-growth story seemed to occur in the case of the United States, which avoided direct participation in the world conflict until December 7, 1941. Nevertheless, a complex 125,000-pound airplane

Facing page:
The Boeing B-17G bomber routinely flew at 65,500 pounds gross weight, and B-17Fs even went up to 72,000 pounds. The development of the B-17 was largely a story of weight growth. The Model 299 prototype of 1935 weighed 38,000 pounds, the Y1B-17 of 1938 weighed 42,600 pounds, the B-17B of 1939 weighed 47,900 pounds, and the B-17E of 1941 weighed 53,000 pounds. From the Model 299 of 1935 to the B-17G of 1945, gross weight increased by 27,000 pounds, mostly as a result of increased defensive armament, new and larger tail assemblies, more armor and fuel tanks, and new electronic radar navigation and bombardment systems. The wing area of 1,420 square feet remained unchanged, so that wing loading increased from 27 to 46 pounds per square foot. All this was made possible by a 60 percent increase in available engine horsepower achieved over eight years—from four 750-horsepower Pratt & Whitney R-1690-E Hornet engines in the Model 299 to four 1,200-horsepower Wright R-1820—97 engines in the B-17F and G models.

The National Air and Space Museum's restored Messerschmitt Bf 109G *Gustav* is one of the finest examples of the Luftwaffe's dominant front-line fighters of World War II.

The Boeing B-29 Superfortress was the largest heavy bomber built during World War II.

The performance of the original B-36As and Bs with six piston engines (381 mph) left some room for improvement, and so four General Electric J47 engines were mounted in the outer wing pods of 64 older-model B-36Bs to make them B-36Ds. All subsequent aircraft of this line had the jet pods added. The B-36D had a top speed of 439 mph after the modification.

such as the Boeing B-29 Superfortress bomber, which finished the Pacific War in 1945, had its preliminary specification drawn up in 1938, was refined in 1939, had its prototype contract let in August 1940, and first flew in September 1942. The six-engine Consolidated B-36 bomber, which did not fly until 1946 and is ordinarily considered a postwar airplane, had its preliminary contract drawn up in 1940 and was representative of design studies prepared in 1938 and 1939 and refined during the war.

One of the most significant consequences of World War II was the building of hundreds of airfields throughout the United States and the world where none had existed before, most of them paved with all-weather surfaces. The war established an infrastructure for domestic and global air transportation. Although the sudden creation of this infrastructure cannot be

On August 10 and 11, 1938, Captain Alfred Henke and a crew of three flew the Focke-Wulf Fw 200 airliner D-ACON from Berlin to New York (3,985 miles) nonstop. The Fw 200 was a 32,000-pound airplane that carried 30 passengers. On this flight, its payload was 15,580 pounds of fuel. Here Henke's Fw 200 flies over Bergen Beach shortly after taking off from Floyd Bennett Field for the nonstop return flight to Berlin. The Fw 200 Condor saw extensive wartime duty with the Luftwaffe.

The Bloch SE.161 Languedoc was a 50,000-pound airliner with seats for 33 passengers. Its normal range was 650 miles. Although it first flew in 1939, most of its production and operations occurred in the postwar years 1946–1954, by which time it was an obsolescent relative to the 62,000-pound Douglas DC-4, the DC-6, and the Lockheed Constellation.

underestimated, its many profound effects on the airplane, aviation, and communications are invariably ignored.

Before the war broke out in 1939, gigantic American, British, Japanese, French, and German flying boats seemed predestined to be the *Queen Marys* of the transoceanic airways while the four-engine transports—such as the D.H. 91 Albatross, Boeing 307, Focke-Wulf Fw 200A, Farman 2000, Junkers Ju 90B, and Bloch 161—were just entering service. However, the postwar availability of new airfields, along with the wartime development, production, and extensive use of the Douglas DC-4, Boeing 307 and Lockheed L.049 Constellation, signaled the dramatically sudden end of the big flying boat. Great water expanses were a complication the airplane never needed, and seaplane operations were filled with many technical, mechanical, and natural headaches and hazards. The seaplane provided versatility only

The prototype of Lockheed's four–engine L.049 Constellation ("Connie") civilian airliner appeared as a military transport, a C-69 (serial number 43-10309), and first flew on January 9, 1943. Howard Hughes later flew the aircraft nonstop from Burbank, California, to Washington, D.C., in under seven hours. The Connie had its greatest impact on coast–to–coast commercial air service when TWA put it in service on its Los Angeles–New York route in March 1946.

where there were inadequate airfields ashore. It is popularly believed that the superior characteristics of the land plane put the flying boat out of business, but it is more correct to say that the bulldozer and Portland concrete vanquished the flying boat. Seaplanes still exist, but since the 1950s they have become very rare birds of marginal utility.

Jets: The Beginning of a New Era

Although the gas turbine engine is often thought to be a product of World War II, this is merely a chronological coincidence. Its invention dates from Frank Whittle's conceptions of the late 1920s and his historic British patent No. 347,206 of April 16, 1931. Others, earlier, had vaguely envisioned a gas turbine turning a propeller; Frank Whittle's genius conceived it in terms of a self-contained unit of pure thrust. Almost concurrently there was the more immediately fruitful work of Hans von Ohain and Anselm Franz in Germany.

Whittle was repeatedly frustrated by timid financiers and a somnolent British aviation bureaucracy. He had an engine running on a test stand in 1937, but no British airplane flew with a gas turbine until May 15, 1941. Von Ohain was more fortunate. He obtained the patronage of Ernst Heinkel, an airplane manufacturer who wanted to establish himself in the aero engine

The Gloster E.28/39, fitted with Frank Whittle's WIx turbojet engine, first flew on May 15, 1941. The engine is on display in the National Air and Space Museum's Jet Gallery.

WHITTLE WIX, 1941

The Lockheed C-130 Hercules is one of the most durable and successful medium-size military transport aircraft ever built. The first two C-130 prototypes were built for the U.S. Air Force in 1951 and equipped with four Allison T56 propeller-turbines with three-bladed variable-pitch propellers (which were soon replaced by more advanced four-bladed propellers). By 1987, Lockheed-Georgia had built over 1,800 Hercules transports which served in numerous air forces throughout the world as tactical troop and cargo carriers, aerial tankers, gunships, and electronic reconnaissance and warfare aircraft.

business of the future. On August 27, 1939, at Marienehe, Germany, while Frank Whittle was still pleading with the grand panjandrums of the British Air Ministry in London, test pilot Erich Warsitz opened the throttle of a Heinkel He 178 and sent it screaming into the air. This was five days before Adolf Hitler's legions invaded Poland, initiating a European war that became World War II. A small machine of 4,400 pounds, the He 178's only function was to provide a testbed for von Ohain's He.S-3b gas turbine, and in so doing it became the world's first jet airplane.

Although knowing that best results would be obtained from an engine with an axial compressor, both Whittle and von Ohain sought immediate results by developing engines with a centrifugal compressor. This was the quickest way to demonstrate proof-of-concept. The centrifugal compressor's shortcomings were that its large diameter increased an airplane's frontal area and that the air had to change direction at least twice before

The Junkers Jumo 004 axial-flow turbojet engine of World War II was used in the Messerschmitt Me 262 jet fighter. Air entered at the left, was compressed in the eight-stage compressor, and was exhausted into combustion chambers where fuel was injected and burned. The hot gases were exhausted through a turbine wheel that turned the eight compressor stages and then were exhausted through the jet nozzle at the right.

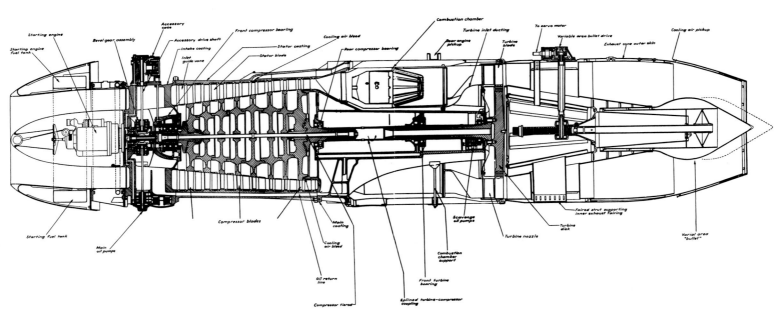

As Nazi Germany collapsed in the spring of 1945, many advanced secret weapons, production plants, and operational bases fell into Allied hands. Allied airmen were particularly interested in Messerschmitt's Me 262 jet fighters and bombers, which were soon thoroughly examined and flight tested. Here, Army Air Forces' test pilot Major Russ Schleeh flies a Me 262A-1a *Schwalbe* (Swallow) fighter that the Germans had not even painted prior to its seizure by American forces.

reaching the gas turbine's combustion chambers. In an axial turbine, the air is compressed through a series of small stages, the air's passage is "straight through," and the unit's cross section is substantially smaller. The axial-flow gas turbine was considerably more complicated to design, develop, and manufacture, but it was the turbojet of the future.

Almost concurrent with von Ohain's work, Anselm Franz of the Junkers Engine Company developed the Jumo 004, the world's first axial-flow turbojet. The Messerschmitt Me 262 fighter plane was designed for this power plant; the plane first flew in July 1942, but did not enter combat service until October 1944. The Me 262's maximum speed in level flight was 541 mph, faster than propeller-driven airplanes could achieve in a dive.

If available in numbers in October 1943, the Me 262 would have severely complicated the Allied bomber offensive against Germany in 1944–1945. American B-17s and British Lancasters labored along at 210 to 250 mph under their heavy loads of bombs and defensive machine guns and ammunition, escorted by fighters that cruised at 350–400 mph. Armed with four 30mm cannon, the Me 262s would have enjoyed a tremendous advantage in speed and firepower. But this was not to be. After the successful cross-channel invasion of June, 1944, the Allies had scores of fighter bases in Europe for their thousands of propeller-driven fighter planes. Quantity can overwhelm quality, and by means of new tactics and sheer weight of numbers, the Allied air forces simply overpowered the few hundred operational Messerschmitt jet fighters available to the Luftwaffe by late 1944.

During the war, propeller-driven fighters often reached speeds approaching 500 mph, where they were troubled by the phenomenon of compressibility. Local airflows on the body of the aircraft were accelerated to sonic speeds, creating shock waves that often locked control surfaces or damaged the structure, or both. Up until this time, only power-plant designers had to be concerned with sonic speeds, taking care to hold propeller tip speeds substantially below the speed of sound. It had been convenient for aerodynamicists to treat air as a medium similar to water, an incompressible fluid; now it had to be treated in terms of the compressible medium it is.

In the 1930s Italy's government sponsored annual conferences honoring the Italian scientist Alessandro Volta (1745–1827). The subjects of these conferences varied from the arts to political theory. The Italian Macchi-

The B-47 became the mainstay of the Strategic Air Command's medium bomber force from the early 1950s through the mid-1960s. The 160,000-pound B-47A shown here was one of only 10 special-production replicas of the XB-47 built at Boeing's Wichita, Kansas, plant and first flew on June 25, 1950.

The XB-47 Stratojet was redesigned for swept-back wings after Boeing designers visited German research establishments after 1945. The XB-47 first flew on December 17, 1947, the forty-fourth anniversary of the Wright brothers' first flight.

Castoldi M.C.72 seaplane had recently set successive world speed records, including a new one at 440.68 mph (Mach 0.57) in October 1934, leading to 1935's Volta Conference, which dealt with high-speed flight. This Volta Conference also gave the world Mach Number as the basic measure of speed relative to the speed of sound. The term honors the Austrian physicist Ernst Mach (1838–1916), whose work in ballistics revealed the change in airflow around a body moving at supersonic speed. Since 1935, Mach 1 had been the speed of sound. However, because the speed of sound varies with atmospheric pressure and temperature, it is a relative measure.

The new spectrum of thrust becoming available from turbojets liberated the airplane from the propeller's inhibiting disc, opened the speed envelope toward the supersonic, moved flight into the realm of Mach numbers, and reduced mph to a ground-bound measure. However, the demands of flight at high Mach numbers also changed the shape of the airplane.

Using the turbojet in a new generation of combat planes was an obvious application, and the end of the war saw a large variety of experimental jet fighters and jet bombers. Typically, they combined tomorrow's thrust unit with yesterday's aerodynamics; they had straight wings and multiengine designs, but had their engines mounted in nacelles similar to piston engines. All these airplanes met with difficulties while trying to fly at high, subsonic Mach numbers.

At 1935's Volta Conference the German physicist Adolf Busemann (1901–1988) theorized that sweepback in a wing would delay the onset of compressibility and the creation of shock waves. In 1935 this was interesting but useless information. However, being first on the scene with jet airplanes, after 1939 the Germans were the first to face the thicket of problems created by high-speed flight. They perceived an application for Busemann's theory, and by 1945 had developed a wealth of technical data. The end of the war deprived them of an opportunity to apply it, and these data passed into the hands of the victorious Allies, who found the far-reaching implications of the German materials rather mind-boggling. The most valuable immediate function of some of the German data was to validate new research and design work under way in the United States and to a lesser extent in the Soviet Union and Great Britain.

The B-47

The most dramatic and influential airplane of the 1945–1950 era was the Boeing B-47 bomber. Rolled out for public view in September 1947, the B-47 Stratojet not only possessed the startling aspects of a futuristic flying machine drawn from the pages of a science fantasy magazine of the 1930s, it looked more like an oversized fighter than a bomber. Atop its slender fuselage, the pilot and copilot sat in tandem under a teardrop plexiglass canopy. Its thin, high-aspect ratio wings were swept back at a breathtaking 35 degrees; the six General Electric J47 engines in streamlined nacelles suspended from pylons beneath the wings jutted forward, adding to the optical illusion that the airplane might be in motion even as it sat parked on the ground.

The mighty B-29A bomber of World War II and the new Stratojet were vastly different aircraft. The B-29 had a gross weight of 141,000 pounds, load-to-tare ratio of 50:50, and a wing loading of 77.6 pounds per square foot. As finally developed, the B-47's gross weight was 206,700 pounds, its load-to-tare ratio 61:39, and its wing loading 144.7 pounds—each of which would have been regarded as absurd only 10 years earlier. Whereas a B-29's maximum speed was 360 mph, the B-47 cruised at 550 while capable of accelerating to more than 600 mph, Mach 0.9, at altitude. The B-47's

The Boeing YB-52 intercontinental bomber first flew on April 15, 1952, and the second proto-type, the XB-52, flew on October 2, 1952. After the first prototypes and three B-52As, seven major series (B through H) were built that grew from 405,000 to 488,000 pounds (525,000 pounds after in-flight refueling). A total of 742 production model B-52s were built by Boeing in Seattle and Wichita, Kansas, and the last B-52H was delivered to the U.S. Air Force in October 1962. This B-52G carries two North American GAM-77 (later AGM-28) Hound Dog standoff missiles on pylons beneath the wings.

Facing page (bottom):
An elegant airplane of 114,640 pounds, the Sud-Aviation SE-210 Caravelle, which first flew on May 27, 1955, was the first short-haul jetliner and the airplane that introduced rear-mounted engines. The Caravelle was also the first Euro-pean jet airliner to break into the American market when United Air Lines bought 20 of them. Introduced to service in 1961, the Cara-velle made it possible to commute daily by jet between Chicago and New York.

technology was subsequently extrapolated into the B-52 Stratofortress, the 488,000-pound intercontinental giant that first flew in 1952 and whose latest variants, the B-52Gs and Hs, were on front-line operational duty with the U.S. Air Force's Strategic Air Command as of 1989.

A most unusual aspect of the B-47, for 1947, was the design of its engine installations: in nacelles suspended from pylons beneath the wing and sited well forward of the wing's leading edge. This installation created a "clean" wing and provided a number of other important advantages. The engine inlets and most of the nacelle were outside the wing's aerodynamic pressure system. With the engines far removed from the fuel systems, fire hazard was greatly reduced; in the event of a fire, the isolated engine could burn itself away and fall off, with minimum damage to the wing. Because they were sited forward of, and below, the wing's center of lift, the B-47's engines acted as mass balances that resisted divergence. Other advantages were that the engine units were convenient to the ground and easily serviced, and most of the airplane did not have to be taken apart to change an engine.

Historically, the most significant aspect of the B-47 was that it, like the Lockheed Orion and Douglas DC-1 of 15 years earlier, established a new generalized shape for the airplane that has endured from that day to our own. There would be no similar contribution to a basic reshaping of the airplane until the French introduced rear-mounted engines with the SE.210 Caravelle, a 101,400-pound airliner that first flew in 1955.

For almost a quarter of a century after 1947, engines in suspended nacelles sited well forward of the wing were practically a trademark of

The installation of the B-47's six jet engines on underslung pylons is clearly visible in this photograph of a B-47E.

Among the many advantages of the underwing installation of the B-47's jet engines, ease of maintenance and replacement was very important. A U.S. Air Force ground crew and civilian contractors work on one of the B-47's GE J47 engines.

The Avro Vulcan was a delta-wing strategic nuclear bomber that entered service with the RAF's Bomber Command in the 1950s and was used on Argentinean targets in the Falkland Islands during the 1982 conflict. The four Bristol Siddeley Olympus engines that powered the 200,000-pound bomber were buried in the wing roots deep inside the fuselage and could push the bomber to near Mach 1 speeds.

Facing page (top):
This British Overseas Airways (BOAC) de Havilland Comet 1 shows the location of the four jet engines in the wing root area, in marked contrast to the pattern pylon mounting that was established with the Boeing B-47.

Facing page (bottom):
The Tupolev Tu-104 entered airline service with *Aeroflot* in September 1956 on the Moscow-Irkutsk route. Directly developed out of the mid-wing Tu-16 bomber, the early model Tu-104A (SSSR-L5421) shown here was a 167,000-pound low-wing monoplane powered by two AM-3M axial-flow turbojets, each with 19,180 pounds of thrust. The wing-root installation of the engines was a simple design that did not attempt to fair the engine into the wing, which would have required a thicker wing structure.

American multiengine jet planes. The British preferred to streamline their engines into the wingroots, as done in the de Havilland Comet airliner and the Vickers Valiant, Handley Page Victor, and Avro Vulcan bombers. This form promised what clearly appeared as aerodynamic cleanliness, but it involved complicated engine inlet designs, the problem of unusual thickness at the wing root and of tapering it to the tip, and the disadvantage of heavy structures to carry the wing around the engines. Furthermore, engine accessibility for maintenance or replacement was less than simple. In the 1950s the Soviets also demonstrated a preference for wingroot installations, exemplified in the Tupolev Tu-16 medium bomber and Tu-104 airliner, and the Myasishchev Mya-4 bomber. However, since 1959 engines in the wingroot of large, multiengine aircraft have not found acceptance anywhere.

After 1945 there was no mad scramble to hurry civil air transportation into the jet age. The early turbojets had voracious appetites for fuel, and only an intensive development of in-flight refueling techniques and tanker aircraft made long-range bombers practicable. For airliners it was assumed that the turboprop, a gas turbine turning a propeller, would be more efficient, and that this would be a straightforward development. However, the development of a reliable reduction gear necessary between the high-speed turbine and the low-speed propeller proved to be full of headaches. Paradoxically, refinements in the turbojet preceded widespread availability of turboprops by almost 10 years.

The de Havilland Comet

With their postwar lead in gas turbine technology, the British rushed the world into transportation at high subsonic Mach numbers with the de Havilland D.H. 106 Comet, which flew on July 27, 1949. On May 2, 1952, BOAC inaugurated the world's first commercial jetliner service on its London-Johannesburg route. The Comet 1 was 107,000 pounds, with seats for 36 passengers. Its cruising speed of 450 mph (Mach 0.68 at altitude) was almost twice that of the Douglas DC-6B, also 107,000 pounds and the most versatile piston-engine airliner of the 1950s. But the Comet 1's range with necessary fuel reserves was only 1,750 miles. Although slower, the DC-6B carried almost twice as many passengers and, with fuel reserves, its range was 3,000 miles. In competition with a DC-6B between Chicago and San Francisco, 1,860 miles, a Comet's speed would be lost by the necessity of stopping for en route refueling. However, de Havilland was planning "stretched" variants, including a Comet 3 with trans-Atlantic range.

Unfortunately, the Comet had too many lethal engineering and design problems. Within a year, two Comets were lost in accidents related to a wing stalling condition during takeoffs. Once identified, this problem was fixed, but three other Comets disintegrated in flight within a few minutes of takeoff, during climb-outs to their 35,000-foot cruising altitude. The first accident was attributed to a thunderstorm, a circumstance that may have masked the real problem. In the next two accidents, the Comets disappeared over the Mediterranean shortly after takeoff from Rome.

The de Havilland D.H.106 Comet 1 was the world's first commercial jet airliner. It entered service with British Overseas Airways Corporation (BOAC) in 1952, and gave the British aircraft industry an enormous advantage over American commercial aircraft builders. That edge disappeared and was never regained when three Comet 1s were lost in 1953–54 and the aircraft were withdrawn from service.

The Douglas DC-6B was one of the most successful airliners of the 1950s.

At first the obvious was suspected: a bomb placed aboard the airplanes. Another theory centered on turbine disintegration, the engine parts being hurled into the fuselage, destroying the pressurized cabin. However, corpses recovered from the sea showed no residue from explosives nor fragmentation injuries, but their condition bore clear evidence of explosive decompression of the cabin shell. Meanwhile, in April 1954, all Comets were grounded.

The possibility of metal fatigue seemed far-fetched; as yet, no Comet had been flown 4,000 hours, and even at 10,000 hours an airplane is still "new." However, the Comet was operating in a wholly new realm of flight. Although airplanes had been flying with pressure cabins since 1940, the cruising altitude of these propeller-driven machines rarely exceeded 25,000 feet. A Comet cruised at 35,000 feet.

Atmospheric pressure at sea level is 14.7 pounds per square inch, but at an altitude of 5,280 feet (the elevation of Denver, Colorado) it falls to 12.3; at 18,000 feet to 7.2; and at 35,000 feet to 3.3. An airplane's pressure cabin never attempts to create a sea-level environment. To do so would result in a significantly heavier and less efficient airplane, and it would serve no useful purpose.

Pressure cabins typically simulate an altitude of 8,000 feet. This results in 4.16 pounds per square inch on the cabin shell interior at 20,000 feet; 5.46 at 25,000 feet; 7.5 at 35,000 feet; and 8.0 at 40,000 feet. Equally important is the pressurization cycle, the number of times the cabin shell is pressurized and depressurized. With each cycle the cabin's structure expands and contracts, inflicting wear on its materials. In a service between London and Johannesburg a Comet flew through six cycles. The minimal maintenance

This Aloha Airlines Boeing 737 lost part of its fuselage skin over the Hawaiian Islands in April 1988.

The malfunctioning of a cargo door latch on this Boeing 747 resulted in the loss of a large section of the fuselage skin in February 1989.

required by a gas turbine gave the Comets a much higher utilization rate than piston-engine equipment, and their high cruising speed acted to put them through more pressurization cycles per hundred hours than a piston-engine airplane. Routine wear was accelerated.

In an epic salvage operation, the Royal Navy recovered 70 percent of one Comet's wreckage from the ocean floor. Concurrently, the Royal Aircraft Establishment acquired a Comet, built a tank around its fuselage, filled both with water to contain a possible explosion, and subjected the cabin shell to an accelerated cycling of pressurizations. After 3,057 cycles the test-tank Comet's fuselage failed. In terms of six cycles a day, 300 days a year, this amounted to 19 months of actual operation.

A comparison of this controlled test-tank failure and the wreckage brought up from the ocean floor showed striking similarities between the two cabin failures. Once the cabin experienced local failure, it immediately propagated itself throughout the structure. In flight, the airplane would be shredded within seconds. This was the inspiration for rip-stop construction: frequently occurring strongpoints designed into the cabin framing and shell that prevented a local failure from becoming catastrophic.

A dramatic demonstration of the effectiveness of rip-stop construction occurred in April 1988, when an aging Boeing 737 of Aloha Airlines started shredding its skin at 25,000 feet above the Hawaiian islands. Although the loss of cabin shell had mind-boggling dimensions, the airplane retained its structural integrity and the pilot was able to fly it to a safe landing.

In late February 1989, a Boeing 747 departing Honolulu for New Zealand lost a lower forward cargo door due to a lock failure. This caused a rapid decompression and the loss of a 10- by 20-foot section of the forward cabin and the power in two engines. Nine passengers were swept to their deaths. As with the Aloha Airlines 737, the aircraft retained its structural integrity, and the pilot was able to maneuver the plane back to the airport.

The Boeing 707

Although British gas turbine technology remained a world leader, as a result of the Comet's flawed design, Great Britain lost its lead in jet airliners. Totally redesigned, the Comet did not reenter airline service until late 1958. Meanwhile, Boeing came on the scene with its 707. Initially a design that not only spawned a formidable series of Boeing products, it established a label for an entire generation of airline equipment. Regardless of nationality or manufacture, the expression "707 Generation" describes all subsonic turbojet airline equipment weighing less than 500,000 pounds and built since 1955.

One aspect of the 707's technology transfer occurred in the early 1960s. After customer airlines have flown their airliners away from the factory, major manufacturers continue to keep track of their airplanes; the feedback from operations is vitally important for tomorrow's product. Boeing soon became aware that a 707-320 sold to Air France had "disappeared." The airplane was not operating, had not been destroyed in an accident, and could not be found anywhere. Inquiries to Air France elicited evasive replies. A year later this 707 suddenly reappeared in airline service. Perplexed, Boeing inaugurated its own investigation. Eventually, it was determined that this airplane had been flown to Toulouse, a center of aircraft manufacturing in the south of France, where it had been totally dismantled and its components subjected to detailed study.

There is nothing reprehensible about such dismantling. Given the opportunity, all smart manufacturers do so to a competitor's products; all intelligent nations do so to the military products of other nations whenever

The Boeing Model 717 (55-3118) prototype for the U.S. Air Force's KC-135A Stratotanker is in the foreground; a 707 prototype turns away in the background.

A Strategic Air Command EC-135 airborne command post from Ellsworth Air Force Base, South Dakota, is one of the variants of the KC-135 that still serve in the U.S. Air Force.

THE 707 PHENOMENON

Boeing's jetliner studies started in 1950 when it scouted the possibility of grafting Mach 0.8 aerodynamics to the fuselage of its Model 367, which the Air Force was buying as its piston-engine C-97 transport and KC-97 aerial tanker. The Air Force needed a jet-powered tanker that could operate at a B-47 bomber's cruising altitude of 40,000 feet. A heavily laden KC-97 could rarely climb above 25,000 feet, forcing B-47s to descend for in-flight refueling; thousands of tons of fuel, costing millions of dollars, were being expended annually by B-47s climbing back to their cruising altitudes.

A "jetified" C-97 would have produced a quick-and-dirty jet tanker and transport, but Boeing knew such an airplane would have no long-term future and that Boeing's engineers could do much better. In 1952 Boeing secretly initiated work on a tanker-transport for the Air Force and a demonstrator for the airlines. To conceal its development from competitors, this airplane was called the 367-80, indicating that it was the eightieth variant of its Model 367, the Air Force C-97. Within Boeing it was known as the Dash 80.

The Dash 80's design, construction, and subsequent operations were not funded by the Air Force, and no airline contributed to its development. This airplane was Boeing's own multimillion-dollar speculative investment.

A 190,000-pound airplane, the Dash 80 flew on July 15, 1954, inaugurating three years of vigorous testing. In 1955 the Air Force ordered 29 greatly upgraded, 297,000-pound tanker-transport variants of the Dash 80. This was Boeing's Model 717, which the Air Force designated its KC-135A Stratotanker. Eventually, the Air Force bought over 600 KC-135s and its various special offspring such as EC-135s, RC-135s, C-135s, and so on.

However good a flying machine it was, the ultimate success of the Boeing 707 was in the increase in diameter of its "tube," or fuselage, by a few inches. Whatever diameter tube an airliner design starts with, it will be the same years later when that airplane goes out of production. The redesign of its fuselage cross section is tantamount to redesigning the entire airplane. A fuselage may be "stretched," that is, lengthened, but once an airliner is in production, its diameter is never widened.

The Dash 80 design had a fuselage diameter of 132 inches, while the KC-135 was 144 inches wide. In an airliner this was enough for 2 + 3 seating, but the airlines wanted space for 3 + 3 seating.

Meanwhile, Douglas came on the scene with its prospec-

This photo of the Boeing Model 367-80, or Dash 80, prototype clearly shows its debt to the B-47 and B-52 series, with its sweptback wings and pylon-mounted underwing engine pods.

tive DC-8. Unlike Boeing, Douglas was not locked into a frightfully expensive flying prototype and costly tooling. The DC-8 was a "paper airplane"; with only the flick of an eraser Douglas could promise the airlines anything, and the DC-8 promised a cabin cross section of 146 inches. Fortunately, the 707 was not yet locked into tooling, and Boeing chose to go "two better" and redesigned the 707's fuselage again, now in terms of a 148-inch cross section. This meant losing commonality with the KC-135's fuselage, the necessity of a second production line, and much higher production costs.

The difference of two inches distributed among six seats may sound ridiculous, but where it paid off was in the width of the aisle between the 3 + 3 seating. The willingness to make this change also sent a signal to the airlines that Boeing was deadly serious about the 707 and not simply trying to squeeze an airliner out of its tanker-transport production. As it turned out, Douglas sold 556 DC-8s before the airplane went out of production in 1972, whereas Boeing sold more than 900 of its 707s to the airlines.

Operationally, the 707's 148 inches have stretched across a quarter of a century and will certainly stretch a long way into the twenty-first century. Although most passengers are oblivious to it, when they are travelling in a Boeing 707, 720, 727, 737, or 757, they are all seated in a 148-inch fuselage.

The unusual commonality of tubing among these Boeing airliners inspired an apocryphal story that might be called "The Great Fuselage Machine of Seattle," meaning that Boeing has a machine that turns out one continuous fuselage and production personnel simply slice off however many feet they need for any particular airplane.

The first flight of the 707-120, a 257,000-pound airplane, was made on December 20, 1957. Apparently the same but in fact so different that it required its own production line, the 707-320 intercontinental version, 335,000 pounds, flew on February 15, 1959. Although out of production as an airliner, the 707 is still being produced as a tanker-transport for foreign air forces and as the Air Force E-3A, the Airborne Warning and Control System (AWACS) airplane. As of 1989 some 980 variants of the 707 had been produced.

The most enduring aspect of the Boeing 707 is the name it coincidentally gave to a generation of airline equipment and its technology. Whereas the piston-engine airplanes built between 1936 and 1957 are usually known as the DC-3 Generation, the jet airliners built since 1957 are usually categorized as the 707 Generation.

After careful testing, the addition of more powerful and fuel-efficient turbofan jet engines greatly improved the performance of the later-model Boeing 707s, such as the 120B and intercontinental 320B/C.

Body Cross Section Evolution

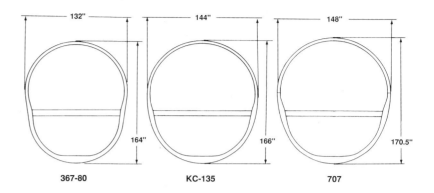

367-80   KC-135   707

These first two production-model 707s on a Civil Aeronautics Administration certification flight in May 1958 near Mount Ranier, Washington, shortly received full approval for civil airline operations.

possible. Nor does it necessarily involve "copying"; for that matter, the "copyist" often improves the original product. For the French this 707 provided a valuable learning experience. A great deal of 707 technology was subsequently worked into the French-sponsored Airbus A300, a 300,000-pound airplane that flew in 1972. The Airbus at first appeared to be a loser. However,

BIGGEST AND BEST—THE BOEING 747

By 1959 a typical gas turbine engine produced 16,000 pounds of thrust. This was 13 times the thrust of the unit that powered the Heinkel He 178 of 1939. Engines of 30,000 and 40,000 pounds thrust were already in prospect and the U.S. Air Force started studying the possibility of a million-pound airplane, a transport capable of lifting a payload of at least 250,000 pounds across 8,000 miles.

In December 1964, the Air Force initiated a design competition among Lockheed, Douglas, and Boeing for an airplane to meet these requirements. In August 1965, Lockheed won the contract, the result being the 769,000-pound Lockheed C-5A that flew 34 months later in June 1968. Pan American Airways went to the losers, Douglas and Boeing, seeking an airliner of similar capabilities. At this time Douglas was already in a debilitating corporate confusion that al-

most sent the company into bankruptcy and did result in a merger with McDonnell in 1967. Boeing ran away with the Pan Am business, the result being the Boeing 747, which went on contract in April 1966, and flew 34 months later in February 1969.

Although the 747 was somewhat smaller than the Lockheed C-5A and not burdened by the C-5A's many military complexities, it was nevertheless an initially troubled airplane. This related to an overweight condition relative to available thrust, but was eventually solved. The 747 introduced the "wide body" airplane to the world. Whereas a 707's cabin cross section measures 148 inches, the 747's measures 255 inches. This cross section was determined by the width of two 8-by-8-foot cargo containers because a primary factor in the 747's design was its versatility as a freighter. That the same volume provides many comforts for 350-some passengers is a happy coincidence.

Since introduced to airline service 20 years ago, the 747's design has gone from strength to strength, from the original 747-100 model of 710,000 pounds with seats for some 350 persons, to 1988's 747-400 of nearly 900,000 pounds, with seats for over 400 passengers. The Boeing 747 has become the *Mauretania*, *Queen Mary*, and *Normandie* of the airways; the essentials of its design may still be in production in the year 2018, half a century after its first flight.

This cross-section comparison chart shows why the 747 was called a "wide-body" commercial air transport.

Airlines introduced the initial 747-100 series in 1970.

The Boeing 747-400 on a test flight.

after 1978 it not only established a new family of airline equipment, but also a multinational foundation for a truly European aircraft industry.

Going Supersonic

While air transportation was groping toward flight by subsonic Mach numbers in the 1950s, military establishments were already rushing toward Mach 2. On October 14, 1947, the Bell X-1 rocket-powered research airplane was flown beyond the speed of sound to Mach 1.06. This was an exhibition of primitive brute force, a triumph of thrust over aerodynamics. Six years later, on November 20, 1953, the more sophisticated Douglas D-558-2 Skyrocket research plane reached Mach 2. Concurrently, a first generation of supersonic fighters started coming off production lines.

Although most fighter planes of the later 1950s were called supersonic, all this really meant was that they had a "dash" capability of a few seconds. This supersonic dash was practically in the category of combat emergency power and had to be used judiciously. Otherwise, fuel consumption became so extravagant it was quickly exhausted and the pilot found himself sitting in the midst of a terrible silence, at the controls of a miserable glider. In regard to fuel consumption, supersonic flight is an emphatic luxury.

When the first Boeing 707 was delivered to Pan American in 1957, the world's speed record belonged to a McDonnell F-101 Voodoo fighter at 1,207 mph (Mach 1.8), but a year earlier, on September 17, 1956, the Bell X-2 research plane had flown at Mach 3.2. The North American X-15 research plane for the exploration of Mach 6 was already on contract. In 1956 the Convair B-58 Hustler—a four-engine bomber of delta wing planform, weighing 175,000 pounds, and capable of Mach 2—entered its test program. Also in 1956, the U.S. Air Force contracted with North American Aviation for the XB-70 Valkyrie, a Mach 3 high-altitude bomber, which was a titanium and stainless steel giant of 520,000 pounds.

The Convair B-58 Hustler was capable of supersonic speeds but had to be refueled every 60 to 90 minutes of supersonic flight.

By 1956 the world was clearly looking far into the realm of supersonic flight. Mach 1 was history; Mach 2 was a fact. All things seemed possible. Optimists chanted: "Mach 2-4-6-8; how far will we accelerate?" Not "Can we?" but "Will we?" However, a supersonic dash was one thing; sustained supersonic cruising was a wholly different matter. The B-58 bomber had only a dash capability. For every hour of flight at Mach 2 it had to be refueled in flight.

Jet fuel, essentially a high-grade kerosene, typically weighs 6.75 pounds per gallon. In quest of a magic fuel that would yield more energy per pound than ordinary hydrocarbons, in the 1950s the U.S. Air Force explored various chemical fuels, generally known as zip fuels. Chief among them was a fuel based on boron. A chemically fueled bomber was supposed to represent the wave of the future. Unfortunately, liquid boron is poisonous to its handlers, its viscosity tends to clog any channel or orifice that can be clogged, and its combustive products are toxic. The "chemical bomber" was a billion-dollar fiasco.

An equally expensive effort was make to develop the technology to use liquid hydrogen as airplane fuel. It required a few years to determine that a useful airplane and liquid hydrogen are simply incompatible. For one thing, liquid hydrogen has to be stored at a temperature close to absolute zero ($-459.67°$ F) and requires a heavy refrigeration plant. For another, it requires a cylindrical vessel for its storage, which tends to be an airplane's fuselage, thereby pre-empting the space ordinarily occupied by payload. The weights demanded by these accommodations negated the advantages of hydrogen's intrinsic lightness. Finally, in terms of military applications, to attempt in-flight refueling with liquid hydrogen was worse than impracticable.

On the eve of the twenty-first century, the airplane's gas turbine continues to be energy dependent on hydrocarbon fuels that weigh 6.75 pounds per gallon, and extravagant fuel consumption remains the voracious *bête noire* of supersonic flight.

A further problem is that in translation from subsonic to supersonic flight, an airplane experiences a shift in its center of gravity from forward to aft. Fighter planes were small enough and their supersonic flight regime short enough that this could be trimmed out aerodynamically, but in large airplanes designed for sustained supersonic cruising it necessitated incorporation of trimming tanks, and pumping tons of fuel from forward to aft, to correct this condition. An alternative was changing the shape of the airliner to a canard, using a foreplane—a horizontal controllable surface at the nose—as did the Wright brothers in their early airplanes.

A gas turbine will not accept supersonic air. Techniques had to be devised to reduce the supersonic flow at the lips of the engine inlet to a subsonic speed at the turbine's face. A cone-shaped spike that moved back and forth at the engine inlet and movable ramps within the engine inlet were designed to create shock waves that dissipated the supersonic air's excessive energy before it reached the blades of the engine's first-stage compressor. Engine inlet design became a fine art unto itself.

Up to Mach 2.2 it is possible to build most of an airplane from aluminum alloys, but beyond that point friction heating of the skin to 500°F or more has a deleterious effect on conventional aircraft materials. For cruising at Mach 3 and beyond, titanium and stainless steel alloys are required. Although titanium is commonly distributed among the earth's materials, tons of it must be processed to produce a few pounds. The industrial processes for titanium's reduction are costly, making it inordinately expensive. And although stainless steels are common enough, working the material into the thin sheeting required by aircraft and tailoring it to the unusual shapes of an airplane is difficult and costly.

Supersonic flight accelerated everything except the speed of human thought required to operate an increasingly complex machine in an increasingly unforgiving environment. Inevitably, a multiplication of systems became necessary in the control loop between the pilot and his airplane, all of which added to complexity and costs.

Compared to flight at Mach 0.85 (560 mph), everything about supersonic flight is inordinately expensive. The only cheap aspect of supersonic flight may be the pilot, because requisite training and experience is not much more than that required for flying a subsonic airplane of similar sophistication.

The Concorde: Supersonic Airliner

By 1960, as the Europeans watched the Americans run away with the world market for subsonic jet airliners, the British and French independently initiated studies of a supersonic airliner. While the Americans were busy producing for Mach 0.85, the British and French planned to preempt them in the realm of Mach 2. These efforts were more complex and expensive than anticipated, promising to overtax each nation's resources; therefore, on November 29, 1962, Great Britain and France concluded a formal treaty aimed at the joint development of a supersonic airliner. This was the Aérospatiale—British Aerospace Corporation's Concorde, which turned out to be a Mach 2.2 airplane of 390,000 pounds with seats for 125 passengers.

The United States viewed this Anglo-French effort as a challenge, and eight months later in June 1963, President John F. Kennedy announced a national project to develop a supersonic transport—the SST, as the American project would be called. It would go one better than the Anglo-French project by aiming for a Mach 3 giant of some 750,000 pounds, with seats for 290 passengers.

The Anglo-French Concorde represented a massive investment on the part of Great Britain and France. Although only 14 aircraft were built, the Concorde's development has paid numerous dividends to the aerospace industries in both countries.

This British Airways Concorde Supersonic Transport (SST) was a technological triumph but a commercial failure because of its great cost, limited seating capacity, and high operating expenses.

The Aérospatiale–British Aerospace Corporation Concorde first flew in March 1969. Meanwhile, the Soviets had developed their own supersonic airliner, the Tupolev Tu-144, of 286,000 pounds. Obsessed by a need to score historic firsts, the Soviets hurried the Tu-144 into the air on December 31, 1968, nominally a year before the Concorde's first flight. Although cloaked by typical Soviet secrecy, it seems that more than a dozen Tu-144s were built. One was destroyed in a spectacular accident at the Paris Air Show of 1973. No Tu-144 entered airline service except for a limited freight service between Moscow and Alma Ata in 1977–1978.

The Concorde required some extensive redesigning and a production model was not ready until 1972. When it came time for the airlines of the world to exercise their options on ordering Concordes in February 1973, none did, but the British and French governments strong-armed their respective national airlines into ordering Concordes. British Airways and Air France each signed up for seven. By means of convoluted financial arrangements, the governments practically made a gift of the airplanes to their airlines and guaranteed a subsidy for operation of them.

The years after the Yom Kippur War of October 1973 saw a series of global energy crises that doubled, quadrupled, and further multiplied the price of oil and jet fuel. The airlines that declined to buy gas-guzzling Concordes in February could feel very pleased with themselves after that October.

Seven years after the Concorde's first flight, British Airways and Air France inaugurated scheduled services with their supersonic airliners on January 21, 1976. The child who was born when the Anglo-French Concorde treaty was signed in November 1962, was almost 14 years old when these services were inaugurated. More significantly, the 20-year-old engineers who joined the British or French aircraft industry in 1962 were now 34, with 14 years' experience working on the cutting edge of advanced aerotechnology. These time frames point out that the monetary costs of the Concorde were ridiculously high, perhaps as much as $20 billion in all for only 14 airplanes, but its national benefits were many.

The Supersonic Boeing 2707

Meanwhile, the ambitious American SST had long since been consigned to aeronautic's trash basket. Because not even a consortium of private corporations could muster the multibillion-dollar financing for an SST, the U.S. government orchestrated the entire drama. It was December 1966 before a design competition between Boeing and Lockheed was decided in favor of Boeing. It is said that the Lockheed engineers enjoyed a hearty laugh, remarking that "Boeing deserved it!"

The Boeing 2707 supersonic transport was overloaded with novelties, chief of which was a variable-geometry "swing-wing." The wings could be swept forward to provide a high-aspect ratio that shortened its takeoff run, reduced landing speed, and provided efficient subsonic cruising. They could be swept back for supersonic flight. At the dawn of the 1960s, variable geometry seemed to "square the cube" between the requirements of

SST Configuration Evolution

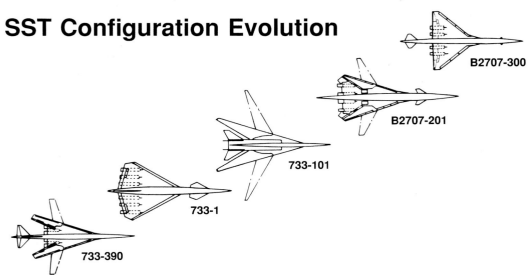

The evolution of Boeing's Supersonic Transport, the B2707-300, shows the various variable geometry and delta wing configurations that were considered in an unsuccessful effort to find an economical and efficient design. Escalating costs led the U.S. Congress to cancel the SST's development.

The first of only two 520,000-pound XB-70 Valkyrie supersonic bombers was completed by North American Aviation in 1964, three years after the U.S. government canceled the B-70 program when it was decided that an aircraft flying at 75,000 feet and three times the speed of sound stood little chance of penetrating enemy defenses successfully. NASA and the U.S. Air Force conducted important flight research with the two prototypes until one crashed after a midair collision. The other XB-70 is now at the Air Force Museum at Wright-Patterson Air Force Base, Ohio.

The Rockwell International B-1B was originally developed as a manned strategic bomber to replace the U.S. Air Force's B-52 fleet. President Jimmy Carter terminated the B-1's development in 1977, and in 1981 President Ronald Reagan revived the bomber as the B-1B. The B-1B has had numerous problems with its various subsystems. At a cost of $250 million per aircraft, the B-1B is the most expensive operational aircraft ever procured by the U.S. Air Force. A large part of the cost is attributed to the complex variable-geometry wings and the operational requirement for supersonic flight capability.

subsonic and supersonic flight. However, every innovation involves drawbacks, and in the 2707 it was the horrendous weight of the hydraulics that actuated the wings, as well as the added weight of a reinforced fuselage that had to carry everything. Estimates varied from 25 to 40 tons for these additions.

Meanwhile, the XB-70 Mach 3 bomber had been canceled. Only two prototypes were built, and in 1966 the one that had been heavily instrumented to produce test data was destroyed in a midair collision. Soviet air defenses, especially the lethal surface-to-air missiles (SAMs) that had claimed Francis Gary Powers and his U-2 in May 1960, had driven the U.S. Air Force out of its wild blue yonder to low-level profile missions where fuel was expended in greater quantities. The B-1 bomber that was intended to replace the B-52 went on contract to Rockwell International in 1970. It was designed to fly supersonic at high altitudes and then to penetrate enemy air defenses in the dense, turbulent air among the treetops. At the very moment Boeing was giving up on the swing-wing, it was made a conspicuous feature of the new B-1 so that the plane would have maximum capabilities in all flight modes. When it finally entered production in the early 1980s, the B-1B was another milestone—the most expensive aircraft ever built, at nearly $250 million each. However great its theoretical appeal, variable geometry remains a weighty luxury that only military airplanes can afford.

After two years of variable geometry nightmares, Boeing scrapped the swing-wing. The 2707 design was revised in terms of a straightforward delta wing similar to the Lockheed proposal the government had rejected. When the Concorde flew in March 1969, Boeing was back at square one.

However simplified, even the revised SST design generated nightmarish problems. Structure weights went up, more thrust was required to carry the new weight, more fuel was necessary to feed the increased thrust, and at the rate of 675 pounds per hundred gallons the fuel invariably meant more weight. The design was trapped in an upward series of fuel-weight spirals with development costs estimated at about $5 billion when, in May 1971,

Congress refused to appropriate any more funds for its development, and the SST was dead.

Many knowledgeable observers in the United States and Europe quietly feared that the Concorde would eventually develop Comet-like problems, but the Anglo-French engineers have built well. In terms of its cost effectiveness, the Concorde is a mediocre airliner, but it is a magnificent piece of technology. Since 1976 the British and French Concordes have provided regular supersonic service between Paris and London and New York, Washington, D.C., and Miami—for those who can afford it. Although the Concorde once flew to the Middle East and Latin America, today only the North American routes remain. In 1989 the one-way Concorde fare from New York to Europe was $2,300.

Boeing 747: Wider Rather than Faster

What the Anglo-Europeans of the 1960s did not realize, and the Americans did not fully appreciate, was that the way to go in airline equipment was not forward with more speed but sideways with more space. Boeing was doing this with its 747, which received its go-ahead in 1966, flew in 1969, and entered airline service in 1970. Ironically, the sizing of the Boeing 747 was determined by its prospective use as a freighter. In contrast to 14 Concordes, 715 Boeing 747s have been delivered through early 1989 and several hundred more are on order.

Given the many expensive complexities of a supersonic airplane, the absence of a fuel that weighs less than 6.75 pounds per gallon, the finite characteristics of global energy reserves and inevitably higher energy prices, it seems likely that once the Concordes are retired, flight beyond Mach 1 will be the exclusive preserve of military aircraft. In spite of speculation about international efforts to develop a new supersonic airliner and even a hypersonic airliner that will fly at Mach 6 or more, at Mach 0.85 the typical air traveller is probably flying as fast as he or she is going to.

The B-2 Stealth Span-Loader

Between 1903 and the 1930s, the airplane was transformed from a vegetable product to a mineral product. On the eve of the twenty-first century, an increasing use of fiberglass, epoxy resins, carbon fibers, boron fibers, and polymers to reduce the weights of airframe materials without any sacrifice in strength is moving the airplane toward a product of modern chemistry. Besides substance, even the form of the subsonic airplane may be on the eve of a dramatic change.

The all-wing span-loader is experiencing a tenuous revival. On November 22, 1988, the Northrop B-2 Advanced Technology Bomber (ATB) "Stealth" aircraft, a subsonic, all-wing airplane with a wingspan of 172 feet and weighing some 300,000 pounds, was unveiled to the public. The B-2 claimed one record almost immediately—it is the largest aircraft ever built mostly of nonmetallic materials. If it enters production in numbers, it will set another record—at an estimated cost of $500 million apiece, the B-2 will be by far the most expensive aircraft ever built, nearly doubling the per unit cost of the B-1B. However, costly stealth (low observables) technology, designed to prevent detection by hostile air defenses, has no function in the civil airplane that, given an increasingly crowded airspace, must be as conspicuous as possible. However, the B-2's all-wing planform has revived interest in the span-loaded airplane.

The conventional airplane carries its payload in a fuselage that is practically suspended from a wing's midpoint, where all loads come to a focus. The span-loaded airplane distributes the load across the wingspan; it has no fuselage or empennage and is popularly known as a flying wing. A practical span-loaded airplane was not possible until a wing could be built thick enough to create the volume necessary for distribution of the payload inside the wing. This required an airframe of such size and weight that it was not practical until the shelf technology of the 1940s became available.

The first successful span-loaded airplanes of practical dimensions were the Northrop XB-35, a four-engine propeller-driven bomber of 209,000 pounds that flew in 1946, and the YB-49, a jet-powered variant of 213,000 pounds that flew in 1947. However, in 1949 the U.S. Air Force canceled further development and production of the YB-49 in favor of the Convair B-36, a piston-engine propeller-driven behemoth that was notorious for its internal complexities and relative slowness. Unfortunately, this controversial decision had the unwanted consequence of condemning the span-loaded all-wing airplane as a generic type. In the continuing quest for more efficient subsonic cruising over intercontinental distances, the twenty-first century may witness a revival of the span-loaded airplane. Indeed, the U.S. Air Force has already turned to the Northrop B-2 ATB, a modern descendant of the YB-49, as its strategic bomber of the future. Ironically, both Northrop bombers have exactly the same wingspan—172 feet.

In the years since Wilbur Wright's dramatic demonstration at Hunaudières, a fragile and unreliable machine of questionable utility has spawned a new and awesome technology that has, for better or worse, touched most aspects of everyday life. In the second half of an as yet unfinished twentieth century, the advances in aviation have been staggering. How we will fly, and in what aircraft, when the first century of flight comes to a close continues to be dazzling to contemplate.

The Northrop B-2 "Stealth" bomber, an all-wing airplane, has approximately the same dimensions and weights as does the Northrop YB-49 bomber that was abandoned in 1949. This military revival of the all-wing, span-loaded airplane may spur its development for commercial uses.

Facing page:
Jack Northrop's XB-35 piston-engine flying wing flew in 1946 but was soon replaced by the YB-49 jet-powered version. Controversy still surrounds the U.S. Air Force's cancellation of the YB-49 in 1949 in favor of Convair's B-36. Today's B-2 is directly descended from Northrop's flying-wing bombers of the late 1940s.

THE LITERATURE
Dominick Pisano

Humanity's continual quest to push back the parameters of flight—to go higher, faster, and farther and to build bigger and better aircraft—is perhaps the most prominent characteristic of the history of aviation. Indeed, it is remarkable that in a little more than three quarters of a century since the invention of the airplane, the technological face of aviation has changed in undreamt of ways.

During this relatively short time, the airplane has been transformed from the stick-and-wire Wright *Flyer*, capable of carrying the pilot 852 feet in 59 seconds, to the streamlined, jet-powered passenger airliner, capable of traveling routinely at three fourths the speed of sound, carrying payloads of 300 to 400 passengers and attaining ranges of 8,000 miles.

More recently, high-speed, high-altitude reconnaissance and research aircraft like the Lockheed SR-71 and North American X-15, with the help of jet- and rocket-powered engines and advanced design features, have reached speeds of three to six times that of sound and altitudes of 15 to 60 miles.

And, at a conceptual level, there are ideas like the hypersonic aircraft, which after takeoff would be able to reach speeds 25 times greater than the speed of sound, orbit in space, then glide or be propelled back to earth.

The unprecedented technological growth of aviation, however, did not and does not take place in a vacuum. Although the literature of aviation has always been large, in the past it has tended to focus primarily on technological progress, and thus rarely does it take into account the broader framework—the social, cultural, political, and, in current times, environmental context in which the events took place.

Despite the intellectual limitations of the literature itself, I have endeavored in this essay, whose format is too limited to allow a comprehensive coverage, to include those works that the authors themselves consulted and to direct the reader to other useful sources. I have further attempted to key the essay to the individual chapters in this book and to provide sources for bibliographic and general studies.

BIBLIOGRAPHY AND GENERAL STUDIES

Readers interested in additional titles that relate to the history of aviation should consult Dominick A. Pisano and Cathleen S. Lewis, *Air and Space History: An Annotated Bibliography* (New York: Garland, 1988). See especially Peter L Jakab, "General Histories" (pp. 28–32); F. Robert van der Linden, "Aircraft" (pp. 60–75); Rick Leyes, Deborah G. Douglas, and William A. Fleming, "Propulsion" (pp. 86–109); Thomas J. Noon and Howard Wolko, "Aeronautical Engineering" (pp. 110–131); Von D. Hardesty, et al., "Military Aviation" (pp. 132–155); R. E. G. Davies, "Air Transportation" (pp. 156–187); Samuel B. Fishbein, Thomas J. Noon, and Dominick A. Pisano, "Navigation, Communication, and Meteorology" (pp. 204–215); Samuel B. Fishbein and Thomas J. Noon, "Events" (pp. 238–255); and Dominick A. Pisano, Von D. Hardesty, and Samuel B. Fishbein, "Aviation Industry" (pp. 283–292).

Studies of a general nature include: Charles H. Gibbs-Smith, *Aviation: A Historical Survey from Its Origins to the End of World War II* (London: Her Majesty's Stationery Office, 1970), a work that is particularly strong on the early history of powered flight; Roger E. Bilstein, *Flight in America, 1900–1983: From the Wrights to the Astronauts* (Baltimore, Md.: Johns Hopkins University Press, 1984), a fine survey of the field; C. R. Roseberry, *The Challenging Skies: The Colorful Story of Aviation's Most Exciting Years, 1919–1939* (Garden City, N.Y.: Doubleday, 1966), a solid account of aviation's "Golden Age"; and John W. R. Taylor and Kenneth Munson, *History of Aviation* (New York: Crown, 1972), a good introduction to the essential personalities and events.

Also of general interest is the 23-volume *Epic of Flight* series produced by Time-Life Books from 1980 to 1984, which covers, among other subjects, the early history of flight, military and commercial aviation, long-distance flying and aerial exploration, and aircraft design and testing.

More technical in nature are John D. Anderson, Jr., *Introduction to Flight*, 3d ed. (New York: McGraw-Hill, 1989), an introduction to aerospace engineering that combines a historical and technological perspective; and Laurence K. Loftin, Jr., *Quest for Performance: The Evolution of Modern Aircraft* (Washington, D.C.: National Aeronautics and Space Administration, 1985), which traces the development of the airplane from World War I to the present.

CHAPTER 1: FARTHER by Terry Gwynn-Jones

David Nevin, *The Pathfinders* (Alexandria, Va.: Time-Life Books, 1980), provides an overview of long-distance flying in the 1920s and 1930s, especially the numerous attempts to cross the At-

OF AVIATION

lantic. Louis Blériot's English Channel crossing in 1909 is covered admirably by Tom D. Crouch, in *Blériot XI: The Story of a Classic Aircraft* (Washington, D.C.: Smithsonian Institution Press, 1982, pp. 26–43). Igor Sikorsky's long-distance flight from St. Petersburg to Kiev is recorded in K. N. Finne, *Igor Sikorsky, The Russian Years*, eds. Carl J. Bobrow and Von Hardesty, trans. and adapted by Von Hardesty (Washington, D.C.: Smithsonian Institution Press, 1987), and Igor I. Sikorsky, *The Story of the Winged S: An Autobiography* (New York: Dodd, Mead, 1938).

Although there are many fine secondhand accounts that chronicle the attempts to fly the Atlantic, those rare firsthand accounts, like Harry G. Hawker and K. Mackenzie Grieve, *Our Atlantic Attempt* (London: Methuen, 1919); Charles A. Lindbergh, *The Spirit of St. Louis* (New York: Charles Scribner's Sons, 1953); and Italo Balbo, *My Air Armada* (London: Hurst and Blackett, 1934), are particularly pleasing.

Alan J. Cobham's various flights to Africa, the Middle East, Southeast Asia, and Australia are recounted in *A Time to Fly* (London: Shepheard-Walwyn, 1978). Bert Hinkler's 1928 solo flight from England to Australia is outlined in Roy Mackenzie, *Solo, The Bert Hinkler Story* (Sidney: Ure Smith, 1962). Charles E. Kingsford-Smith and Charles T. P. Ulm chronicle their 1919 trans-Pacific flight in *The Flight of the Southern Cross* (New York: Robert M. McBride, 1929).

A descriptive account of the first flight around the world by the U.S. Army in 1924 will be found in Lowell Thomas, *The First World Flight; Being the Personal Narratives of Lowell Smith, Erik Nelson, Leigh Wade, Leslie Arnold, Henry Ogden, John Harding* (New York: Houghton Mifflin, 1925). A description of Wiley Post's around-the-world flight in 1931 is contained in Wiley Post and Harold Gatty, *Around the World in Eight Days: The Flight of the* Winnie Mae (New York: Rand McNally, 1931; reprinted by Orion Books, 1989). Amelia Earhart, *Last Flight* (New York: Harcourt, Brace, 1937), arranged by her husband, George Palmer Putnam, and told through her dispatches, letters, charts, and logs, describes her attempt to fly around the world and subsequent disappearance in 1937. Donald L. Barlett and James B. Steele, *Empire: The Life, Legend, and Madness of Howard Hughes* (New York: W. W. Norton, 1979), contains information on Howard Hughes's around-the-world flight in 1938.

The rise of Pan American Airways is chronicled in Robert Daley, *An American Saga: Juan Trippe and His Pan Am Empire* (New York: Random House, 1980), and in Marylin Bender and Selig Altschul, *The Chosen Instrument* (New York: Simon and Schuster, 1982).

CHAPTER 2:   HIGHER AND FASTER by John D. Anderson, Jr.

So much of what was achieved in making aircraft fly higher and faster could not have been possible without the efforts of test pilots, who often placed their lives in jeopardy so that information could be gathered and technological improvements made. Richard P. Hallion, *Test Pilots: The Frontiersmen of Flight* (Garden City, N.Y.: Doubleday, 1981; revised and updated by Smithsonian Institution Press, Washington, D.C., 1988), is the best all-around source. Hallion dispels most of the myths about test pilots and points out that theirs "is a story without end" because "the frontiers of the sky can only be pushed back, and are never closed."

The pursuit of altitude and speed in aviation began with the efforts of the Wright brothers to develop a practical airplane. Marvin W. McFarland, ed., *The Papers of Wilbur and Orville Wright: Vol. 1 (1899–1905), Vol. 2 (1906–1948)* (New York: McGraw-Hill, 1953) is the standard reference for the Wrights. Other useful sources are Fred C. Kelly; *The Wright Brothers: A Biography Authorized by Orville Wright* (New York: Harcourt, Brace, 1943); Fred Howard, *Wilbur and Orville: A Biography of the Wright Brothers* (New York: Alfred Knopf, 1987); and Tom D. Crouch, *The Bishop's Boys: A Life of the Wright Brothers* (W. W. Norton, 1989). A series of technical essays on the Wrights's 1903 machine will be found in Howard Wolko, ed., *The Wright Flyer: An Engineering Perspective*, Proceedings of a Symposium Held at the National Air and Space Museum, December 16, 1983 (Washington, D.C.: Smithsonian Institution Press, 1987).

The standard biography of Glenn Curtiss is C. R. Roseberry, *Glenn Curtiss: Pioneer of Flight* (Garden City, N.Y.: Doubleday, 1972). Peter M. Bowers, *Curtiss Aircraft, 1907–1947* (Annapolis, Md.: Naval Institute Press, 1987), outlines the development of Curtiss aircraft from the earliest days to just after World War II.

Design aspects of World War I aircraft are extensively explored in Laurence K. Loftin, Jr., *Quest for Performance* (pp. 7–66). One of the best books on the Schneider Cup races is David Mondey, *The Schneider Trophy: A History of the Contests of La Coupe D'Aviation Maritime Jacques Schneider*

(London: Robert Hale, 1975). Edward P. Warner, *Technical Development and Its Effect on Air Transportation* (Northfield, Vt.: Norwich University, 1938), is a lucid interpretation of technological progress in commercial aviation. Douglas J. Ingells, *The Plane That Changed the World: A Biography of the DC-3* (Fallbrook, Calif.: Aero Publishers, 1966), is a thorough treatment of one of the most significant airplanes ever built.

Two standard works on Lockheed aircraft are Richard S. Allen, *Revolution in the Sky: The Lockheeds of Aviation's Golden Age*, rev. ed. (New York: Orion Books, 1988), and René J. Francillon, *Lockheed Aircraft Since 1913* (Annapolis, Md.: Naval Institute Press, 1987). Wiley Post's pressure suit and his around-the-world flight in the Lockheed Vega he called *Winnie Mae*, after the daughter of the aircraft's sponsor, are the subjects of Stanley R. Mohler, *Wiley Post, His* Winnie Mae, *and the World's First Pressure Suit* (Washington, D.C.: Smithsonian Institution Press, 1971). Barlett and Steele, *Empire: The Life, Legend, and Madness of Howard Hughes*, contains a chapter on the development and testing of the Hughes Racer, as well as on Hughes's other aviation ventures.

Air racing is covered in Terry Gwynn-Jones, *The Air Racers: Aviation's Golden Era, 1909–1936* (Sydney: Lansdowne Press, 1984); Don Dwiggins, *They Flew the Bendix Race: The History of the Competition for the Bendix Trophy* (Philadelphia: J. B. Lippincott, 1965); and Reed C. Kinert, *Racing Planes and Air Races: A Complete History*, 13 vols. (Fallbrook, Calif.: Aero Publishers, 1967–69).

A fine introduction to the era of modern jet-propelled aircraft will be found in Walter J. Boyne and Donald S. Lopez, eds., *The Jet Age: Forty Years of Jet Aviation* (Washington, D.C.: Smithsonian Institution Press, 1979; updated 1989). Richard Hallion, *Supersonic Flight: The Story of the Bell X-1 and Douglas D-558* (New York: Macmillan, 1972), is still the foremost account of breaking the sound barrier. Jay Miller, *The X-Planes* (Arlington, Texas: Aerofax, 1988), is the best survey of experimental aircraft to date.

CHAPTER 3: BIGGER by James R. Hansen

A general survey of large aircraft will be found in Michael J. H. Taylor and David Monday, *Giants in the Sky* (London: Janes, 1982). Norman Bel Geddes, *Horizons* (New York: Dover, 1977, pp. 109–121), and *Miracle in the Evening, An Autobiography*, ed. William Kelley (Garden City, N.Y.: Doubleday, 1960. pp. 274–302), describe the famous industrial designer's ideas for a multiengined flying wing capable of making regularly scheduled trans-Atlantic flights in luxurious comfort.

The story of Samuel P. Langley's experiments with the manned *Aerodrome* is told in Tom D. Crouch, *A Dream of Wings: America and the Airplane, 1875–1905* (New York: W. W. Norton, 1981), chapters 7 and 12: Igor Sikorsky's *Il' ya Muromets*, the world's first large four-engined aircraft is detailed in Finne, *Igor Sikorsky, The Russian Years*, and in Sikorsky, *The Story of the Winged-S*.

See G. W. Haddow and Peter M. Grosz, *The German Giants: The Story of the R-Planes, 1914–1918*, 2d ed. (New York: Funk and Wagnalls, 1969), for an informative discussion of the "Riesenflugzeuge" (giant airplanes), developed in Germany during World War I, and Arthur Baumann, "Progress Made in the Construction of Giant Airplanes During the War," NACA Technical Note 29 (Washington, D.C.: National Advisory Committee for Aeronautics, 1920), for a technical view of these early large aircrafts.

Barlett and Steele, *Empire: The Life, Legend, and Madness of Howard Hughes* (pp. 113–125, 156–160), outlines the ill-fated HK-1 *Spruce Goose* flying boat project. Richard C. Knott, *The American Flying Boat: An Illustrated History* (Annapolis, Md.; Naval Institute Press, 1979), surveys the development of the flying boat in the United States. Richard K. Smith, "The Intercontinental Airliner and the Essence of Airplane Performance, 1929–1939," *Technology and Culture* 24 No. 3 (July 1983, pp. 428–449), is a contextual interpretation of the history of the flying boat. Laurence K. Loftin, Jr., *Quest for Performance* (pp. 163–216), contains an excellent technical analysis of flying boats.

For a technical discussion of large aircraft, see H. Roxbee Cox, "Large Aeroplanes," *Journal of the Royal Aeronautical Society* 42 (July 1938, pp. 591–595); F. A. Cleveland, "Size Effects in Conventional Aircraft Design, *Journal of Aircraft* 7 No. 6 (November-December 1970, pp. 483–512), AIAA Very Large Vehicle Conference, *A Collection of Technical Papers* (New York: American Institute of Aeronautics and Astronautics, 1979); and Richard K. Smith, "The Weight Envelope: An Airplane's Fourth Dimension," *Aerospace Historian* 33 (Spring 1986, pp. 30–44).

The evolution of the commercial airliner to recent times is detailed in Ronald E. Miller and David Sawers, *The Technical Development of Modern Aviation* (London: Routledge and Kegan Paul, 1968), and Peter W. Brooks, *The Modern Airliner: Its Origins and Development* (London: Putnam, 1961; updated and revised in 1982 by Sunflower University Press, Manhattan, Kans.).

The development of the Boeing 747, the first so-called wide-body aircraft is detailed in Laurence S. Kuter, *The Great Gamble: The Boeing 747; The Boeing–Pan Am Project to Develop, Produce, and Introduce the 747* (University, Ala.: University of Alabama Press, 1973) and Douglas J. Ingells, *747: The Story of the Boeing Super Jet* (Fallbrook, Calif.: Aero Publishers, 1970). Also, chapter 6 of John Newhouse, *The Sporty Game* (New York: Alfred A. Knopf, 1982), "Bigger Is Better," contains a lively description of the genesis of the Boeing 747.

CHAPTER 4: BETTER by Richard K. Smith

Improving aircraft technologically became the *raison d'être* for aviation in the twenties and thirties and the National Advisory Committee for Aeronautics led the way. For various discussions of NACA's pioneering work, see John V. Becker, *The High-Speed Frontier: Case Histories of Four NACA Programs, 1920–1950*, NASA SP-445 (Washington, D.C.: National Aeronautics and Space Administration, 1980); James R. Hansen, *Engineer in Charge: A History of the Langley Aeronautical Laboratory, 1917–1958*, NASA SP-4305 (Washington, D.C.: National Aeronautics and Space Administration, 1987); and Alex Roland, *Model Research: The National Advisory Committee for Aeronautics, 1915–1958*, 2 vols., NASA SP-4103 (Washington, D.C.: National Aeronautics and Space Administration, 1985), although the latter is more a political history of NACA than a technological one. See also Fred E. Weick and James R. Hansen, *From the Ground Up: The Autobiography of an Aeronautical Engineer* (Washington, D.C.: Smithsonian Institution Press, 1988), for the story of one of the leading NACA designers and engineers in the interwar period.

Other titles that explore the technological development of aircraft include Peter Brooks, *The Modern Airliner: Its Origins and Development*; Alexander Lippisch, trans. Gertrude L. Lippisch, *The Delta Wing: History and Development* (Ames, Iowa: Iowa State University Press, 1981); E. T. Wooldridge, *Winged Wonders: The Story of the Flying Wings* (Washington, D.C.: Smithsonian Institution Press, 1983); Loftin, *Quest for Performance*; and Miller and Sawers, *The Technical Development of Modern Aviation*, although the latter is somewhat preoccupied with the economics of airliners.

The aviation industry, unfortunately, is a subject that has not been given the attention it deserves in the literature. Nevertheless, John B. Rae, *Climb to Greatness: The American Aircraft Industry, 1920–1960* (Cambridge, Mass.: MIT Press, 1968), and Gene R. Simonson, ed., *The History of the American Aircraft Industry: An Anthology* (Cambridge, Mass.: MIT Press, 1968), provide a useful introduction.

The literature of military aircraft in World War II is vast, but a few titles will suffice to give the reader a general outline of the subject. See especially, Kenneth Munson, *Aircraft of World War II* (Garden City, N.Y.: Doubleday, 1972); John W. R. Taylor, ed., *Combat Aircraft of the World from 1909 to the Present* (New York: G. P. Putnam, 1969); Gordon Swanborough and Peter M. Bowers, *United States Military Aircraft Since 1908* (London: Putnam, 1971); Gordon Swanborough and Peter M. Bowers, *United States Naval Aircraft Since 1911*, 2d ed. (Annapolis, Md.: Naval Institute Press, 1976); John F. Taylor, *British Aircraft of World War II* (New York: Stein and Day, 1976); J. R. Smith and Antony L. Kay, *German Aircraft of the Second World War* (London: Putnam, 1972); René J. Francillon, *Japanese Aircraft of the Pacific War* (Annapolis, Md.: Naval Institute Press, 1988);

and Jean Alexander, *Russian Aircraft Since 1940* (London: Putnam, 1975).

Developments such as wind tunnels, jet propulsion, fuels, and propellers, which contributed substantially to the development of the modern airplane are topics covered by Donald D. Baals and William R. Corliss, *Wind Tunnels of NASA*, NASA SP-440 (Washington, D.C.: National Aeronautics and Space Administration, 1981); Boyne and Lopez, eds., *The Jet Age: Forty Years of Jet Aviation*, which contains valuable essays by jet pioneers Frank Whittle and Hans von Ohain; Edward W. Constant, *The Origins of the Turbojet Revolution* (Baltimore, Md.: Johns Hopkins University Press, 1980); Robert Schlaifer and S. D. Heron, *Development of Aircraft Engines; Development of Aviation Fuels—Two Studies of Relations Between Government and Business* (Boston: Harvard Graduate School of Business Administration, 1950); and George Rosen and Charles A. Anezis, *Thrusting Forward: A History of the Propeller* (East Hamilton, Conn.: Hamilton Standard and British Aerospace Dynamics Group, 1984).

The history of British contribution to supersonic flight is chronicled in Charles Burnet, *Three Centuries to Concorde* (London: Mechanical Engineering Publications Ltd., 1979). The debate over the Boeing supersonic transport project is thoroughly analyzed by Mary E. Ames in a chapter titled "The Case of the U.S. SST: Disenchantment with Technology," (pp. 49–82) in *Outcome Uncertain: Science and the Political Process* (Washington, D.C.: Communications, 1978). Kenneth Owen, *Concorde: New Shape in the Sky* (London: Jane's, 1982), is a solid discussion of the Concorde technology that takes into account some six years of actual scheduled flying.

Finally, although the literature of the technological development of aviation is vast, it will be possible through the aforementioned sources to become familiar with some of the basic literature. Those interested in delving deeper will find that each individual source usually provides a comprehensive bibliography.

INDEX

Italic page numbers refer to illustrations or their accompanying captions.

303

PHOTOGRAPHY CREDITS